THE PROMISE CONTINUES

EMPIRE STATE COLLEGE
THE FIRST TWENTY - FIVE YEARS

Empire State College expresses sincere appreciation to those who have helped mold the institution's distinguished history and who have helped underwrite this very special chronicle.

Kenneth T. Abrams
Jane Altes
Academy for Learning in
Retirement at Saratoga Springs
Joseph E. Aulisi
Anne R. Bertholf
Kathleen and George Bragle
Fernand Brunschwig and
Jennifer Herring
Robert B. Carey
Ronald D. Corwin
Doreen DeCrescenzo
Dennis R. DeLong
Amy Durland and Robert Mains
Joyce E. Elliott
Doris C. Etelson
Maureen Farese

J. David Ferris, Ph.D. '84
Michael Fortunato
Dr. Mary Ellen Giblin
Justin A. Giordano
Lewis and Colleen Golub
Hugh B. Hammett
Ellen G. Hawkes, Ed.D.
Marlene Herr and Paul Lutz
June and Lester Hoeflich
Margaret Boston Jackson
Drs. Carolyn and Randy Jarmon
Bernice and Howard Kahn
Marjorie W. Lavin
Patricia J. Lefor
Timothy and Ann Lehmann
Helene D. Locke
Robert and Phyllis MacCameron

Robert P. Milton
Mary Nell Morgan and
William Lee Brown
Dr. Moses and Myrtle Musoke
Mae M. Ngai
Daniel I. Peters and friends
Richard T. Othmer, Jr.
Mary F. Reed
Robert E. and Patricia O. Ross
Sal Rubino
Edward Saueracker, Ph.D.
James H. and Joan N. Savitt
Linda Ann Scura
Dr. Carolyn C. Shadle
Sondra and David Silverhart
Dean Marie J. Wittek

THE PROMISE CONTINUES

EMPIRE STATE COLLEGE
THE FIRST TWENTY - FIVE YEARS

BY RICHARD F. BONNABEAU
FOREWORD BY ERNEST L. BOYER

THE
DONNING COMPANY
PUBLISHERS

To the founders and pioneers of Empire State College—
State University of New York and to those who follow.

Copyright © 1996 by State University of New York Empire State College

All rights reserved, including the right
to reproduce this work in any form whatsoever
without permission in writing from the publisher,
except for brief passages in connection with a review.
For information, write:

The Donning Company/Publishers
184 Business Park Drive, Suite 106
Virginia Beach, VA 23462

Steve Mull, General Manager
Debra Y. Quesnel, Project Director
Tracey Emmons-Schneider, Director of Research
Mary Jo Kurten, Editor
Chris Decker, Graphic Designer
Dawn V. Kofroth, Production Manager
Teri S. Arnold, Marketing Assistant

Library of Congress Cataloging-in-Publication Data:

Bonnabeau, Richard F. (Richard Francis), 1943—
      The promise continues : Empire State College—the first twenty-five years / by Richard F. Bonnabeau.
           p.   cm.
      Includes bibliographical references and index.
      ISBN 0-89865-966-3 (alk. paper)
      1. Empire State College—History.   2. Distance education—New York (State)—History. I. Title.
LC5806.N7B65   1996
378'.03—dc20   96-4381

                                                  CIP

Printed in the United States of America

Contents

Foreword

American higher education, with several thousand campuses, has taken great pride in what we like to call "the diversity of the system." And in some respects there's reason to feel satisfaction in the special nature of each campus with its own heritage, its own traditions, and its own distinctive climate. Surely what undergraduates experience at Berkeley is far different from life at the College at Geneseo in New York or even what goes on at Santa Cruz, another campus of the University of California.

But many years ago, while a young administrator, I began to discover that higher education, with all the talk about diversity, was, in many ways, a hugely imitative system and that the nation's colleges and universities, in spite of their claims of distinctiveness, are far more than we are ready to admit busily engaged in cloning one another. This fact came home to me dramatically when I attended my first curriculum committee meeting at a small college where I had just become academic dean. We were defining our requirements for general education, and rather than discuss what was best for our own students, we turned immediately to the Pomona College catalog, a more prestigious institution down the road. And when I asked, "Where does Pomona get its standards," the registrar rather jokingly replied, "Probably from Harvard." And that brief exchange, which occurred forty years ago, gave me more insights into the culture of higher learning than any I've ever had.

This imitative approach to academic planning applies, of course, not just to curriculum requirements, but to how many units it takes to complete a baccalaureate degree, and even to how many times each week a class should meet and what the length of each class should be, with forty-five to fifty minutes being the revealed truth.

None of this is necessarily evil, of course. Tradition does have its place, and it's obvious that within these rigidly imposed arrangements, learning can and often does occur. And surely by having standardized procedures, it's easy for students to complete a credential and move on to further learning or the world of work.

Simply stated, I've never felt that the current system of American higher education can or should be radically overhauled, although improvements surely can and should occur. Still, one does wonder about the educational efficacy of the rigid system that now dominates higher learning—the depressing similarity in academic practice— whether it be a massive land-grant college in the Midwest or a Baptist college in the South. Check the catalogues. Students, regardless of where they go, will be asked to jump through the same bureaucratic hoops even though the mandates are based more on tradition than tests of excellence. And even today it's virtually impossible to find a college in America that is, in fact, marching to a different drummer, St. John's College perhaps being one of the very few exceptions.

All of this was very much on my mind when I became chancellor of the State University of New York, a complex cluster of campuses which had, at the time, seventy-two separate institutions. There were specialty institutions such as medical schools, a college of ceramics and the like, but below the surface the core assumptions at almost all of the State University campuses were essentially the same.

I began to speculate about the possibility of organizing within this network of traditional colleges a new kind of institution based on student learning. It was a time of unprecedented turmoil in higher education. Many felt the very survival of the University was at risk and the conviction grew that this may be precisely the time to start such a new college—a non-campus institution that would not depend on the rigidity of the calendar or class schedule but on the creativity of the students, with faculty serving not as academic managers but as mentors.

Still, I had reservations. This also was a time when the University urgently needed to be pulled together and many believed, especially key legislative leaders, that the State University had grown too large. What, in fact, would be the reaction if a new chancellor, as his first major policy act, proposed to start yet another campus—and a very curious one at that.

I consulted first with my friend and colleague, Sam Gould, who was retiring as chancellor, and Sam, predictably, gave the idea unqualified support. Chancellor Gould had always been a bold, innovative planner and he agreed without hesitation that a new non-campus college for SUNY was an idea whose time had come.

But what about the trustees? I should not have worried. At that time, the State University was led, thanks to Governor Nelson Rockefeller, by the most educated and most enlightened board I have ever encountered in higher education. These public servants understood precisely their role as guardians of the public trust—no grandstanding, just a deep determination to serve the people of New York and most especially the student. The idea of creating a college where learning was the goal around which all other arrangements would be organized, while novel, was for all trustees enormously appealing.

As to the Governor, he loved the idea from the very first. My problem was not getting him to endorse the College, but to hold him back. The Governor had his own great ideas about what such a college could be—even though the baby, so to speak, had not yet been born. But again, my concern was not with the novelty of the idea, but with a deep conviction that higher education should be far more attentive to teaching and learning than to procedures and that this country would be greatly enriched if we could build a truly diversified system of higher education.

And so it was Empire State College was created. Kay, my wife, and I talked late into the night about what name would suit the new institution, considering such possibilities as "University College," but one night it occurred to me that "Empire State" seemed to capture precisely the spirit and purpose of the institution the trustees were endorsing.

Giving birth was, of course, only the beginning. Endless years of planning and creative leadership were required to bring it all together. And it is with an unrestrained pride and admiration that I have read Richard Bonnabeau's superb history of Empire State College which reflects twenty-five years: early euphoria, followed by agonizing struggle, the march to maturity, and, finally, remarkable success. Reading this beautiful narrative I frequently was reminded of fascinating events I had long since forgotten. For example, the truly intense intellectual encounter between two of my most cherished friends, Arthur Chickering and Loren Baritz, as they sought to define, with clarity, the age-old tension between the content and process of education. This vigorous intellectual debate, occurring as it did during the early days of Empire State College, surely created a much more educational and intellectually vigorous institution, as Professor Bonnabeau so wisely points out.

I was struck, too, in reading this outstanding history, about just how difficult it was (and is) to create a college with no buildings, no traditions, and no procedures to guide people through the day. Indeed, I was impressed by just how much the faculty, in the early days, was deeply divided about what Empire State College was and should become, with many joining the institution more convinced of what they opposed in higher education than what they supported.

Bringing all of this together called for almost superhuman leadership ability—a rare blend of wisdom, courage, and patience, with a larger vision and deep streak of patience and persistence. Nominees for the president of Empire State College came pouring in from academic leaders all across the country. But something was not right.

We needed a new person with a new vision and I kept returning, time and time again, to a young colleague in our own office. Jim Hall, while limited in traditional administrative experience, still seemed to bring together all of the qualities we needed, plus he was creative, well organized, and had a vision and a deep commitment to better learning for all students.

No decision I made proved to be more consequential—and more unqualifiably successful. Jim Hall, as president of Empire State College, has, throughout the years, made all the difference. He took a dream and gave it shape and direction and inspiration. It was Jim who shared the agony of the early conflict, listening and wisely mediating and helping to form a college with its own sense of direction and, ultimately, a deep sense of confidence as well.

Beyond building cohesion, President Hall was a brilliant strategist. He understood, intuitively, the politics of education, but, above all, he understood the purposes of Empire State College, moving quickly to make the College a statewide institution. He clarified the role of mentors, boldly sought and achieved national accreditation, and used this recognition to consolidate the College's internal governance arrangements, and, in the process, quickly built an institution with international distinction.

Even more remarkable, Jim Hall introduced changes within an already innovative institution—with special institutes, art centers in the cities, a resource center for faculty, and more recently a bold commitment to new technology. President Hall, as a visionary, understands how the new electronic age will transform teaching and learning, how students can be in touch with networks of knowledge all around the world and yet, in the Empire State tradition, mentors will have a crucial role to play to assure that students sort out the trivial from the consequential and move from information to knowledge and, ultimately, to wisdom.

It is truly remarkable that Empire State College, in its twenty-five-year history, has had just one president to give it shape and policy direction and constancy. And I am more grateful than I can ever say that Jim Hall has been that leader. I have unrestrained admiration for what he has accomplished and I am absolutely confident that no one in America could have built so solidly and so brilliantly this new college which has, during the past quarter century, emerged as one of the world's most distinctive and most prestigious institutions.

I find it curious that, after all these years, most of higher learning still remains more imitative than creative. More independent study programs have emerged and adults are coming back to college in large numbers, but still there remains an inclination for campuses to give out credits like "green stamps."

I am convinced, however, that the twenty-first century will bring a sea of change to higher education. Through technology, students increasingly will be able to direct their own learning, accomplishments in education will be measured in terms of knowledge acquired, not time served. In the end, the success of learning will be based upon the empowerment of each student.

And Empire College will have helped lead the way.

Ernest L. Boyer, President
Carnegie Foundation for the
Advancement of Learning

Years ago, so long ago I can't remember precisely, I said to James W. Hall, founding president of Empire State College, "Someone should write a book about the College." In 1990, I became the College historian and archivist. The book followed. But first I spent a number of years conducting an oral history project because I was concerned that the College might lose much of its history, which is unique and worth telling. I interviewed pioneer faculty and administrators as well as a number of State University of New York (SUNY) System administrators, including former SUNY Chancellor Ernest L. Boyer, whose first major act in office was to initiate the planning for what became Empire State College. The oral history transcripts, including materials found in the Empire State College Archives, among them many reports prepared by the Empire State College Office of Research and Evaluation, established the factual basis for this history.

This book was written mainly for the Empire State College community, present and future. The curious reader and those interested in nontraditional education might find value in some of the things recounted here about a college that is unique to American higher education. Although I did my best to reflect the richness of the programs the College created over the past two and a half decades, I was neither able to discuss the majority of them in great detail, nor was I able to recount the unique history of each learning center. But this book, which is the first history of Empire State College, I hope, has broken ground for subsequent works.

The book has a factual texture, deliberately so. I wanted to capture the spirit of Empire State College, especially the early years—the personalities, the passion of beliefs played out in various fora, the substantiality of what was accomplished—and to do this in large measure through the voices of the people who brought this College into being. They speak to future generations, and I hope, in this remembrance, that they will encourage those who follow to sustain the commitment to the principles that informed the existence and gave special purpose to professional lives of the founders and pioneers of Empire State College.

This story is more biography than institutional history. I say that because the College has a palpable being—a personality. I am amazed, always, whether we gather in small groups for College-wide governance or for the annual All-College Conference, which brings together faculty, professional personnel, administrators, clerical staff, and students from the disparate parts of New York State, how close we are, how bound we are by the values we share about Empire State College. It is not that we agree on everything. In fact, you will see that we have disagreed heartily, at times. But we all have, which I believe explains our unity and success, a unique commitment to students despite the variety of programs and the vast distances that separate us. For this reason, Empire State College, though undergoing many programmatic changes this past quarter of a century, is essentially the same institution. It is so because the College has made a student-centered approach to learning a priority in all its undertakings. It might sound trite but it is true.

Preface

Acknowledgments

I am indebted to many individuals who made this undertaking possible. I owe special thanks to Dr. Ronald Grele, director of the Columbia University Oral History Research Office, for his sound guidance in organizing the Empire State College Oral History Project and for his advice about interviewing techniques. The interviews provide much of the substance of this book. I am indebted to the following participants in the ongoing oral history project: Kenneth Abrams, Loren Baritz, Robert Barylski, Ernest L. Boyer, George Bragle, Arthur Chickering, F. Thomas Clark, Ronald Corwin, Forest Davis, William Dodge, Jane Dahlberg, George Drury, Peter Gilbert, Joseph Goldberg, James W. Hall, John Jacobson, Timothy Lehmann, Sanford Levine, John Mather, Albert Serling, and Harry Spindler. In many respects they are my coauthors.

I very much appreciate the support of my fellow historians at Empire State College who encouraged me to launch the oral history project and to break this new ground in my professional development; they include Nicholas Cushner, Tomasz Grunfeld, Hugh Hammett, Helen Hopper, Robert MacCameron, Frank Rader, Robert Seidel, Steven Tischler, and Wayne Willis.

Arthur E. Imperatore merits special thanks for providing the endowment to the Empire State College Foundation which made the oral history project possible. I am proud to be included among Empire State College faculty who have received the Foundation's Imperatore Community Forum Scholar award.

I am greatly indebted to the Empire State College Foundation, which supported the publication of this work.

I wish to thank, also, Carolyn Broadaway, Nancy Bunch, Jean Carpenter, Thomas Dehner, David Elliott, Daniel Granger, Larry Greenberg, Douglas Johnstone, Curt King, Elizabeth Lawrence, Rita Kelly, Barbara Marantz, Kathy McCullagh, Thomas Rocco, and Evelyn Ting. They were kind enough to respond quickly to my inquiries, mostly by electronic mail. Many of their responses, and fittingly so, dealt with the section on technology.

Special thanks go to Jane Altes, vice president for academic affairs, for forwarding documents of historic import to me and for her words of encouragement; to William Ferrero, vice president for administration, and to Dennis Belt, assistant vice president for budget and finance, for creating two graphs on the College's budget, and for helping me to gather information on the history of the budget; to Sharon Grigsby, alumna and assistant for student affairs at the Genesee Valley Center, for sending historic documents and photographs to the College Archives; to Keith Elkins, an early mentor at the Niagara Frontier Learning Center, for sending archival materials he had collected while a member of the Pierce Society; to Robert Barylski, founding mentor at the Genesee Valley Learning Center for sharing his sketches depicting issues of the early days of the College; and to Rhoada Wald, founding mentor of the Long Island Regional Learning Center, for sharing her research on mentoring.

I owe a special debt to the former staff members of the Office of Research and Evaluation. Although the ORE no longer exists, the studies they produced offer a treasury of historical information. The staff included Ernest Palola, assistant vice president for research and evaluation; Paul Bradley, director of institutional research and evaluation; Timothy Lehmann, director of program evaluation and subsequently associate vice president for research and evaluation; Jack Lindquist, research associate who became president of Goddard College; and Richard Debus, associate for cost analysis.

My thanks go to former and present colleagues who read parts of the manuscript. They are Joseph Boudreau, George Bragle, Robert Carey, Arthur Chickering,

10

Dennis DeLong, Mary Folliet, Carole Gillmore, Ellen Blake, Robert Hassenger, Douglas Johnstone, Douglas Long, George McClancy, Rhoda Miller, Lois Muzio, Albert Serling, and Julie Smith. I am deeply indebted to Kenneth Abrams, Timothy Lehmann, Hugh Hammett, and Robert Seidel who helped to edit the manuscript, as well as to James W. Hall who read the manuscript in its entirety.

Special thanks go to State University Secretary Martha Downey for locating important documents for the Empire State College Archives, to Ruth Maynard of International Programs for her technical wizardry in preparing various iterations of this volume for circulation among my colleagues, and to Peter Princep, retired South East Region director for the British Open University and sometime consultant and plenipotentiary from the BOU to Empire State College, for his thoughtful advice.

To Monica M. Bonnabeau, I am deeply indebted for her resolute support for a project she greatly subsidized with patience, understanding, and encouragement.

I owe a debt of thanks to Mentor Mel Rosenthal whose many fine photographs helped to illustrate this history of the College.

I should not fail to note my gratitude to President James W. Hall. His foresight in establishing the Office of the College Historian and Archivist and his support for the Empire State College Oral History Project were necessary first steps in getting this book underway.

President Hall deserves much credit for the success of Empire State College. He had a major role in planning it, in getting it off the ground, in helping it to mature organizationally and programmatically, and in guiding it through many crises these past two and a half decades. His genius as a leader has been knowing instinctively where the College should be headed and knowing when and how to nudge people along. Jim has kept us out there, at the cutting edge.

Introduction

This book is about one of the most important experiments in American higher education in the latter part of the twentieth century, Empire State College—State University of New York.

This nontraditional college, created at a time when many other experimental colleges and programs came into existence, survived—indeed flourished—while others perished. To understand Empire State College's success, this book asks the reader to consider many factors, including the unique quality of its educational practices which draw upon the special faculty role created by the founders of Empire State College—the mentor; and the continuity of leadership—the College has had the same president since its founding in 1971.

It is the mentor, working with students individually, who draws upon the resources from each student's community, from the resources of other State University of New York campuses, and from the resources generated by the College through its Center for Distance Learning to plan and execute individual programs of study. It is the mentor as coordinator who administers satellite programs at community colleges or the mentor as entrepreneur who develops programs serving special student populations, ranging from community-based programs for minority students to programs for corporate managers. The combined efforts of hundreds of mentors in community-based or program-based operations or in the large regional learning centers across New York State have made the College as Ernest L. Boyer envisioned it to be, "truly . . . a college of the Empire State."

Empire State College has nurtured an environment that promotes planning at all levels. Beginning in 1972, the College has had a master plan and periodically revises it, incorporating the judgments of the faculty, professional employees, Administrative Council, and College Council. In the 1980s, Hall instituted strategic planning at the center level, connecting it to budget formulations, and in 1994 Hall, sensing a sea change about to take place in the competitive environment faced by Empire State College, brought a team of senior administrators from center to center to lead discussions about how best to position the College for the future. It is this passion for planning conjoined with the unique flexibility of the Empire State College educational model which explains much of the College's programmatic diversity, recounted in great detail in this book, and, of course, its extraordinary success.

The book, which analyzes major themes chronologically, provides a detailed account about the planning for the College by State University of New York Chancellor Ernest L. Boyer and his special task force; the first critical years of the College's existence, marked by aggressive growth, even during a period of contracting state revenues, and marked by the heated struggle over the mission of the College between key figures in the College's central administration; and the extraordinary ability of the Empire State College since its founding to continue to provide sound and meaningful programs of study to students who have no other access to college and graduate level education. The last section examines how the College has made connections with technology and with the corporate world and discusses a host of other critical junctures that have made Empire State College unique to American public education. This section is followed by a chapter providing an overview of first principles and enduring achievements. It is based on a chapter that I coauthored with Hall. It appeared in *Important Lessons from Innovative Colleges and Universities,* edited by V. Ray Cardozier and published by Jossey-Bass in 1993.

Because President Hall had such a key role in the planning of the College and seeing it through its first twenty-five years, I asked him to imagine how Empire State College might evolve over the next quarter-century. And so he has provided his vision of the future, looking back from the year 2021—the year of the fiftieth anniversary.

1970–1971

1

GENESIS

Dr. Ernest L. Boyer (right), then chancellor of the
State University of New York, with Dr. James W. Hall
at President Hall's inauguration. It was held at the
Canfield Casino Museum, Saratoga Springs, New York,
September 5, 1972. In his address, Boyer said,
"Empire State College is . . . built on firm assumptions,
and these assumptions shall endure."

The Epoch: "The Loss of Authority and of Confidence"

Empire State College was established April 1, 1971, less than a year after Ernest L. Boyer became chancellor of the State University of New York (SUNY). This was a moment of great social and political turmoil. It was a time when citizens questioned the legitimacy of every major American institution; an era when colleges and universities found themselves at once a forum for massive protests against the war in Vietnam and under attack by the very people to whom they gave sanctuary. Martin Trow, writing about the embattled university, the theme for the Winter 1970 *Daedalus* edition, observed:

> *The loss of authority and of confidence in that authority is nowhere more evident than in our colleges and universities. The constant attacks on the universities for their "irrelevance," their neglect of students, their "institutional racism," their implication in the war in Vietnam and in the "military-industrial complex" have deeply shaken the belief of many academic men in their own moral and intellectual authority.*[1]

Educators called for major reforms to restore the legitimacy of higher education. Like so many other colleges and radical experiments sponsored by traditional campuses created in the late 1960s and early 1970s, Empire State College sought to bring about meaningful change, to make higher education relevant and accessible. It was this search, courageously undertaken by the founders, administrators, faculty, and staff of Empire State College, that put it, from its inception, on the cutting edge of innovation in American higher education.

Boyer and the Planning Task Force: All Hallows' Eve Reflections

Ernest L. Boyer, long a member of the progressive movement in education, wanted significant reform. Obliged to balance competing demands, he chose to create a new SUNY college to offer alternatives to traditional education rather than try to reform the entire State University system, the largest in the United States. This new institution would be a college to serve both adults and students of traditional college age, including those students from other SUNY campuses who might chose to pursue their degrees in a nontraditional forum.

Perhaps feeling the pressure of rivals seeking funding for nontraditional programs, Boyer moved very quickly after becoming chancellor to devise a plan and to seek external funding. In fact, Alan Pifer, president of the Carnegie Corporation, in the fall of 1970 had recommended creating two kinds of nontraditional, degree-granting universities. Furthermore, Ewald Nyquist, New York State Commissioner of Education, had announced at his inaugural address in September 1970, the possibility of the Regents offering an external degree.[2]

Boyer convened a special two-day planning session of top SUNY System staff, including Merton Ertell, his deputy vice chancellor who became the chief planning officer for the project. The group met October 30 and 31. James W. Hall attended in his capacity as assistant vice chancellor for policy and planning. Boyer already had given a good deal of thought to what a SUNY nontraditional college might look like and even discussed it with his predecessor, Chancellor Samuel Gould. In fact, Boyer and Gould had reviewed a number of options, revisited in the planning session, ranging from the British Open University (BOU) to the tutor/mentor model. Initially, the group discussed the British Open University, a program designed specifically for the adult learner. It was similar to SUNY's State University of the Air but minimized the use of television and focused more on high quality, print-based independent study materials. Although there were a number of aspects about the BOU that caught the attention of the group, the BOU's fixed curriculum and packaged courseware lacked the flexible, student-centered approach to learning that ideologically energized American educational reform in the late 1960s and early 1970s. The BOU, therefore, was not an attractive option for Boyer, although he had decided even before he convened the planning session to have, much like the BOU, "free-standing learning centers all across the state."[3]

Hall "quickly became a very active and valuable participant."[4] In fact, Boyer asked him to draft an outline of the ideas Hall had put forward during the planning session about a tutor/mentor-based model. Hall spent All Hallows' Eve at home preparing the outline. Only one page in length, it contained "some key ideas" of what was to become Empire State College, including the first use of the term "mentor" to define an innovative faculty role.[5]

Merton Ertell immediately formed a SUNY planning task force to flesh out the ideas presented at the retreat.[6] The other members included John Mather, deputy assistant chancellor; William R. Dodge, acting university dean for continuing education; Harry K. Spindler, assistant vice chancellor for finance and management; Gordon A. Christenson, university dean for educational development; Robert W. Spencer, director of master plan development; and Hall. Acting University Counsel Sanford H. Levine served as liaison to the task force. Many of the task force members had participated in the special planning session. The group met on November 3, 1970, just three days after Boyer's planning session. The next day, Ertell submitted to Boyer a proposal for three alternative programs. Because of the crush of time these were roughly sketched outlines and presented without specific recommendations. The three consisted of a SUNY-wide version of the SUNY at Brockport's extended baccalaureate degree in liberal studies, which required students to spend some time on campus; a version of the British Open University; and an extended tutorial program housed mostly on SUNY campuses. Ertell attached Hall's All Hallows' Eve reflections which detailed how the mentor model might work. Ertell observed, "All three models are obviously related. Indeed, they may be only variations on the same theme, and combinations may be both desirable and possible."[7]

Ertell liked the tutor/mentor model, a more flexible program than the Brockport or the British model. In addition, the program could "be centrally administered through a network of collegiate tutorial centers, many of which might be located on a [SUNY] campus. . . . [and] easily extended to adults."[8] It was this more student-centered proposal, incorporating the finer elements of the others, that over time became the focal point of further deliberations.

Artist Kurt Feurherm, a founding mentor of the Genesee Valley Learning Center, with a guest at the Center's open house.

A Visit to the British Open University: "Different as Chalk and Cheese"

The launching of the United Kingdom's British Open University (BOU) offered Chancellor Boyer an opportunity to promote a SUNY nonresidential college. Just a few months before the BOU became operational, Boyer sent four of his staff to England, headed by Ertell, to examine the program more closely. In 1963 British labor leader Harold Wilson had proposed a nontraditional university for adult students as an alternative to the United Kingdom's elitist education.[9] Ertell reported the team's findings to the SUNY Board of Trustees in mid-December.[10] The BOU, although the least interesting of the models presented to Boyer the month before, had over 40,000 applicants, which demonstrated that there was an immense interest in a degree-granting nontraditional alternative, especially for adults. If such demand existed in the United Kingdom, it surely existed in New York, so the thinking went. Moreover, as

17

task force member Harry K. Spindler noted, the United Kingdom was an example of a society willing to gamble on a "huge departure" from traditional education.[11] But the task force still championed a program based on an individualized curriculum, jointly devised by the student and mentor, which veered sharply away from the imposed curriculum of the British Open University. As Lord Perry, the BOU's first vice chancellor put it, the two programs were "as different as chalk and cheese."[12]

Carnegie and Ford: A Race for Funding

Chancellor Boyer moved quickly to capture funding from the Carnegie Corporation and the Ford Foundation. About this time, New York State Education Commissioner Ewald Nyquist was preparing to submit a proposal for an examination-based external degree, one of the two models recommended by Alan Pifer.[13] Boyer needed external funding because of SUNY's deteriorating fiscal situation. It would be difficult for him to go to the SUNY Board of Trustees for approval to launch a new college without major grants. On December 8, 1970, Boyer sent a brief proposal to Carnegie and Ford, requesting $1,830,755 for a period of two years.[14] Less than two weeks after submitting the proposal, Boyer heard from Alan Pifer who encouraged him to begin "on a more modest scale."[15] Boyer agreed.[16] This cleared the way for Ford and Carnegie to give "an earlier and more substantial start" to Regents College.[17] Ford and Carnegie together granted the New York State Education Department $800,000 and the State University of New York $1,000,000.

The Board of Trustees: Unanimous Support

With both Carnegie and Ford moving quickly to award grants of $500,000 each by January, and with the anticipated funding from Governor Rockefeller, Boyer was able to go to the SUNY Board of Trustees on January 27, 1971, to request a resolution to establish "a nonresidential, degree-granting college."[18] The Board meeting was charged with excitement. The State University was "coming out of a discouraging period. For three years, at least, the Board had confronted student unrest and legislative threats to close down campuses because of drugs and riots. So the very fact that an educational innovation had come along was refreshing."[19]

The Board unanimously supported the resolution. It called for an independent college that would "draw upon the resources of the entire university to devise new patterns of independent study and flexible approaches to learning thereby providing accessibility for young people and adults for whom an off-campus individualized instructional pattern will be most effective."[20]

Blueprint: *Prospectus for the New University College*

With the Ford and Carnegie grants in place and the SUNY Board of Trustees resolution in hand, the task force prepared a blueprint for the new college. *Prospectus for the New University College* was ready by February 1971. The *Prospectus* incorporated many of the elements in Hall's mentor/tutor-based model. It outlined the major components of what became Empire State College. No subsequent publication of note in the early history of the College failed to mention the force of its guidance. The *Prospectus* provided the first clear articulation of a college transcending the "constraints of space, place, and time" that would serve "individuals of all ages, throughout society, according to their own life-styles and educational needs."[21]

[The College] will seek to transcend conventional academic structure which imposes required courses, set periods of time, and residential constraints upon the individual student.[22]

[The College] will rely on a process rather than a structure, of education to shape and give it substance as well as purpose. This emphasis will place the central focus upon the individual student learning at his own pace with the guidance and counseling of master teachers.[23]

This process will place the responsibility for learning on the student in return for his freedom to pursue his education according to his individual needs and interests.[24]

Through appropriate counseling and advisement, a program of study will be designed for each student to meet the individual's particular educational objectives, taking into account fully his then current educational experience.[25]

Of particular note was the vision of the flexible use of resources and approaches to learning, ultimately to become the hallmark of Empire State College. To emphasize this openness and to contrast it to the "closed system" of the British Open University, the *Prospectus* italicized the following sentence: *"It [Empire State College] will provide the resources both for structure, if necessary, and for individual creative learning, if desirable."*[26]

The *Prospectus* roughly outlined the College's organization, a series of well defined regional learning centers coordinated by an administrative core. The cloudy musings about service centers on SUNY campuses found in earlier plans were replaced by the concept of a more independent institution with a statewide presence reaching from Long Island to Buffalo. It was to be a college "within reasonable commuting distance of every resident of the state."[27] The regional learning centers would "provide the locus of instruction and . . . provide facilities for advisement, counseling and tutoring, and a communication link to the admissions, records, and testing services of the administrative center."[28] By the third year of operation, the *Prospectus* projected ten thousand full-time equivalent students and much larger numbers in subsequent years. Included in these numbers were students who had been denied access to traditional education because of race, culture, or geography.[29]

The administrative headquarters staff would consist of the president, three vice presidents, a dean for academic programs, a dean for program design, and their supporting personnel. An important component proposed for the administrative center—a parallel to the British Open University—was the program design group, headed by a dean or administrator of equivalent rank, which would comprise what was to be known as the Learning Resources Center. The Center would have a key role, providing "the direction and competence for the future development of the academic program and curriculum . . . and . . . have functional responsibility for curriculum and media development."[30] It would be responsible also for developing and acquiring structured learning resources to support the instructional programs of the regional learning centers.[31] This proposed central role in the development of the academic program, as we shall see, caused immediate friction in the College.

The task force believed that the survival of this unusual College called for an extraordinary faculty. The *Prospectus,* therefore, recommended recruiting individuals who had "excellence in motivating others to learn; integrity of commitment to perceived values; and personal security to face risks of the unknown."[32] In addition to recruiting faculty from traditional disciplines, the *Prospectus* foresaw hiring professionals and paraprofessionals as well as individuals with "other work experiences." Such faculty would be "responsible for students in experiential learning arrangements [internships] . . . in research institutes, industry, museums, etc."[33]

Dr. Arthur Chickering during a pensive moment. As founding academic vice president, Dr. Chickering brought to Empire State College many years of experience in nontraditional education. His book, *Education and Identity,* published in 1969, won the National Book Award from the American Council on Higher Education.

Council of Outside Educators and the Fear of Balkanization

On February 9, 1971, Chancellor Boyer convened a prestigious council of educators to review the *Prospectus.* They spent the day with Boyer, Hall, and other members of the task force. They included Stephen Bailey, director of the Syracuse University Research Corporation and regent of the University of the State of New York; John C. Crandall, vice president of State University College at Brockport; Calvin Lee, vice president of Boston University; Warren Martin of the Center for Research and Development in Higher Education at Berkeley; Dr. Walter Lowen, dean of the School of Advanced Technology at the State University of Binghamton; Dr. Marshall Robinson, the Ford Foundation's vice president and program officer for higher education; and Arthur Chickering, visiting research scholar of the American Council on Education.[34] The council gave the *Prospectus* a "tremendously positive" endorsement: "This is terrific. This is forward-looking. Let's do it. Go ahead. We urge you to do it."[35] There was only one exception. Stephen Bailey of Syracuse University, who later became president of the American Council on Education, said, "Well, I think it's just wonderful, this Statewide institution; and, of course, it should be, with the single exception that you shouldn't do this in Syracuse."[36] Boyer declared, "This will be a statewide institution. There will be no exceptions to it."[37] Boyer's objection was a critical point, and one that Hall kept in mind. He "worked very hard and fast" to make Empire State College "statewide before anybody could Balkanize the College through regional limitations." Boyer faced a similar challenge a year later when the SUNY Faculty Senate "pressed vigorously for the control of Empire State College." Boyer declared "without equivocation, that this was a free standing college within the university system and that no faculty could direct the work of Empire State any more than the faculty at Brockport could control academically the Stony Brook program. The debate ended."[38]

Governor Nelson A. Rockefeller: Enthusiastic

Chancellor Boyer needed Governor Rockefeller's support. Boyer had an excellent relationship with the Governor. Rockefeller, who invested much of his energy in creating a strong public university system, was enthusiastic about the proposal.[39] On March 16, 1971, Rockefeller noted his approval of the Board of Trustees' amendment to include Empire State College in the State University Master Plan. He wrote, "This idea appeals to me very much, and I have included $200,000 for planning the experimental college in my Executive Budget. I do not know how this will fare with the Legislature, but I will do all I can to support the program."[40] At first, the Division of the Budget (DOB) rejected the supplemental funding request. Boyer called upon his deputy assistant John Mather to do the legwork for securing state funds. Mather, a member of the task force, had a major role in developing the grant proposal for Carnegie and Ford; he arranged a meeting with Perry Duryea, Speaker of the Assembly; Will Stevens, Chairman of the Assembly Ways and Means; and Irving Friedman, a staff member. They agreed "in less than 45 minutes" to the amount requested in the supplemental budget. Duryea then worked successfully with Senator Warren Anderson to change the DOB's position.[41]

Naming the College After the Empire State

Finding a suitable name for the College was an interesting challenge for Boyer. The tradition in SUNY was to name a campus after its location. "Here was a college that had no 'place'; it would be everywhere."[42] Because the College would serve all of New York, the Empire State, Boyer settled on a name that New York State had made famous through such bold undertakings as the Erie Canal, linking New York to America's heartland in the early nineteenth century, and the construction of the Empire State Building—a symbol of irrepressible hope during the Great Depression.[43] Boyer's statement about the new college at a press conference on February 16, 1971, held at the Governor's Office in New York City, hinted at a name for the College. Boyer referred to the new nonresidential college as "truly . . . a College of the Empire State."[44] At the next SUNY Board of Trustees meeting, February 24, 1971, the Board officially designated the nonresidential college, "State University of New York Empire State College."[45]

Empire State College: "A Turning Point in Boyer's Tenure"

The press conference was a turning point in Boyer's tenure as chancellor. The announcement of SUNY Empire State College "was front page news all across the state."[46] As Boyer put it, the "new college was a winner with the media. . . . Because of student unrest, every press conference I had was preoccupied with crisis issues. The reporters now wanted to know about the College."[47] For Boyer, "it was like a breath of fresh air. For the first time, I was able to talk about education—about adult learning, about a new way for people to be educated. And that led to other questions. . . . In the midst of a crisis, with Empire State College, suddenly, I was in control. From that event I could talk about education more broadly. It was a lesson I never forgot."[48]

James W. Hall: "Bring this Unusual Institution to Life"

With the grants and state funding secured, the development of the College moved into an operational stage. On April 1, 1971, Boyer appointed planning task force member James W. Hall, then thirty-three, acting director, giving him the responsibility "to bring this unusual institution to life."[49] Hall moved quickly to recruit a nuts-and-bolts planning staff. He wanted "people who had powerful ideas about what was important to change in higher education." Hall believed that "the depth and complexity" of the College mission called for "different major viewpoints" to be brought together "into one institution—for the benefit of the student—so that [Empire State College was not] a single mode institution. . . . a monomodal craft that would have to fly only on that wing."[50] In addition to planning task force member William R. Dodge who had already come on board, Hall recruited Arthur "Chick" Chickering as well as Loren Baritz, a noted SUNY at Albany historian, to serve as key staff to further define the academic mission.

Arthur Chickering: "Eleven Years of Concrete Working Experiences"

Arthur Chickering's enthusiastic contribution to the February meeting had impressed Hall, who "became a very ardent proponent for his potential role in the College."[51] Chickering was an admirable choice. He "had been very much involved all during the 1960s at Goddard College in Plainfield, Vermont, which was an innovative, progressive institution."[52] He directed a federally funded research project on thirteen small American colleges to study the impact of colleges on students and their "influence on attitudes and impact on personality characteristics."[53] His book on the project, *Education and Identity* (1969), won the National Book Award from the American Council on Education. Chickering liked what he saw in the Empire State College *Prospectus:* It "had a lot of . . . principles that . . . were all entirely consistent with [his] experiences at Goddard College and . . . experiences with the Union for Experimenting Colleges and Universities" as well as principles he saw operating at Antioch and Monteith. Chickering's contributions to the February meeting of the council reflected "eleven years of concrete working experiences in institutions and with students."[54] In 1963, he was at Goddard when it "started the first adult degree program in the country, which was a mix of two-week residential experiences and then six months of independent study working with . . . mentors."[55] Goddard had become famous for guided independent study, which students undertook after their freshman year, and student-created degree programs. In the spring of 1971 Chickering began working as a consultant for the College, and on July 1, Boyer appointed him academic vice president.

Loren Baritz: Scholarship and "Brilliant Teaching"

Loren Baritz was a colleague of Hall in the SUNY at Albany history department, where Hall held a joint appointment. Baritz was a respected scholar and a popular

Dr. Loren Baritz (right), provost for instructional resources and subsequently executive vice president, with Dr. John Neumaier, former president of State University College at New Paltz. Neumaier joined the faculty of the Metropolitan Learning Center, located in Manhattan, in 1972.

teacher who used multimedia to enrich his classes. Baritz was "aware of a kind of deadness that had developed" in American college classrooms.[56] He "was really interested in an approach to curriculum that would motivate students to learn . . . much more dynamically." He "was interested in brilliant teaching, using every means at hand. And he . . . saw at Empire State College and also in the [use of] media—print materials and so on—the way to create something more dynamic."[57] Hall anticipated that Baritz as provost for instructional resources would attract nationally recognized scholars to develop independent study modules.[58]

Chickering and Baritz: "The Anvil of the Conflict"

Chickering and Baritz, both strong-willed individuals, soon clashed. But Empire State College "became a stronger institution, because it was hammered out on the anvil of the conflict" between them.[59] Though they differed strongly, their polar opposite views created a wide spectrum of ideas in which Empire State College's mission would flourish ultimately, but not without heated debates that accompanied the interaction between two strongly committed individuals.[60] For Chickering, Empire State College had the potential to be a more refined version of Goddard. The *Prospectus* spoke to "responding to students as individuals." Chickering viewed in such language the invitation to devise an individualized curriculum for each student through contract

Dr. William R. Dodge, a member of Chancellor Boyer's planning task force and founding dean of the Center for Statewide Programs with Dr. Virginia Lester, founding associate dean. Dr. Lester was later named president of Mary Baldwin College. In 1979 Dodge became dean for World University's branch in Miami, Florida, and later Rockland County Community College's vice president for academic affairs.

learning.[61] "He saw, having been at Goddard College where they had this individual contractual model, a way to try that idea but on a much broader scale."[62] Goddard was a private college. Empire State College "was an opportunity in the public sphere, where, too often, education was treated almost as batch processing in a huge . . . university like SUNY."[63] Chickering, "who was very concerned with education as the central tool of human development and growth," recognized the opportunity "to take this idea, this very personal individual approach . . . [and] . . . thereby improve the quality of education." He did not want a "preestablished curriculum," believing that "once you define a curriculum, no matter how creative it is, that becomes the driving force and the individual must be subordinate to it. . . . The individual approach to designing a curriculum was truly revolutionary."[64]

For Baritz, "responding to students as individuals did not mean going beyond meeting their intellectual needs," nor did it mean "constructing individualized curricula."[65] Although Baritz shared with Chickering the mission of creating student-centered alternatives to traditional education, he questioned the readiness of most students to pursue individualized study. Baritz disagreed with Chickering that every "curriculum had to be individually constructed through a contract with an individual student."[66] As Baritz noted, he "didn't know . . . how the student was going to get a general education and not just follow his nose."[67] He brought this concern to overseeing the first "learning contracts that were coming out of the various centers and scribbling little notes to people [mentors] about why they were criminals—doing a bad job."[68] Baritz believed, therefore, that structured independent study modules, often interdisciplinary in organization and designed by "some of the most high powered intellectuals in the country" was the best approach.[69]

Chickering, in opposition, totally rejected the concept of modules. Student purposes were paramount. "He envisioned an evolving individual study program—an individual curriculum as the centerpiece, achieved through planning and goals established for a single student."[70] Moreover, Chickering was fearful of "the forces of regression" that existed in the system. He believed "that they would continually push Empire State in a more and more conservative direction."[71] Chickering, therefore, was "determined to take the institution as far out as possible."[72] "Later this division provoked some misunderstanding of what the mission of the institution was."[73] The conflict worked its way through the fabric of the institution as newly hired faculty, often recruited by either Chickering or Baritz, took sides in the controversy.

The different "major viewpoints" of Chickering and Baritz "explains the depth and complexity of Empire State."[74] But as Chickering and Baritz battled to impose their particular viewpoints on the mission, their discord "created nights [when Hall stared in frustration] at the ceiling trying to figure out how . . . to get this thing to work smoothly."[75] Hall stuck to the original intent of the *Prospectus* as he planned for the September opening of the College: "The mission, clearly from the beginning, was to create alternative models of education other than the classroom, basically the old lecture and seminar method, and to experiment with other models, keeping the student at the center."[76] The individualized curricula did not originate with the task force, but the group established, "in a broader sense, the statements having to do with responding to students as individuals . . . drawing together such educational resources as they might require."[77]

William R. Dodge: "Practical Experience"

William R. Dodge, acting SUNY dean for Continuing Education, was, with Chickering and Baritz, the third of Hall's associates. Dodge had worked for the SUNY

Independent Study Program and was "the only one on [Boyer's task force] . . . who had the practical experience of creating materials and working with the adult learner."[78] He did not, however, push to have the SUNY Independent Study Program incorporated in any major way in the College mission. Although Dodge's program at its peak had enrolled six thousand students, its completion rate was disappointingly poor, less than 25 percent. Students had as long as a year to complete their courses, but they remained isolated from their SUNY tutors who worked on an overload basis and were generally more committed to campus-based students. Dodge thus saw correspondence course materials "as supplemental to a contract but not as the main vehicle" of the alternative education model that Hall had envisioned.[79]

Contract Learning: "Focusing on Learning"

The purpose and design of contract learning, mentioned in the *Prospectus* and intimately connected with the role of the mentor, began to take shape in the early conversations that eventually formed Empire State College's learning process. To Chickering, the term contract learning was much more appealing than the concept of independent study:

Mentor Peter Gilbert (left) joined Empire State College in July of 1971 as assistant for continuing education and then became a founding faculty member of the Center for Statewide Programs. Now retired, Gilbert was one of the first employees of the College.

Governor Nelson Rockefeller's (right) enthusiasm for Chancellor Boyer's proposal to create a nontraditional SUNY college was critical to the early success of Empire State College. He greets Alexander Aldrich at an awards ceremony in the early 1970s. Happy Rockefeller is standing next to the Governor. At the time, Aldrich was the Governor's executive assistant. Now, as coordinator for public policy studies at the Center for Distance Learning, Aldrich brings his many years of experience in public service to mentoring and curricular planning.

There was a lot of variability around independent studies in terms of their degree of rigor, the degree to which they had explicit objectives, the degree to which there was tough-minded evaluation. Often independent study meant . . . a reading list and . . . a paper. We were quite clear that we wanted something that was tougher, that was more rigorous, that would really be in the nature of a binding agreement between the institution and the individual; because this was what the educational program was going to be and the basis of the person's enrollment. So, the language of contracts between the institution and the individual, and the reciprocity there, was appealing, and we were focusing on learning.[80]

Most important, the contract could encompass a whole range of learning activities:

Any kind of instructional material that was organized and appropriate both in complexity and level of learning should be grist for the mill of a contract. . . . All we knew was that there was a lot of learning materials in libraries, in colleges, in universities, at work, in cultural organizations, and in government—a lot of learning materials that could be drawn on, but we had no idea how to go organizing them at that point . . . [The contract] was an organizing structure for marshalling these resources within the community, both academic and social and governmental and cultural.[81]

In summary, the learning contract became the equivalent of a syllabus for individual guided study. It specified the amount of credit, purposes, the learning activities, and the criteria and methods of evaluation. Although a contract could be amended, its binding force and legitimacy were underscored by the signatures of the student, mentor, and associate dean.

The Mentor: "A Flexible Response to Students"

Initially, the mentor role was the subject of much debate. Mentors were presented in the *Prospectus* as an important part of a wide spectrum of Empire State College learning options, but their role as "master teachers" was not fully articulated, neither were their guidance and counseling functions, nor the Socratic dimensions of mentoring. In fact, Hall and his associates were not completely satisfied with the term mentor, because its traditional use was "a little more hierarchical and paternalistic" than they would have preferred. Nevertheless, it had greater merit than the term professor, which had "a didactic dimension, [and] teacher was too general in terms of the range of meanings it had."[82] In the end, mentor was as good as any other term they could conceive of to "signify the special kind of quality of an Empire State faculty member in a special kind of relationship" with students and to indicate a break with the past.[83]

Although a fine sculpting of the mentor role awaited the experience of mentors

interacting with students, "there were some things that [Hall and his associates] knew what they wanted":

> *First, we wanted a relatively egalitarian role. Egalitarian in that . . . two individuals that were coming together whose purpose was to create a series of learning experiences. These would be helpful to the student entering this relationship, and probably the mentor would learn too. We recognized that the faculty member was knowledgeable, was going to be a resource person and ought to have very wide, broad-based expertise—because he or she would be dealing with a wide range of students—rather than great depth in a narrowly defined area. We wanted a person who was very good at listening, who would be skillful in helping people clarify the purposes for their degree programs and their contracts and who would not have a pre-packaged set of objectives or assumptions to impose on students. So they had to have a flexible response to students with very diverse backgrounds. That was important.*[84]

Initially, the absence of a clear definition created "a tendency to want to invite people who were primarily counselors to become mentors." But Hall resisted this, and there "were very angry discussions." He wanted "faculty . . . to put the student in the

Dr. Ernest Boyer with spouse Kathryn Boyer at the reception following President James W. Hall's inauguration in the Canfield Casino. Mrs. Boyer is a graduate of Empire State College and a longtime member of the Empire State College Foundation. In 1994 the Foundation established a bequest society in honor of the Boyers.

center; but they also had to *know something*."[85] The confusion, really a duality or tension, about the role originated in the thinking "of the late sixties about teachers as facilitators, advisors, and counselors."[86] Hall and his associates decided ultimately not to hire people with degrees in counseling, but to seek professionals with "that perspective and those skills, who were [also] really very, very strong in a broad area of subject matter."[87]

Regional Learning Centers: "Administrators and Faculty Worked as a Team"

The suggestion to have a statewide college composed of centers was first mentioned in Merton Ertell's November 4, 1970, memorandum to Chancellor Boyer. The visit to the British Open University strengthened the importance of regional centers. The BOU planners had identified a series of regional learning centers to bring faculty and students in easy reach of one another.[88] This idea appealed to the task force. They had ample evidence of the dismal consequences of isolating students from faculty in the traditional correspondence study programs. Moreover, the statewide presence of SUNY provided a network to establish centers in strategic locations around the state.

The Empire State College centers were planned to accommodate hundreds, rather than thousands, of students to meeting one-to-one with their mentors and tutors. Also, the size of the College centers—each had a core of ten or more mentors and a few administrative officers—was "small enough so that administrators and faculty worked as a team, not in opposition. They would all know each other and then they would know all of the students connected with the center on a fairly personal basis."[89] In effect, this "created . . . a series of organizational modules which fit together into what was actually a large organization, but which operated with a tremendous amount of individual involvement, personal commitment and capability."[90] They were uniquely responsive to their particular community environments.

Center size was "a strong organizational principle" for Chickering because of his research on small colleges and his experience at Goddard, where "a quantum change in the dynamics" among student, faculty, and administration occurred when enrollments dramatically increased.[91] "It was important," Chickering reminisced, "that the faculty be able to sit down together and talk about students and educational programs, understand each other and know each other's students to the extent that students wanted to move from one faculty member to another."[92] This convinced him of the importance of creating units of 250 or 300 students served by "a small core faculty that really would have to work together with administrative leadership"[93] This viewpoint nicely dovetailed the recommendations of the *Prospectus*.

Hall and the others foresaw, at the same time, that the learning centers "would tend to create a culture." They "worried that [centers] might go flying off in all kinds of directions."[94] As much as they wanted the centers to have "a lot of autonomy," they still recognized the importance of creating a "reasonable consistency" among them, so that "the quality of the product, the nature of the product, had to be somewhat similar, within reason."[95] It was important, therefore, to recruit faculty and deans who were committed to "the basic educational principles of the College."[96]

By early summer, the planning neared completion. On July 6, 1971, Hall sent Chancellor Boyer a detailed account of the status of the project. In fact, Hall's tenure was almost over. In June, Boyer requested, however, that Hall continue "providing top leadership during the next thirty days or so."[97] In the July 6 memorandum, Hall reported that he anticipated that the first learning centers, one in Albany and the other in Rochester, would open on October l, 1971. In addition, he noted plans to open other centers in the coming years: Westchester County (January 1972), Rockland (April–June, 1972), Nassau (July 1972) and Suffolk (1973), as well as centers in Syracuse (October 1972), Buffalo (1972–73), and Binghamton (1972–1973).[98]

The Labor Center: "Political Dynamism"

The schedule for opening learning centers, however, was subject to the state's budgetary climate and available funds. The Albany Center would open its doors before the Rochester Center, and a center for labor studies located in Manhattan—not anticipated by Boyer's task force—came into existence with great fanfare in early September 1971. The center, popularly known as the Labor College, became part of Empire State College as a consequence of an elaborate compromise worked out by Harry Van Arsdale Jr., a highly respected and powerful labor leader, Governor Rockefeller, and Chancellor Boyer. Van Arsdale wanted Rockefeller to find some way to create the nation's first accredited college program in industrial and labor relations for trade union membership. Yet Cornell's School of Industrial and Labor Relations (ILR), a SUNY institution, had frustrated the New York City Labor Council with its unwillingness to grant credit for ILR courses offered in New York City.[99]

Rockefeller went to Boyer, who quickly realized that Empire State College could offer a solution. Boyer proposed to Hall that Empire State College accept credits from ILR courses as advanced standing toward associate and baccalaureate degrees in industrial and labor relations.[100] Hall agreed, believing that the program fit the mission of the College. He was unaware of the "political dynamism" behind the request and felt no pressure from Boyer.[101] On September 8, 1971, Hall joined Boyer, Rockefeller, Attorney General Louis Lefkowitz, and others to celebrate the opening of the Labor College in Manhattan, at 130 East Twenty-fifth Street. Harry Van Arsdale Jr., with son Tom, had arranged for a seven-story building, owned by the Electrical Workers Benefit Society, to house the program, for a rent of $1 per year.[102]

In the July 6, 1971, memorandum to Boyer, noting the progress of identifying facilities for the College, Hall moved away from the notion of campus-based access articulated in the *Prospectus*. In Hall's thinking, Empire State College would be at once both a community-based and statewide college. It was a remarkable way to envision the structure of the College. Hall described it in this way:

> *The success of Empire State College is not based upon the reliability of construction schedules or the ability of the Bond market to support ever higher levels of building. Empire State will require relatively modest quarters throughout the state, and will utilize existing structures (shopping centers, church education buildings, schools, public buildings, existing University facilities) in establishing its Learning Access Centers. This eliminates delays in program development, and places the emphasis squarely on the educational objectives of the College.[103]*

Saratoga Springs: A "Divinely Ordained" Location for the Coordinating Center

Chancellor Boyer struggled with the problem of where to locate the College's coordinating center. He did not want Empire State College in Albany, where it could be viewed as the "Chancellor's college" or "overshadowed by SUNY-Albany."[104] Then one day it occurred to him that "Saratoga, a wonderful community, was just up the road. It had a wonderfully important historic name, easy access to an airport, and there was no SUNY campus there. So it seemed to be divinely ordained" as a place to locate

President Joseph Palamountain (left) of Skidmore College with President Hall at the inauguration reception. Palamountain welcomed the arrival of the new college to Saratoga Springs. He made arrangements for Empire State College to lease a number of Skidmore's buildings which had been vacated when Skidmore moved to its new campus north of the city.

Political scientist Dr. Jane Dahlberg, dean as well as a founding mentor of the Metropolitan Center, resigned her post as a dean at Sarah Lawrence to join Empire State College.

experience faculty gained from the first few months of mentoring was critical to the development of the academic program. From this mentors began to develop "a set of principles" to inform the design of "contracts and degree programs." As Chickering saw it, "the most important decision . . . in creating Empire State College . . . was to begin immediately with students and faculty."[131]

That is totally contrary to what one might expect. . . . But I [Chickering] had watched other institutions, e.g., Hampshire College and Evergreen State, spend two years planning. And they'd bring together some dynamite faculty and administrators. The problem was that once they got in business with students, they were so wedded to those forms they'd created that it was very hard to change those in response to their experiences with the students. So, we chose to take our chances and get going and create the institution. . . . At one level it was an expression of the fundamental philosophy of the institution, to pay attention to the students and be responsive to them, but it also programmatically was a wonderful way to create a new institution.[132]

A pioneer mentor, Jane Dahlberg, who had resigned from Sarah Lawrence to join the Metropolitan Center, illustrates Chickering's point:

My very first student, a young man, walked in. He had read about Empire State College. He'd gone to the University of Chicago and was missing one credit because he would not take ROTC. He had, then, travelled around the world and was writing a book. . . . MacMillan had given him an advance on the book and Columbia [University] had accepted him for his doctorate, but he needed one credit [to complete the baccalaureate degree]. We had no idea at the time how to do prior learning [assessment]. . . . And so I asked him if he would take a Graduate Record Exam. He said, "I'll take four subjects as well." And he got 100 in all four subjects. Then I said, "We certainly could give him a degree." And then [Mentor Joseph Goldberg and I] talked, "Well no, it's not our degree. He has to do something for us." We didn't have 32 credits [as a residency requirement]. . . . We hadn't formulated that. . . . So, I drew up a contract for him.[133]

Mentor Dahlberg's experience with degree program planning demonstrates the interaction of a seasoned academic mentoring a mature student and the pragmatic approach to developing procedures in the first few months of the College's existence:

The first degree program I did—again, I didn't know what I was doing—was for one of the labor students. . . . She brought me all the certificates for subjects she had studied. . . . I took them home and spread them out in my study, all over the floor and desk. I put them all together eventually and decided that this batch of certificates—adding up the hours and asking her what she read and she had done and so forth—equalled a certain amount of credits. And that was the first portfolio. . . . We didn't have a committee. There were only the two of us. . . . I sent that up to Saratoga, and Arthur Chickering . . . said, "This is very good. This is the way we're going to do it. Let's try to follow this format." So we started.[134]

Retrospect and Prospect

From these experiences and that of other mentors, the College moved quickly to bring the academic program into focus. By early 1972, Chickering gathered a number of task force committees, composed of faculty and administrators, to forge their experiences into procedures and policies. Experience, however, was a difficult, and uncertain path. As we shall see, Empire State College did not travel the quixotic and, ultimately, fatal path taken by other nontraditional colleges and programs which had been created in the 1960s and 1970s. Many were radical departures which became bereft of any good standard of pedagogy and either failed to attract new students or, if anchored in traditional campuses, fatally alienated their powerful hosts. Rather,

Empire State College moved along a less traveled path, a conservative direction, that addressed as much the importance of academic quality as it did developing meaningful alternatives to traditional education.

Launching the College was, in the end, the gamble that ultimately paid off. As Boyer put it, "The odds were hugely against this strange new institution."[135] As if to underscore the metaphor and the risks involved, Hall was inaugurated president at the historic Canfield Casino Museum in Saratoga Springs on September 5, 1972.

Carmen Cornute (center), one of the first students, meets College Council Chair Elliott Goodwin at the inauguration reception. Goodwin served as chair for ten years. Ronald Corwin, founding dean of the Long Island Center, stands next to her. Corwin is currently the vice president of the American Stock Exchange.

Striving for Consensus

Empire State College began enrolling students while it was constructing an academic program, somewhat akin to laying track fast enough to stay ahead of the locomotive. The College had scant time to experiment, indeed it had little time to waste because it had to devise quickly a program that at once would satisfy students and, just as critical, accrediting agencies. This task would be difficult enough for a college existing as a solitary campus. But Empire State College was spread across New York State. Some learning centers were separated from each other and the coordinating center by hundreds of miles. The College even had a unit on the other side of the Atlantic. The potential was great that the academic program would fragment in all sorts of pieces as each center implemented its own interpretation of the College mission. It was especially critical, therefore, in the first months of the College's existence that faculty and administrators agree about fundamentals of good mentoring practice and its administrative supports. While the *Prospectus* provided a blueprint, it was just a sketch of what the College might become. The *Prospectus* and the euphoria of undertaking a pioneering venture in public education were necessary for launching the College. But by themselves they could not hold the enterprise together for long.

The September 1971 Inaugural Workshop, held at the Institute of Man and Science in Rensselaerville for pioneer faculty and administrators, was just the beginning of a process of attempting to reach consensus. There was no guarantee that faculty would not reject the administration's interpretation and propose a more radical vision. The strong reaction to the emphasis on learning modules was surely an indication of a faculty at odds with elements of the blueprints presented at the Inaugural Workshop. The atmosphere in the nation and in higher education, as well, was charged with the fervor and energy of high-spirited individuals who believed in the need to rescue people from the institutional tyranny of batch processing and warehousing, whether it be the tyranny of government, asylums, or universities. Empire State College drew such individuals to its faculty, and they were innately suspicious of plans presented ex cathedra.

In fact, just a few months after the Inaugural Workshop, an Albany Learning Center faculty member issued a call to the College community that a new college be created. The "tormented mentor," as he characterized himself, invited students and faculty to meet on December 14, 1971, to "deschool our school . . . for the creation of the college, for seizing a rare time in the life of this college for preventing it from becoming the drab, unimaginative environment that we cannot live and work in."[1] He called for an immediate moratorium on a host of activities until a new college was created, including such things as hiring new faculty, admitting new students, instituting any policies regarding tuition, degrees, and evaluation of credit for prior learning. He wanted a moratorium on anything that was "not at least in part or in spirit originated in the student and faculty sector of the College," including attending "command performances (hastily called and obviously set up to give the appearance of democratic agreement to administrative whim)."[2] Also, he called for eliminating "*all imposed* review" of learning programs.[3] Underscoring the newness of the College and the potential to recreate itself, the mentor requested participants to bring furniture to Room DO-16, which had been stripped bare by previous occupants.[4] Nothing radical emerged from the proposal, nor the meeting, but it did indicate the College faced faculty dissent.

Task Force Committees: "Starting Points, Not Ultimatums"

Chickering continued to move quickly in building consensus on the academic program. The Inaugural Workshop was the first step. Yet he and President Hall recognized that agreements had to emerge from the faculty's experience, albeit brief, of working with students, as Chickering noted, in "face-to-face contact." Consensus and the policies and procedures that would flow from it had to be constructed by faculty and administrators working together.[5]

In February 1972, Chickering established two College-wide committees, composed of faculty and administrators, to hammer out statements about these issues. Unlike the Inaugural Workshop, where faculty received the wisdom of consultants, each committee had a strong faculty voice, and faculty now spoke from the experience of working with students. Mentors and administrators could at this point begin to codify what constituted good practice. To underscore the power of the committees, Chickering referred to each as a task force. They were the Task Force on Contracts, Records, and Transcripts and the Task Force on Assessing Prior Learning. The "tormented mentor" from the Albany Center joined other faculty in the Task Force on Contracts, Records and Transcripts. Chickering chaired both committees and wrote the report on Learning Contracts, Records, and Transcripts. He stated, "I want to emphasize that these recommendations are starting points, not ultimatums."[6] Nevertheless, Chickering's report included directions for students, and by inference mentors, on how to write contracts and the forms to use. It read more like a directive than a letter.

Task Force on Learning Contracts, Records, and Transcripts: "The Months of Groping . . . Were Over"

The task force called for sharply delineated learning contracts and their digests and evaluations—narrative evaluations which served as part of student transcripts. The months of groping for a systematic way to plan and record learning were over. Mentors now knew in a structured outline what was expected. Learning contracts had to include "a brief description of the student's long-range plans, aspirations, or interests; . . . the specific purposes to be served by that particular Contract; . . . the readings, writings, tutors, courses, outside agencies and other learning activities and resources to be used; and the arrangements for evaluation . . . set in a time framework which indicates general sequence."[7]

Chickering fully expected that students would write their own contracts "after the first [one] or two."[8] Although this practice fell by the wayside as mentors succumbed to the pressure to produce well-written contracts in a timely manner, the structure of learning contracts has remained essentially the same: topic of study, learning activities, and means of evaluation. The document for the evaluation of learning contracts— digest and evaluation—had to be a narrative with three major components: purposes, major learning activities, and evaluation. It would be essentially the learning contract rendered in the past tense. In 1996, these components are topics of study and evaluation. The digest and evaluation had to include evidence to support the recommendation for credit, including reports from tutors, supervisors, grades for courses taken at other colleges, and evaluative commentary for written assignments or for other activities. "The student's performance is evaluated in relation to his own purposes and in relation to the College objectives which are pertinent to the particular activities undertaken, or to the processes by which they were pursued."[9]

One remarkable practice regarding evaluations was the omission of failures in the student's permanent academic record. Only successes were recorded for public consumption. Records of incomplete contracts or outright failures were for internal use only, for the mentor to keep note of a student's progress and to plan subsequent satellites as well as specialized programs. Together they served almost three thousand students. The number of locations and students for such a young college was remarkable. In the process of growth, the College began serving a large number of labor and community organizations.

The Long Island Center, for example, made a "special effort to relate closely with agencies and industry, utilizing their intern and apprentice programs, laboratories, specialized libraries, and other facilities for meetings and office space."[44] The Long Island Center established programs with the Suffolk County government, the Creedmor and Central Islip state hospitals, Head Start in Hempstead, and the Clearwater Drug Rehabilitation Program. The Rochester Learning Center, later to be known as the Genesee Valley Learning Center, established a program at Attica prison, a New York State Correctional facility that had been just a few years earlier the site of one of the country's worst prison riots. The program, which had a mentor on site one day a week, served both inmates and prison employees. Programs serving correctional facilities were established also by centers in other parts of the state.[45]

Making connections with other colleges, both public and private, was another notable accomplishment. Many State University faculty served as tutors, and a number of faculty joined the College on a temporary basis, on terms ranging from three months to a year. Some enjoyed the experience so much that they became permanent members of the Empire State College faculty. SUNY colleges made their libraries available to Empire State College students and hundreds of Empire State College students cross-registered at other SUNY campuses. The ability to do so was especially important to students who needed to qualify for certification in programs not available through the College. SUNY campuses, such as Suffolk Community College, State University College at Old Westbury, State University College at Buffalo, and State University College at Plattsburgh, made facilities available for Empire State College programs. Private colleges were supportive as well, providing many excellent tutors from their faculties.[46]

In the spring of 1973, the College separated the labor program from the Metropolitan Center and created the Center for Labor Studies. This permitted more effective administration of the labor program. As a fully-constituted center, with a dean and associate dean as well as a separate faculty, including faculty from Cornell's Industrial Labor Relations program, the Center for Labor Studies, which offered classroom-based instruction, could focus its attention on the needs of students from powerful union constituencies.[47] The Center increased its enrollments quickly and expanded its instructional sites from downtown Manhattan to the World Trade Center II and to Hicksville, Long Island.[48] This change also made it possible for the Metropolitan Center to focus on contract-learning programs, both for individual students and students participating in agency-based or similar outreach programs.[49] In fact, thanks to a 1975 Carnegie grant, the center established a satellite program in Bedford-Stuyvesant, at the Commercial Center Complex of the Bedford-Stuyvesant Restoration Corporation and its partner, D & S Corporation, a nonprofit organization devoted to developing "the leadership and management skills of area residents."[50] The program attracted employed minority women, mostly African-Americans between the ages of twenty-four and forty, who pursued degrees mostly in business, community and social services, and the social sciences. A study by the Empire State College Office of Research and Evaluation indicated that the students "rated themselves higher than other ESC students [their age] in leadership abilities and drive to achieve."[51] Today, the Bedford-Stuyvesant satellite remains an excellent example of the ability of regional learning centers to bring Empire State College to local communities. Bedford-

Stuyvesant recently celebrated its twentieth anniversary.

The Urban Studies Center, another program that strengthened the College's presence in New York City, was part of the Center for Statewide Programs, formerly the Division for Statewide Programs. Its faculty were dispersed among satellite programs throughout the state, including Manhattan and rural regions. Statewide's headquarters were in Saratoga Springs but separate from the central administration. The programs in New York City were expressly designed to take students out of State University classrooms and to expose them to the cultural resources unique to the City. "Religion and the City," coordinated by Robert Carey, drew "specifically on the rich mix of religious communities and traditions." This program quickly evolved to include Empire State College students, mostly Hispanics and African-Americans, preparing for the ministry by earning degrees in community and human services as well as in urban studies with Carey and Mentors Shelly Halpern and Beverly Smirni. As the program developed many students came from the New York Theological Seminary and the Institute of Theology at the Cathedral of St. John the Divine. The word spread that here was a State University program where one could complete a religious studies major. Eventually, closer working ties were established both with the Institute of Theology and New York Seminary. With the latter, Carey, and others in the program obtained a grant from the Eli Lilly Foundation. This created a series of support programs for New York Seminary students who enrolled in the Urban Studies program to complete their degrees.[52]

"Art and the City," coordinated by Sumner Hayward, focused on the performing arts. A key and initial feature of this program was to serve students from SUNY campuses, scattered about rural New York, who wished to live and learn in the city. Eventually, as in the instance of "Religion and the City," participants included matriculated students pursuing associate and baccalaureate degrees through Empire State College.[53]

In time, other programs making special use of New York City's unique cultural resources followed. In the visual arts, New York had become the "international center of the contemporary art world," where the presence of so many distinguished artists, critics, dealers and collectors "provided extraordinary opportunities for learning experiences of the highest order."[54] Mentor Irving Kriesberg, with the support of the National Endowment for the Arts, initiated a studio arts program in cooperation with the Council on the Art Department Chairpersons of SUNY and the University-wide Committee on the Arts. The program made it possible for advanced undergraduate art students from all over the State University to study painting and sculpture at the Wesbeth studios in lower Manhattan. Students worked at the studios under the guidance of the program coordinator with distinguished visiting artists and critics. All students attended weekly seminars in Greenwich Village, SoHo, and at colleges in New York City to discuss a host of topics related to the world of art and their career interests. Students also had the opportunity to have apprenticeships with distinguished artists.

George McClancy, who has coordinated the program since 1976, increased the fields of study to include graphic design, photography, filmmaking, critical theory, and philosophy. Under his leadership the program has increasingly attracted graduate students, both from SUNY and from "universities around the country and . . . all over the world."[55] As one might expect, many of the students have become distinguished artists themselves. In 1996, the Studio Program continues to be one of Empire State College's stellar accomplishments.

Dr. Robert Carey, a founding faculty member of the Center for Statewide Programs, coordinated the "Religion in the City" program. He subsequently became a mentor at the Metropolitan Center and, for a time, associate dean. Photograph by Lloyd C. Woodcock Photographers.

Other programs begun by the College in its first years, and no less exciting for their significance and accomplishments, included "Media and Communications in the City," the latter coordinated by former London satellite chief Kenneth Abrams. Most of the students were already employed in various fields of the communications industry: film, radio, television, journalism, and professional writing. Earning a degree through Empire State College, which often incorporated advanced standing credit for experiential learning, helped graduates to hold on to their jobs, further career goals, and gain recognition for their professional achievements. Among the graduates are a well-known movie producer, a famous dancer who became a dance critic, and a number of teachers who had lacked bachelor's degrees and were now able to keep their teaching positions in New York City colleges.[56]

The Plattsburgh satellite, established in the latter part of 1972, was Statewide's first program serving rural New York. "For the first time the University with this form of teaching and learning could get into areas where it had not been, the more rural, inaccessible kinds of places."[57] Dean Dodge arranged for office space at the State University at Plattsburgh campus. The coordinator, Scheffel Pierce, was on leave from Plattsburgh. Pierce developed a program that employed faculty from his college as tutors as well as faculty from Clinton Community College, North Country Community College, and qualified tutors from the community. Loren Baritz was a strong advocate for the creation of the Center of Statewide Programs. He provided Learning Resources Center faculty, who were "heavily involved in orientation sessions for new students as well as tutors."[58] The Learning Resources faculty provided instructional support and served on faculty assessment committees for Plattsburgh students. Not surprisingly, learning modules were a featured part of educational delivery. In fact, faculty in remote satellites tended to be heavier users of learning modules than faculty in regional centers. In time, satellites were added in Binghamton, New Paltz, Saratoga, Syracuse, Utica, Westchester, and Watertown. By mid-year 1975 the Center had the second highest enrollments in the College.

Of special note in this period of robust growth was the Albany Center's program, launched in 1973, to provide degrees for employees of Eleanor Roosevelt Developmental Services (ERDS). Headquartered in Schenectady and serving five upstate counties, ERDS was an innovative program launched by the Department of Mental Hygiene in the mid-1960s to serve people with developmental disabilities. Under the direction Canadian psychiatrist Hugh LaFave, ERDS returned hundreds of individuals from huge state facilities to live as close to normal lives as possible in their own communities. Among their numbers were severely disabled children and adults whose parents had been persuaded by mental health professionals to commit them to state hospitals.

LaFave, a pioneer and nationally prominent leader in his field, had recruited an energetic and idealistic staff, though many lacked sufficient educational credentials to satisfy New York State Civil Service requirements for permanency. Wanting staff who reflected the communities of ERDS's clients in terms of class, gender, and race, LaFave had hired many women and African- Americans. But they lacked college degrees, and, at times, even high school diplomas. For LaFave, Empire State College was the solution to satisfying the New York State Civil Service, keeping his employees, and enhancing their professional development. ERDS employees could receive credit for experiential learning and pursue their degrees while they continued to work. To encourage them, LaFave persuaded the Department of Mental Hygiene to give employees time for time. That is, for every hour they worked on their education, employees were given an hour off from work. For these students, the Albany Learning Center had become a pathway to professional advancement. A number of ERDS employees went on to earn master's degrees and doctorates. The partnership with the Albany Learning Center was central to the success of Eleanor Roosevelt Developmental Services.

One cannot help but note the parallels between Empire State College and Eleanor Roosevelt Developmental Services. Both pioneer organizations in their respective fields, they were staffed by idealists who broke from traditional practices to find ways to treat people as individuals.

Of the programs the College launched in 1973, the New Models for Careers was exceptional for being completely based on external funding. It demonstrated how much national attention the College had acquired. This program, initiated with a $500,000 three-year Kellogg Foundation grant, developed models in four broadly defined career areas: business, allied health, engineering technology, and human services. Essentially, the program aimed at connecting the career plans and prior work-related learning of students "with the larger social, cultural, and intellectual interest which can then provide the basis for an expanded range of exploration and

Dr. Sig Synnesvedt (right of center) founding dean of the Niagara Frontier Learning Center with Loren Baritz (extreme left) and guests at the Center's open house in 1974. Dean Synnesvedt came to Empire State College from the State University College at Brockport, where he chaired the Department of History from 1968 to 1974.

learning."[59] In doing so, students were expected to "take charge of their own career development and life with greater confidence and self-assurance."[60] Headquartered on the campus of Rockland Community College in Suffern, the program coordinated its activities with two-year programs. It cooperated also with employers and unions in the region.[61]

New Models attracted slightly older students than the other Empire State College programs. Students tended to be married, had children, often held supervisory positions, found appealing the ability to earn a college degree while employed, and had the equivalent of associate degrees through their work-related learning. Their objectives about attending college, however, did not differ from other Empire State College students: "They enrolled to learn, to meet requirements for graduate school or for various job oriented reasons."[62] Students reported a "perceived growth in areas of intellectual competence and personal development."[63] In 1975, the College joined New Models, headquartered in Suffern, with other units in the Hudson Valley—Purchase, Yorktown Heights, and Middletown—to create the Lower Hudson Learning Center. Mary Ann Biller, who had been appointed associate dean of the New Models for Career Program the year before, became dean of the new center. Faculty members were Nancy Bunch, Jay Gilbert, Rhoda Miller, and Lois Muzio.[64]

The Buffalo Learning Center, later the Niagara Frontier Regional Learning Center, was one of the last centers created in the College's formative years. Located in office space provided by the State University College at Buffalo, the Center opened its doors in the fall of 1974. Sig Synnesvedt was the founding dean. In 1971, E. K. Fretwell, then president of the State University College at Buffalo, had informed Chancellor Boyer of his institution's intention to develop a regional center that would "carry on the mission of Empire State College in the Buffalo Region" and his wish to cooperate with Empire State College in carrying this out. Fretwell wanted it to be a State University College at Buffalo program, not an Empire State College program.[65] Boyer's response made it clear, however, that the initiative for planning the learning center should come from President Hall. Boyer requested that Fretwell meet with Hall to see how State University College at Buffalo could contribute to the undertaking. This prevented the Empire State College option from being foreclosed, a step that may have been a warning to other SUNY presidents about where SUNY nontraditional education initiatives should originate.[66]

The Buffalo Learning Center, whose name was changed to the Niagara Frontier Learning Center in 1975 to reflect its regional presence, was shaped by the experience of the Rochester Learning Center. John Jacobson, the Rochester dean, had worked with President Hall in planning the center. Rochester faculty, including Robert Hassenger, Allan DeLoach, and Reuben Garner, and support staff member Sally Spencer were founding members of the Niagara Frontier staff. In the first year of operation, the Center focused its energies on Buffalo, including a special outreach program to the sizeable Hispanic community of the city begun by Richard Bonnabeau and continued by Nicholas Cushner, and on developing successful administrative operations. Dean Synnesvedt, however, began discussing with the faculty plans for expansion in the spring of 1975. In fact, President Hall had considered a number of possible outposts in the region, among them Jamestown, Fredonia, Dunkirk, and Niagara Falls. He was especially interested in establishing sites at community colleges. Empire State College's ability to provide baccalaureate programs to community college graduates was a remarkable example of how an innovative college could serve the unique needs of working adults within their own communities.[67]

Mentoring: "My El Dorado"

Who were the faculty drawn to Empire State College? Why did they come? What did they expect to accomplish? A report on mentoring produced by the Office of Research and Evaluation, based in large extent on surveys conducted in 1973 and 1974, revealed much about who mentors were and their motives. It showed much also about the emerging nature of this new faculty role in public higher education.

The average age of mentors was forty and 33 percent were women, 7 percent higher than national figures. Full-time mentors carried an average of seventeen full-time and thirteen part-time students; on average mentors had worked 3.9 years at other colleges and universities, 1.8 years in other educational institutions such as the State Education Department; and 4.5 years in other fields such as business. A significant percentage, 35 percent, had experience as college administrators; 15 percent had held nonteaching research positions at universities; 12 percent had been faculty in nontraditional programs; and almost 60 percent had doctorates or the equivalent, a percentage much higher than the national average for four-year colleges.[68]

Mentors interviewed in 1973 had identified three primary factors which drew them to the College: "the flexible program, the chance to work more closely with students, and the opportunity to try something new."[69] The 1974 survey supported these findings: Over 55 percent of the mentors identified three statements as being "very important" in their decision to come to Empire State College: "the

Buffalo Mayor Stanley Makowski (seated) signs a proclamation designating January 17–23, 1977 as "Empire State College Week." Dr. Robert Hassenger, acting dean of the Niagara Frontier Learning Center, stands left of the mayor. Immediately behind Hassenger is Dr. Robert MacCameron, who stands next to Dr. Nicholas Cusher (center).

interdisciplinary curricular focus, [the] nature of the academic program (flexible location, scheduling, mode of instruction), and [the] educational philosophy of ESC."[70] Another very important reason for coming to Empire State College, quite striking for the high percentage (67 percent) of respondents, was "the dissatisfaction with traditional degree programs."[71] Among the personal goals receiving high percentages were: "to have more direct, personal, individual contact with students" (97 percent), "learn to work with adult, mature, experienced students" (76 percent), "learn to work better with a variety of learning resources within and outside of the College" (84 percent), "learn to work better with students outside my discipline" (70 percent), and "to help develop a new educational concept" (95 percent).[72]

Although the Office of Research and Evaluation reported that there was no "typical" day in the life of a mentor, it did find patterns of activities common to almost all mentors and time estimates for carrying them out: One hour or more for paperwork (writing learning contracts and digests and evaluations, completing forms to track the academic progress of students, preparing degree programs, writing correspondence, etc.); one hour for College committee work; one hour for telephone calls to students or related calls; one to three hours for meetings at the center, group studies, and/or contacts outside the center; and four hours of meetings with individual students, usually of one or more hours in duration. Some mentors grouped activities such as reserving specific days of the week for paperwork or professional development.[73]

Here is how one mentor described his day:

I like to come in early (about eight) and try to spend my first hour or so catching up on my paperwork. I find I can handle about four students a day and try to get one at nine, one at eleven, one at two and one at four. Of course, on Tuesday we have faculty meetings so I am lucky to see any students then. I try to keep my evenings free for my family but a few students can only come in then so it seems that at least one evening a week is spent here too. The rest of my work comes in small swatches and I use it for contacting tutors, talking with colleagues, reading mail: the whole schmear.[74]

The routine masked anxiety about the "several unfamiliar and nonstandard jobs" that had to be learned. The Office of Research and Evaluation quoted one mentor who said, "We must tackle many chores that we know virtually nothing about."[75] Most mentors had spent years pursuing a specific discipline; they were not trained to counsel and advise students, to design degree programs in a multitude of areas of study, to hire and evaluate tutors, to hire expert evaluators for credit by evaluation, to manage a bank of students and the attendant mountain of paperwork, to serve on assessment committees, to tutor students in one-to-one formats, and to treat each student as a unique individual. Few mentors had any theoretical appreciation for learning styles and teaching methodologies as they applied to nontraditional and, for that matter, traditional pedagogy. What most mentors knew about teaching came from observing undergraduate and graduate professors and from teaching in traditional colleges—not readily transferable skills. Empire State College faculty, therefore, had to learn about mentoring from experience, and from each other. The helter-skelter newness of the role was the heart of the challenge mentors faced, the root of their anxiety, but the source of great satisfaction when, at last, mastering its complexity. As Mentor George Drury noted, "For a while there's anxiety and wandering around the halls of a center wondering: 'What is this place? Why am I here? What did I do that brought me to this stage?' Then, after a while, there's a certain swagger: 'I want to tell you about this; I just had this great session with my student.'"[76]

Dr. John Hall, founding director of the Admissions Office, later became president of Goddard College.

The 1975 Office of Research and Evaluation report on mentoring indicated that Empire State College faculty "overwhelmingly endorse the concept" of mentoring, and the report provided a number of quotes from faculty who spoke in enthusiastic terms about the meaning of their work with students:

My greatest sense of satisfaction comes from working with a student through his whole program, seeing him graduate, and move into a new job or new responsibilities. It gives me a sense of completion. . . .

ESC students are the best I've ever had. My students are far superior to upper division students at [my former college]. In fact, they are more like graduate than undergraduate students. . . .

My El Dorado is the best part of what I do now: meet one-to-one with students and deal intensively with intellectual matters.[77]

Mentor Workload: "Empire State College Was Not a Gathering for Oxford Dons"

Mentors soon discovered that Empire State College was not a gathering for Oxford dons. The College placed extraordinary demands on its faculty. Mentors soon realized that they were more facilitators than teachers. They needed excellent organizational skills to attend to the needs of thirty to forty-five full- and part-time students. Mentors who did not were at risk when it came to renewal and tenure, no matter how significant their credentials and scholarship.

Mentors therefore complained especially about workload. Although the 1975 ORE mentor report noted that faculty at Empire State College worked about as many hours as faculty at traditional colleges, over 91 percent of the mentors surveyed noted that they worked more than other faculty, and 61 percent expressed dissatisfaction with the workload. Sixteen percent spoke of the mentor role as "nearly impossible" to do.[78] One mentor was quoted as saying:

It's a heavy load. Think about what happens at a center. One day is killed with faculty meetings. Orientation kills half a day a week. If you have thirty students and you're seeing them once every three weeks (which I think is a low average), that is ten to twenty hours a week. Paperwork, which often consumes a half an hour per student visit, also eats up time. There is little time to read and you always feel that you could be doing a better job if you had the time. It's that kind of pressure that is with you for every student you see and this gives the feeling of being overloaded.[79]

Another said:

I think the strain is lack of sustained time on any particular activity. Having thirty different problems is the problem.[80]

The report, however, pointed to mentoring style as one of the possible causes of workload problems. Many mentors, either from preference or from the lack of resources to hire tutors, were the primary tutoring resource for their students. Some mentors made tutoring arduous: "A new mentor would likely interpret what he or she was doing as giving a class one-to-one and be worn out after five appointments, five classes, and wonder how he or she could get to the sixth, seventh, eighth, ninth, and tenth appointments. Often there was the question, "Why can't I get these people into one place, one room, and have it done with?"[81]

Sociologist Joseph Goldberg, a founding mentor of the Metropolitan Regional Learning Center, formally expressed his concerns to the College Assembly during the fall 1973 All-College Meeting:

I think it's unquestionably true that what [President Hall] said the other day. . . . A miracle has come on the face of the educational scene, namely, that a lot of things have happened in a very short time; and I think no one has any illusions about that. . . . I think that what's happened is that this achievement has come at an enormous cost. I don't think it has to be spelled out in detail that the cost has come at a number of levels. I think it's come at the cost of people, occasionally their sense of pride. It's come, at times, at the cost of their sense of what they should be doing with students and what they are not doing with students. It's come at the cost of completing their own work; finishing their doctorates; producing a certain amount of creative work so they remain alive in their own field. It's come at the cost where they're locked into an institution because they won't be able to transfer because they are not cleaning up their own credentials. It's coming at a cost of not living with their own families because they have to give an inordinate amount of time to this institution and it seems to me, it comes at a cost that is particularly cruel, and I want to make this clear; it comes at a cost where most of us are paralyzed into not being able to

Dr. Robert Barylski, a founding faculty member of the Genesee Valley Center, located in Rochester, and later assistant to the academic vice president, takes a break with a fellow mentor from the intensive deliberations of a 1973 All-College Meeting at Mohonk Mountain House. In 1979 Barylski became dean of New College, an innovative campus of the State University of Florida.

criticize it because the people who lead us really work at the same rate. So we're not in a position of saying, like Charlie Chaplin in Modern Times, *that the guy who is pushing the button to make people speed up their work is reading the comics or doing a crossword puzzle. Everybody is working like a dog. . . . I must say I resent deeply and profoundly being put into a position where no matter how much and what form my work takes, it's never enough.*[82]

Goldberg had expressed his concerns to Loren Baritz soon after the founding of the College. In fact, Goldberg led a delegation of faculty from the Metropolitan Center to complain about the workload and its impact on their professional development. Goldberg said to Baritz, "'Loren, we haven't read a book.' He looked at me with his usual wonderful wide-eyed look and said, 'Haven't read a book? I expect you all to write one!'"[83] Baritz, though, became quite concerned: "I thought they were being deprofessionalized . . . because of the incredibly long hours."[84] "They were withdrawing intellectual capital and they weren't adding to it. That was bad enough, but I thought what of five years from now or ten years from now. And then think that these are the guys who are designing learning contracts. I tell you, I just shook in my boots."[85]

Chickering was particularly concerned about the emotional dimensions of the workload problem, the "basic survival burn-out issue."[86] He saw a parallel between mentors and professionals in mental health. From his own experience at Goddard, Chickering knew that mentors "were going to get in emotionally powerful relationships with students; they weren't just going to be academic relationships." The degree program, for example, "is an emotional document and the learning contract is an emotional enterprise when . . . rooted in important purposes to the students."[87]

THE MYSTERY BLOCK

| "PRISTINE" MARBLE | TRUE CREATIVE MINDS AND HANDS ARE INVITED TO HELP DESIGN AND PRODUCE A MASTERPIECE "VERITAS" "EXCELSIOR" | FALL 1971 |

SECLUDED THINK TANK WHERE ARTISTS ASSEMBLED TO CREATE NEW DESIGNS

"LET 100 FLOWERS BLOOM" BUT THIS RESULTED

"COMPOSITE" DESIGN

THEN YEARS OF DISCUSSION AND EXPERIMENTATION ALL BUSILY CREATING ALL CHIPPING AWAY YET, NO MATTER HOW THEY CHIPPED, THE "COMPOSITE" MASTERPIECE CONTINUED TO EMERGE — IT RESISTED ALTERATION

HINDSIGHT

X-RAY VIEW OF "PRISTINE" MARBLE

Mentor Barylski in this 1973 sketch critiques the planning process at Empire State College. Faculty chisel away at a supposedly pure block of marble only to find a statue that had been carved by the administration awaiting them. The idea for the sketch was inspired by a popular toy of that time.

The administration took a number of measures in the early years to reduce the FTE (full-time enrollment) burden. One was to continually negotiate with the SUNY System headquarters the lowering of FTE targets and increasing the amount of accessory instruction funds. These funds allowed mentors to employ more tutors and carry less of the instructional burden. As dean of the Genesee Valley Center, John Jacobson split additional faculty lines into small fractions and created a large number of adjunct faculty. These adjuncts generated a higher FTE per faculty line and made it possible to reduce the burden of full-time faculty.[88] As vice president for academic affairs, Jacobson devised the lunar calendar, which, in effect, produced a thirteenth-month year. This created an extra month, because the College was on a twelve-month academic calendar, for mentors to devote to research and other aspects of professional development.[89] The administration also continued negotiating the FTE target with the SUNY System Administration. By 1996 the target has been reduced significantly, and now, each mentor is able to negotiate the FTE, translated into credits, on an annualized basis, so that it can vary according to shifting demands during the year. Nevertheless, state budget crises in the 1990s, which are likely to continue, have increased pressure to save on instructional costs by increasing faculty workloads throughout the State University.

Mentoring: "Working Together to Solve Problems"

While the strain of learning a new faculty role was great, collegial relations were remarkably good, especially when one considers the diversity of faculty and learning centers. Each center was more like a miniature college than a department, and the focus of the faculty was on mentoring, not research. This diversity fostered cooperation more than competition, as mentors depended on colleagues, specializing in business or literature, social services or science, and a host of other disciplines, for help with their students.

In 1973, the faculty at one center emphasized their collegiality:

There is a feeling of people working together to try to solve problems.

We like each other. We all like all of the other people here . . . [We have] enormous amount of respect for each other.

We just don't have factions, we don't have people with axes to grind, we seem to get along well.[90]

George Drury, a silver-haired philosopher and founding faculty member of the Genesee Valley Center, was recruited from Monteith College by Chickering. To Drury the learning center was one of the College's most important inventions: "For one thing, it is, as it has evolved, an altogether special form of faculty association. The bond is not disciplinary (still less is it "interdisciplinary"!). The bond is not, however, governance only; it is education."[91]

Faculty Dissension: *The Road to Wellville*

Workload was not the only issue noted in the 1975 ORE mentor report. Despite numerous workshops, task force committees, and other activities that brought faculty together from across the College, faculty interviewed in 1973 felt left out of the decision-making process. The geographic isolation of one center from another and from the coordinating center probably contributed to this alienation. The report mentioned a sketch illustrating faculty frustration. Drawn by a Genesee Valley mentor who called it "The Secret Plan," it depicted mentors "chipping away at a rock only to discover a finished statue inside."[92]

A college that demanded so much of a faculty was bound to invite dissension. The faculty had abandoned traditional education to join a radical experiment in public education during an era when many questioned authority; they found themselves constrained by policies, procedures, paperwork, long work hours, and high enrollment expectations, and close oversight by deans and associate deans. There was, also, a sense, first voiced by some faculty at the Inaugural Workshop in Rensselearville, that the blueprint for the College had been already drawn up, first by Chancellor Boyer's task force and then by the founding administrators and their consultants. This seemed to leave little room for faculty contributions. "There were all kinds of things that people wanted. [But] it was clear, by the end of the year, that the way the State University was operating that the president was totally in control of the operation of the institution, and so people who felt that we were going toward a more egalitarian model found themselves in a traditional institution."[93] This was contrary to other innovative programs of the time; many of them were controlled by faculty and students; yet, sadly, most were short-lived but noble "do-your-own-thing" experiments such as Fordham University's Bensalem.[94]

In fact, Empire State College operated for two years without bylaws, lacking the time it took to draft and approve them, which reinforced this sentiment of faculty lacking a voice. Dodge and Hall had bylaws at the outset, but Chickering rejected them, arguing that they would have no legitimacy. Dodge had argued that they could be changed, but at least would provide a foundation. Whether this would have prevented prolonged wrangling is just a matter of conjecture. Bylaws approval, a two-thirds vote by the faculty, professional, and administrative staff and officers, occurred during a College-wide meeting held in 1973 at the Mohonk Mountain House, a Victorian resort in the Catskills.

Mohonk was recently the setting for *The Road to Wellville,* a movie based on T. Coraghessan Boyle's novel about cornflake inventor Dr. John Harvey Kellogg. His turn-of-the-century sanitarium in Battle Creek, Michigan, a health dictatorship for the rich and famous, cured mostly psychosomatic ills, including melancholy, with bizarre treatments, strict diets, and sexual abstinence. Kellogg's sanitarium was "the bastion of right thinking, vegetarianism and self-improvement, citadel of temperance and dress reform, and, not coincidentally, the single healthiest spot on the planet."[95] In contrast, the Empire State College group was healthy and quite animated. Meetings began with breakfast at 7:00 A.M. and often continued until midnight, and were then followed by a few hours of socializing at the bar.

Mohonk became Empire State College's setting for a showdown between those faculty who wanted greater control of the College—including a radical faction that sought to eliminate all ranks and titles, and institute a uniform wage—and the administration and its faculty supporters. John Jacobson, then dean of the Genesee Valley Center, encouraged his faculty not to support radical proposals and moved quickly to help defeat a faculty motion to institute equal pay: "That was a serious motion. . . . We recessed for lunch before we voted on that, and I [Jacobson] . . . called all the Rochester faculty into a separate room, and I said, 'Now, look guys, this just isn't going to work. We can't do this. If you go backing motions like this, SUNY's going to shut the College down.'"[96]

President Hall was quite concerned about getting the bylaws passed because the College had gone for two years without them and needed a system of governance. SUNY's policy required that the faculty and the president had to agree to a set of bylaws. As John Jacobson saw it, Hall "didn't have much leverage."[97] In fact, the vote in support of the bylaws was feared so close that when a show of hands was called one mentor who had fallen fully clothed into Lake Mohonk was dragged out by her colleagues, rushed to the nearby College Assembly, and with her arm held aloft cast a rather wet vote. The bylaws were approved. These included Hall's proposal that representatives from the administration, professional employees, and students be included with faculty in the College Assembly.

For John Jacobson the meetings at Mohonk—there were two, held six months apart—were a watershed for the College: "Faculty finally decided . . . that they really did want to have a college, and they weren't just going to fall apart. . . . So many of the innovative ventures that were started in the '60s and early '70s simply disappeared because the faculty wouldn't agree on anything."[98]

Learning Modules: The "Hot and Heavy" Political Struggle

Hall and Baritz had hoped that learning modules, which were independent study guides designed to be significant resources for mentors, would become a unifying force in shaping the academic culture of the College. Hall had anticipated that modules would foster some consistency across the College in the quality and content of student work. The module program ran into difficulty even before the College enrolled its first students when a number of faculty at the Inaugural Workshop objected to their use. Chickering, in fact, was steadfastly opposed to their use. Modules soon became a casualty of the "hot and heavy" political struggle between him and Baritz.[99] Chickering believed that modules were "out of touch with where the students were and where their purposes were."[100] So, he refused to subordinate students to prescribed curricula.[101]

In Baritz's view, individualized contracts would yield to wild abandon if care were not taken. There was a good deal of evidence from ruinous programs started in the 1960s to support this position. Students needed structure, Baritz thought, and he felt he had the answer to preserving the academic integrity of the College while maintaining the spirit of innovation.

Learning modules were a creative way of letting the academy know that this was not a college bereft of standards.[102] Though Baritz's program assumed what students needed to know and wanted to know, he understood the shortcomings of prescribed curricula and expected that the learning resources faculty would supply the creativity and intellectual fire that had been absent from the dull, lock-step format of correspondence study. To accomplish this, he recruited a group of scholars, some distinguished, from the State University campuses and from universities throughout the United States and Europe.

He told each that they had long since mastered the arts of teaching and scholarship. And now it would be a fascinating challenge to discover if they could transfer their classroom genius to paper and other media. "You know what you are doing," Dr. Baritz tells the faculty, "but it is all pre-conscious. What I'm asking is that you put it down on paper—the material you use, the sequence in which it ought to be used, the levels of complexity, and the connections between what you are now saying and other areas, the implicit implications."[103]

The modules produced by these scholars had students explore themes, often interdisciplinary in nature, that were completely different from the lectures-in-print approach of correspondence courses that chopped knowledge into disparate three-credit disciplinary chunks. Baritz expected that the modules could be used as part of learning contracts or an "integrated block of learning standing somewhat alone."[104]

To match the bold departure modules had taken from correspondence courses,

The cover of a learning module by Mary C. Lynn (1973).

Baritz produced television programs that abandoned the talking-head format of SUNY of the Air. Instead of reading from lecture notes, scholars were pressed by peers, "often combatively," to defend their points of view.[105] Baritz "was convinced that most previous attempts at putting scholars on television . . . proved unexciting because the camera [had] not caught them doing their job—thinking and conceptualizing."[106] There were insufficient resources, however, to make television more than a show piece for innovation and a medium to engage American scholars in lively exchanges for student televoyeurs. Empire State College could not replicate the British Open University's equally innovative approach to the use of television, which was mammoth in both scope and accomplishment. The BOU had a budget in the millions of pounds sterling for television programs to supplement print-based courses and had the technical resources of the British Broadcasting Corporation at its disposal. Empire State College invested its limited resources primarily in print-based modules, supplemented at times by audio tapes or other media.

The decision to move ahead with the module program, however, continued to run counter to some faculty wishes:

It was like the French Revolution when the Third Estate decided it should be everything. There was a feeling that the mentors should be everything and somehow administrators at the [Learning Resources] Center were trying to usurp this marvelous new faculty authority that was being created in the institution. . . . The fact that Loren Baritz had assembled the great experts of the world on different subjects to write modules struck a lot of us as the great danger to our ability to teach any thing at all.[107]

In the spring of 1976, Assistant Vice President for Learning Resources Robert Pascuillo reported that 8.6 percent of the contracts he had surveyed used modules as a learning resource. Mentors were finding other alternatives to module-based instruction. In addition, the use of modules was uneven. In the period preceding April 1975, five modules, of the hundred or more that had been produced by that time, accounted for much of the sales, among them *Letter to a Would-be Journalist,* written by William Kennedy, future MacArthur Foundation genius award recipient and Pulitzer Prize winner.[108]

Perhaps another reason for the modules not to take hold—though 8.6 percent of the learning contracts using them is significant—was the lack of tutorial support. Mentors had to hire local tutors for modules to provide guidance and evaluation to students. The modules "required very special kinds of tutors. . . . The kind of tutor you needed for some of those modules would be a Renaissance person. It would have to be somebody like the person who created it."[109] In this regard, it was much easier for a mentor to hire tutors for specific subjects than to find tutors for highly specialized studies such as *Modern Culture and the Rebirth of Theology, The Philosophy of Aesthetics: A Phenomenological Approach* or *The Myth of St. Petersburg*—assuming that mentors were both familiar with their contents and able to excite student interest in their relevance. As Chickering noted, "The distance between where most students were and those modules was quite great."[110]

A reconceptualized learning module program, one that provided tutors at a distance, especially for the less intellectually demanding modules such as *Introduction to Political Analysis, The Question of Normality and Treatment, Theory and Personality,* and *Introduction to Social Analysis*—the most popular modules produced—might have created a more central role for the Learning Resources Center, especially if intensive efforts were made to involve mentors in producing modules. In fact, Hall began to devise a new program to circumvent the difficulties encountered by the Learning Resources Center.

Group Studies: The Social Experience of Learning versus Individualization

Chickering was equally uncompromising about any other approaches that smacked of imposed curricula, including group studies. He, therefore, resisted the pressure from deans to have "collective learning":

I [Chickering] fought that tooth and nail. . . . Once faculty members got into the business of creating group studies and building those into their workload, the efficiencies involved as well as being able to shape group studies to their own intellectual interests would drive the whole program. Again, we would find that the curriculum was driven by, increasingly, the faculty's interests instead of the individual student's needs. I knew that initially group studies with the faculty we had would be fairly responsive to individual students, but I had also hung around institutions long enough to know—in a ten-year time perspective—that those courses have a way of becoming very crusty. We quickly start to fit students into those boxes instead of continually shaping and remedying and reconstituting them. We were already having the problem with boilerplate contracts.[111]

F. Thomas Clark, formerly the dean of the Albany Center, recalled a heated exchange with Chickering over the subject of seminars advertised at his center. Clark had been invited to drop by for dinner at the Chickerings' on his way back from SUNY College at Potsdam, where Clark had held a faculty development seminar on contract learning. Chickering accused him of "giving away the tablets in terms of the mode" and trying to take the Albany Center "back to the classroom structure":

I walked into the Chickerings' house. Chick was very upset about something. I could tell that. He immediately started questioning me on what I was doing, in terms of having seminars at the center. I said, "I thought it was a good idea. As I understand from all the written materials and from when we talked in '71 that the purpose of Empire State College is to meet the learner where that learner is. And while the basic mode may be the learning contract, in the context of the contract, you could do a course at another institution, or seminars that occur at the center." And, I said, "Besides, I think there is a real interest among our faculty in doing seminars; there's an interest among our students in doing seminars. . . ."

That was part of the wonder of Empire State College. That you had this continuum from the classroom, albeit at another institution through cross-registration, to the seminar, or the occasional seminar that might be much more freewheeling, to the internship or the job used as part of the learning situation, to almost the tutorial with a very well constructed guide, if you will, called a learning contract. But we [the Albany Center] were seen as deviants: "Well, you're only trying to generate FTEs [full-time enrollment equivalents] by putting people in groups, all of them." I remember saying to Chickering, "Hold it! Hold it! Hold it! Hold it! That is not what we're trying to do." Admittedly, we were way behind in this crazy way of counting FTEs. He was tough. He was a tough cookie. I loved to work with him. He was very challenging, still is.[112]

Within a few years residencies, group studies, seminars, and workshops became a regular part of the academic program in most centers, and in 1975, the College created Extended Programs, the first successful effort to offer degrees at a distance using structured materials.

College on Public Television: *The Ascent of Man*

Of the alternatives for structured independent study explored by the Learning Resources Center, the use of telecourses brought the College into the dawn of a new era of educational television. Telecourses were neither the talking-head television programs of droning professors of the 1950s and 60s, nor the brilliant low-budget exchanges of notable scholars orchestrated by Loren Baritz, but high quality educational television series transmitted by the public television stations located throughout New York State. The first, *Ascent of Man,* and others that followed, cost millions of dollars to produce. Running the length of a semester, this series and others offered approximately an hour's worth of television each week and had broad-based audience appeal. Programs were broadcast at times convenient for adult students. In addition to the television programs, students had a text and study guide. Though to some extent the *Ascent of Man* preserved the talking-head format of earlier efforts to employ television, the scholar-host Jacob Bronowski, a charismatic Polish mathematician and intellectual, took the viewer out of the classroom and on a remarkable odyssey, from the cradle of Africa's Olduvai gorge, where our hominid ancestors learned to fashion primitive tools, to the carnage of Hiroshima, where the evolution of our species and its technology pointed toward extinction.

This "first college-wide attempt to 'harness' another educational resource began in January, 1975."[113] In addition to the ninety-nine Empire State College students enrolled in the *Ascent of Man*, there were forty-two special students who had been attracted by the PTV media blitz and ESC's promotional efforts. Despite this promising start, subsequent PTV telecourses, such as *The Adams Chronicles* and *Psychology Today*, and a second running of the *Ascent of Man*, had only attracted twenty-three students. Almost half of those were generated through the efforts of one center.[114] Educational television, even extravagantly produced, had failed to attract a great deal of interest on the part of students and mentors, possibly because of broadcast scheduling rigidities. In subsequent years telecourses became more a part of the academic program when the advent of video cassette recorders and inexpensive rental services reduced scheduling problems.

Rationalizing Assessment: The Office of Program Review and Assessment (OPRA)

The College by March 1972 had reached what might be thought of as a consensus on the overarching principles of assessment. Creating a process that would insure equity for individual students and procedural integrity throughout the College, however, did not happen overnight. There was a good deal of variability in quality, from center to center, from mentor to mentor.

By 1973, the College needed a central office to develop conventions and to devise systems as well to review and guide assessment activities occurring at the center level. In September 1973 Hall and Chickering hired Albert Serling for one year to establish an assessment office. Serling was the director of the College-Level Examination Program (CLEP) at the Educational Testing Service. He had been involved in the initial planning and development of CLEP and had taught adults at Rutgers for ten years. He saw his task as assuring "that every student who came to the College would get the same shake without regard to which center he or she *happened* to attend."[115]

We were performing the service on behalf of the students. If there were not a legitimate academic process, then the degree would not be as meaningful, and we would suffer in accreditation; we would suffer in what went on subsequently. So, each student gained according to the goodness of the processes. The second thing . . . is that we were developing a codification of the faculty's wishes.[116]

With the faculty in mind, Serling further refined the assessment process by building on the work of the 1972 task force, the accomplishments of individual centers in improving assessment practices, and Chickering's efforts. Serling was careful not to view his role as one of defining "the academic values of the institution." Serling was aware that there was "a lot of distrust and quarreling between faculty and administration." He did not want a more powerful office of assessment to divide the College.[117] For that reason, he proposed a faculty advisory committee with representation from the administration. He wanted the committee to meet frequently, "so that they could bring forward their criticisms about what was going on, their suggestions for change, and also their general recommendations, which we could follow up on and then bring to APLPC [Academic Policy and Learning Programs Committee] or to the Senate for approval or disapproval."[118] Serling proposed the creation of this committee three or four times, but each time it was flatly rejected by the administration.

Separated from faculty, the Office of Program Review and Assessment [OPRA] became "something to get through, to jump over, a hurdle."[119] But it became a

Albert Serling, founding director of the Office of Program Review and Assessment, joined the College in September 1973 from the Educational Testing Service where he had been director of the College-Level Examination Program (CLEP).

necessary one. Mentors, as student advocates, had difficulty discouraging students from seeking unrealistic amounts or categories of experiential learning credit. "So, OPRA was actually doing what the faculty member wanted but had a hard time doing himself or herself. . . . The faculty and student could then blame OPRA. They could work together to beat OPRA, in effect, but there was really a kind of rhythm to the whole thing which was beneficial all the way around."[120]

One of Serling's early reforms was to exclude students from defending their requests for advanced standing at assessment meetings. If evaluations of experiential learning preceded assessment meetings, assessment committees would have no need to question individual students. Instead, committees would examine the quality of credit evaluations and the academic integrity of the degree programs. In addition, Serling wanted experiential learning evaluations that could stand the scrutiny of accrediting agencies. The process had to be able to justify, albeit in rare instances, cases in which students received up to three quarters of a baccalaureate degree from learning acquired outside of the classroom.[121] He did not want "letters of recommendation but evaluations of learning by experts."[122] Serling also began the process of bringing faculty and outside experts together to develop generic credit evaluations, called conventions, for various professions.[123] Such conventions provided, in effect, college-credit equivalents of certain professional training and practice. In addition to saving mentors the time and resources of providing separate expert evaluations for students in the same professions, conventions insured a consistency in the number of credits awarded and a consistency in the quality of the evaluations throughout the College.[124]

Serling understood that it was the faculty whose authority established academic standards and expectations; faculty, not OPRA, had to pass judgment on individual degree programs. "The Office of Program Review and Assessment counted things: Is there enough liberal arts? Can we see the liberal arts?"[125] Serling "fiercely instructed" his reviewers to only ask questions. "We were not competent to say this was liberal study. That's the job of the faculty. We counted everything as best we could. When there was a clear dispute, I [Serling] would enter in on it."[126]

Within a year of his arrival Serling had achieved what he had set out to accomplish. OPRA was fully operational and capable of processing large numbers of portfolios while preserving the assessment process as "a very powerful instrument" for students "recognizing their own knowledge and competence."[127] Most important, OPRA helped to create a College-wide consistency in assessment practices:

> It helped to insure that there was justice and equality in the credit awards by studying and reporting on Center differences in awards over periods of time. Without such central analysis and vigilance, it would be inevitable that a student's credit awards might depend more on which center she or he happened to be enrolled in then on the richness of their college-level learning.[128]

Self-Study Report and Accreditation Review: "A Powerful, Powerful Instrument for Building Consistency"

The administration brought in Serling at a critical time. The month he arrived, September 1973, the College formally launched preparations for the Middle States Association accreditation visit, scheduled to take place in the fall of the coming year. The College was just two years old when President Hall made a bold decision to seek accreditation within three years rather than the customary five. He believed that the process of preparing for the review and the review itself would galvanize the College, make it look closely at the processes and practices it had put in place and come out of the review a stronger institution. Because Empire State College was so new, it would probably be more able to accommodate changes, even root-and-branch changes that Middle States and the New York State Education Department might recommend. As Hall noted, the "first Middle States accreditation . . . was a powerful, powerful instrument for building consistency. And we consciously used it as such. Make no mistake. We used that accreditation to build an institution."[129]

Calculated or not, the quest for early accreditation was a huge gamble, and there was much to be concerned about. The College had to convince a visiting team, mostly composed of individuals from traditional colleges and universities, that its student-centered program of individualized learning contracts and degree programs, and its system for awarding credit for experiential learning were academically sound.

This was not an easy task for a college on the cutting edge. Empire State College had turned education inside out: Student academic goals and interests replaced curriculum committees; tutors replaced classrooms; interdisciplinary approaches to learning replaced disciplinary ones; congeries of disparate faculty in centers replaced departments; vast community resources replaced a single college library; learning centers spread across the state replaced a solitary campus; and individualized examinations for endless permutations of experiential learning replaced standardized tests. Though, at the time, Empire State College was an exciting departure in American public education, it would not be difficult for naysayers to argue that the foundations of this new academic edifice rested on quicksand.

At the same time, concerns were raised within and outside the institution about shortfalls in academic quality. For example, Ronald Corwin, a regional learning center dean who had not supported the contract renewal of a number of Long Island faculty, believed "that there was a lot of stuff that was slipping by that was pretty . . . sloppy, and it would not pass scrutiny of . . . the accrediting commissions."[130]

There were some faculty who were enormously immature. Some of them were angry. Angry at institutions; at higher education. They didn't really understand that the students who came there actually were really 180 degrees out from that. They [students] weren't angry at education; they wanted a degree. Some of them for no reason except they simply wanted the degree. These folks failed to understand that the students really weren't there because they resented [traditional] higher education. And several faculty tried hard to make the students [that way]; and that becomes a kind of demagoguery.[131]

Just prior to the visit by Middle States and the New York State Education Department, SUNY Vice Chancellor for Academic Affairs Bruce Dearing had some strong concerns about the quality of the academic program. As a result, in preparing for the Middle States review, the College was, at the same time, trying to correct the faults Dearing identified. "Both of those events, the need to respond to Bruce Dearing and the need to respond to Middle States, put on fairly powerful pressure to develop common practices from the College."[132] It was not a coincidence that Hall hired Albert Serling to work on assessment just as the College began the year-long preparations for Middle States. Vice President for Academic Affairs John Jacobson and Mentor Fernand Brunschwig, Long Island Center faculty member, co-chaired the Self-Study Steering Committee. It included one representative from each center, either a faculty member or administrator, and a nonteaching professional and one student as well as one representative from the coordinating center in Saratoga.[133]

The College self-study, issued in the fall of 1974, looked critically at its former practices while pointing toward a more conservative direction of development. Assessment, for example, had become more rigorous. The report boasted of "a complex system with checks and safeguards for assessing prior learning and for granting advanced standing toward degrees for learning done in other institutions and outside of formal institutions."[134] The self-study further noted, as a consequence of the pressure to formally register its degrees, the break from the "inductively" designed degree programs of the "early stages" of the College to those designed in reference to curricular areas and modes of study which had been developed by College-wide faculty committees in 1973 and submitted to the State University of New York and the State Education Department in March 1974.

Vindication: Middle States Association Report

The Middle States evaluation team, chaired by G. Theodore Mitau, chancellor of the Minnesota State College system, issued its report in November 1974. The report praised the three-year-old college, calling it an "important, valid, and innovative educational enterprise":

Empire State College has many strengths; we were all greatly impressed with that which has been accomplished. The College has moved rapidly, and to a large degree successfully, to achieve its stated goals. We found the College and its personnel eager to examine what they were doing and to search for ways to continue improvements. The "Self-Study" and other supplementary documents reveal a genuine effort to make critical judgments, to raise tough questions, and to make the hard decisions. You are already addressing many of the issues raised or discussed in this report.[135]

The Middle States team lauded the College for having created a "dynamic, new element in higher education."[136] It recognized that the mentoring role demanded "a great empathetic quality, keen intellectual insight, and breadth of expertise of a magnitude that inevitably poses challenges to its full realization."[137] The team was moved by the accounts of students praising mentors for their "commitment, perseverance, and intensity of involvement."[138] The team shared the concern that mentors expressed about professional development but urged mentors not to view the question only in terms of their disciplines: "The entire process of mentoring represents in itself—with all of its variety and challenge—a new form of professional life. . . . To the extent that they have an opportunity to analyze their role, depersonalize it, and share it with other colleagues and institutions they may make an important contribution to the field of higher education."[139]

Having said that, the Middle States team then focused on the need for the College to create mechanisms to cultivate the role. In addition to a "mentor interchange concerning roles, methods, and performance," they recommended a formal in-training service program.[140] In fact, efforts to address this need had begun in 1974, when the College secured funding from the Danforth Foundation to create the Center for Individualized Education, a program dedicated to supporting the professional development of faculty as mentors and giving mentoring regional and national visibility.

The team expressed concern that the preponderance of mentors in philosophy, history, and the social sciences worked against the interest of students pursuing degrees in other fields, particularly science, technology, and art. The team was not won over by the College's argument about faculty adjuncts, tutors, and cross-registration meeting this need. "The institution needs to be careful that student choices are not limited or discouraged simply by the fact that mentors are drawn more heavily from some academic backgrounds than others."[141] The team, however, cited no instance where this was a problem. Strangely, while praising the College for inventing a new faculty role in American higher education, the team failed to recognize that mentoring liberated faculty from disciplinary mind-sets. The mentor role demanded that faculty gain expertise about a variety of fields to advise students in degree program planning while it forced students to take ownership, namely by researching the expectations of their fields, both academic and professional. Nevertheless, the team recognized that the liberal arts training of mentors in conjunction with the professional experience of the students "made for a fruitful conjunction for selected students: a liberal arts mentor trying to respond intensely to the academic and personal growth needs of these kinds of students."[142]

What the team said about Empire State College students was remarkable:

They are dedicated, articulate, knowledgeable and extremely enthusiastic. Many spoke of the intellectual confidence they have gained and the personal growth they have experienced. The feeling is expressed by many students that they are working harder than that which was required of them in a traditional college, a perception in which they take great pride. Students are finding Empire State College what they expected to find; the college is proving to be, for its enrolled students, what it says it is.[143]

By 1974, the average age of Empire State College students was thirty-three; half were women; 60 percent of the students were full time; and the enrollment projection for 1974–75 was 2,550. The team believed that the College was best suited for adults "who—for the most part—are highly motivated, independent, goal-directed and who have already had substantial experience in more traditional forms of education and in jobs or other career activities from which they have acquired some skills and knowledge."[144] The team asked the College to break away from this "self-selected clientele" and give access to "those less motivated, less experienced (both educationally and occupationally), and less advantaged," a course of action proposed in President Hall's memorandum of September 30, 1974, to the President's Committee on College Development.[145] At the same time, the team recognized that the mentor role could not support the additional workload.[146]

The Middle States team gave the administration high marks. They singled out President Hall as "an extremely able leader who has earned the respect of the profession locally and nationally, and who has surrounded himself with an exceptionally well-qualified administrative staff."[147] The team scolded the College for not meeting its affirmative action goals and urged hiring more women and minority group members into leadership positions. At the same time, the team commended the College for channeling more resources into instruction and less into administration and support services, from 46 to 67 percent.[148] The team noted the tensions existing between the learning centers and the administration as well as the complaint voiced by mentors about the administration having excessive control over the curriculum. Nevertheless, the team deemed these tensions salutary and believed the curriculum was safely balanced.[149]

The Middle States Association issued its letter of accreditation to President Hall on December 13, 1974. Lee Hornbake, chair of the Commission on Higher Education of Middle States, wrote, "You and your colleagues progressed toward making the College the strong institution you wish it to be."[150]

A former faculty member of Goddard College, Forest Davis was the founding associate dean of the Long Island Center. He subsequently joined the Center for Statewide Programs, where he served as the founding coordinator of the Binghamton satellite. His journal, *Philosophy in Motion,* consisting mostly of his dissertations on a whole range of philosophical, theological, and historical topics, became legendary in the College. Mentor Davis retired a number of years ago and continues to distribute the journal but now by electronic mail.

Grappling with Reality: The New York State Department of Education Registration Visit

The New York State Education Department (NYSED) team, which visited the College in the early in fall of 1974, issued its findings in March of the following year. On April 14, 1975, Alvin P. Lierheimer, associate commissioner for higher education, forwarded a letter to Vice Chancellor Dearing registering Empire State College's programs. To President Hall, Lierheimer wrote, "May we wish you every continued success with a bold experiment, which has been a source of great satisfaction to the Department."[151]

The fifteen-member NYSED team, composed of faculty and high-ranking university administrators from American higher education as well as representatives from the NYSED Bureau of College Evaluation, recommended unanimously that Empire State College receive registration. The report recommending registration opened by praising the College's "highly competent, well informed, and dedicated staff deeply committed to a well defined task. They have tackled a difficult assignment with integrity, energy, flexibility, and imagination. In a relatively short time they have made encouraging progress."[152]

Salvos of praise were quickly followed by bombards of criticism, constructively targeted. The NYSED team "found much more to commend than to criticize." Yet they saw the evaluation as an opportunity to shape this bold experiment while still "in a fluid state."[153] Although the team judged the College "according to sound academic practices and . . . not . . . on an equivalency scale with practices in traditional institutions" all of its non-NYSED members, save one, came from traditional universities.[154] They beheld a strange entity and could hardly understand it without reference to the familiar.

What the NYSED team had to say was sobering and valuable: They questioned the lack of adequate liberal arts studies in a significant number of degree programs; the narrowness of some concentrations; the need for students to do introductory learning contracts in areas for which they had received substantial experiential learning credit; the inconsistency in quality of learning contracts; and the lack of progression to "higher levels of achievement" in some learning contracts. The team even questioned the strong voice students had in shaping degree programs.[155] Though finding most of the contracts they reviewed to be "thoroughly acceptable, and some . . . even inspiring," the team encountered contracts lacking "uniformity in standards within and among learning centers" and pointed to "the very limited exchange and development of academic conversions among mentors in the same fields."[156] Noting that the problem of the integrity of academic standards was "pervasive in all education," the team recommended more "stringent quality controls."[157]

The NYSED team was possibly not aware of the pedagogical differences coexisting uneasily within the College regarding individualized (learner-referenced) and structured (criterion-referenced) learning. The team, nevertheless, sensed an inconsistency in pronouncements against structured learning and made a point of finding no fault with a mentor who prepared identical learning contracts for twenty students, comparing it to cross-registering students at a traditional college. The team noted optimistically that "philosophic statements [will] achieve congruence with practices of the College."[158]

This statement, obliquely targeted at Chickering, was an endorsement to continue structured learning approaches to independent study and foreshadowed the creation of two programs based in Saratoga: Extended Programs, launched in the fall of 1975, and the Independent Study Program, based on British Open University "correspondence" courses, started the following year. Both programs were conceived to serve students throughout the College, either those at regional learning centers and units who wanted or needed structured learning options or those who were unable for reasons of geography, work, or physical disabilities to meet with mentors and tutors.

The NYSED team supported the assessment of prior learning as an "appropriate academic function" which the College managed responsibly. Yet they also perceived it as an area of primary concern.[159] The team noted the progress faculty and administrators had made in building a structured process into the review of student degree programs and portfolios. The report praised the work of Albert Serling and his assistant Myrna Miller, who brought to "their task impressive enthusiasm, knowledge, acumen, and honesty."[160] The team recommended that the policies and practices of assessment needed "firm controls and [that] appropriate adjustments should be instituted, if they have not been." The team was concerned primarily about the lack of examinations to evaluate experiential learnings. They believed that if an exam could not be administered to knowledge areas, then "assigning credit for them is highly questionable" and assessment without tests to validate prior learning, in their judgment, was "black magic."[161]

Though there may have been subjective elements in assessment of experiential learning and cases where evaluators were used who lacked appropriate credentials, Albert Serling had spent the year prior to the NYSED visit organizing and standardizing assessment practices. The team's recommendation "that examinations should be incorporated into the process of validating prior learning whenever appropriate tests exist or can be devised" seemed recidivistic and impractical. Standardized exams could not possibly anticipate the complex and wide-ranging learning that students brought to the variety of degree programs the College had already accumulated.[162]

By the time the team arrived, assessment of nontranscripted learning had become a familiar pattern. An expert evaluator orally examined each student's claim, but only after having read the student's essay articulating learning and having examined supporting documentation. This documentation included such materials as letters from supervisors, portfolios of artistic work, and other evidence that helped evaluators frame questions to plumb the depths of a student's understanding. Because learning was often uniquely acquired, and the College was determined to keep these options for students, it was nearly impossible to anticipate prior learning requests with existing standardized exams. The College, therefore, ignored the team's recommendation to devise tests, but continued its efforts to use standardized tests made available through CLEP, CPEP and, later, Thomas Edison College, when they were suitable.

The team's judgment of mentors and mentorship milled about from hosannas to disapprobation. The team liked the faculty's credentials, both academic and experiential, and equated them with the credentials of faculties at "quality" liberal arts colleges. They found mentors "capable, hard working, dedicated, high in morale, and generally satisfied with their roles and their students. Their commitment, energy, and rapport with one another were impressive."[163] But the NYSED team expressed its serious concern about the "pitfalls" of mentoring: "the risk of becoming an academic guru, of being tempted to play God, of allowing advocacy to interfere with reasoned judgment, of allowing fatigue to slip gradually into apathy or disinterest, or, conversely, to allow interest and enthusiasm to run unchecked into ultimate exhaustion, to become so involved that they cease to be managers or facilitators of learning."[164] In addition, some members of the team expressed their concern that the relationship between some mentors and students "had become so intimate, that it threatened the professional relationship that insures academic safeguards and objectivity. This threat to professionalism is intensified by a 'us against the world' mood at some learning centers at least fostered by a faculty group whose antipathy to traditional institutions allies them to a body of students who share the same feeling."[165] Though the team recognized the professional value of a program which required "a lateral extension of knowledge rather than the pursuit of specialized knowledge in depth," it believed that mentors overextended themselves by tutoring beyond their expertise.[166]

Noting that the College "cannot flip people into this very different approach, without thorough retooling to make them effective in this new role," the team recommended that newly hired mentors receive formal training.[167] Formal training had occurred at the Inaugural Faculty Workshop, and faculty hired as mentor interns through the Eli Lilly Foundation post-doctoral fellowship program participated at workshops held at Harvard and the University of Chicago. Yet new mentors, as the team had noted, depended mainly on "learning by doing and the 'buddy system'."[168]

All together the NYSED team made eighteen major recommendations. It was clear from the tenor of the report that the NYSED and its team welcomed Empire

State College as a major initiative in New York public higher education. Despite the roughly hewn nature of the stuff that made the College successful in its first few years, the College could become a first-rate institution. A number of the problems and recommendations identified by Middle States might have been challenged as being grounded in philosophical differences, perhaps the result, as well, of inadequate time to sufficiently understand the College. Yet even things said in error or in exaggeration provided an opportunity for the College to assess where it was and where it was going. Besides, the visitation was not a forum for debate. And the report and its recommendations were not an occasion for denial or capitulation, thrust or parry. In sum, the NYSED report was a completely frank view of how the College operated from the perspective of an external audience of hardheaded advocates who had in mind the prospect of a future report as much as they had the present one.

Taken together with the Middle States report and its recommendations, the NYSED report helped to stimulate an internal dialog in the College. This dialog had its finest expression in the Center for Individualized Education.

Center for Individualized Education: "Seven Little Orthodoxies"

The efforts to create a college culture reached their apex in the Center for Individualized Education (CIE). President Hall first proposed the Center to Chancellor Boyer on March 21, 1974. In an urgent memorandum to Boyer, Hall reported that the Danforth Foundation was charting new directions for its higher education programs section and planned "a series of regional centers for teaching and learning to be established across the United States."[169] Hall reported that Danforth had "expressed an interest in having Empire State College serve as sponsor for one of these centers which would serve as a national center for contract learning and individualized instruction." To demonstrate SUNY's commitment to the project, Hall requested that Boyer commit $5,000 a year from his special fund for innovative projects to supplement a Danforth grant—$50,000 per year for three to five years—and increase the amount by $20,000 in subsequent years.[170] Boyer offered his strong endorsement as well as a promise to provide the matching funds.[171] By mid-May, Chickering had a proposal ready to ship to the Danforth Foundation.[172]

The Center, which would have a national thrust and also serve both Empire State College and the campuses of the State University, needed a director. F. Thomas Clark, the dean at the Albany Learning Center, had helped Chickering in preparing the grant; he was Chickering's choice to head the center. Clark had had a rocky time at the Albany Center and was just beginning to see "a lot of things come together," and so was reluctant to leave his post. But Chickering persisted and Clark compromised trying at first to do both jobs.[173] It soon became apparent that "if [the new job] were going to succeed, it was going to need full-time leadership."[174] The Albany faculty, who originally objected to having Clark as dean or anyone else, "took a vote of no confidence in [Clark's] decision to leave, and . . . had Jim Hall come down and talk." Perhaps surprised, Clark left the Albany center with "a very, very beautiful letter" from the faculty.[175] Clark's success as dean was good preparation for directing a faculty-oriented program.

Chickering, who by this time had become vice president for analysis and evaluation, worked with Clark in bringing the Center to fruition. Chickering was particularly important in providing the faculty theoretical insights to understand the complex cognitive and behavioral dimensions of the adult learner. His work was particularly valuable for those mentors without degrees in education. Such mentors had practical insights gained from their day-to-day work with students and from insights shared with colleagues, but they had no theoretical perspectives to draw from. Faculty intuitively practiced a liberation pedagogy, but without the theoretical perspectives with which to know why mentoring succeeded or how to improve it. Through Chickering's contributions to the CIE workshops, mentors learned about the stages of development and the life cycle, personality characteristics, and the complex motivations of adult students. Most important, Chickering helped mentors to understand some of the interesting behaviors they saw in their students and to recognize individual differences.

Of the five national centers funded by the Danforth Foundation, Empire State College's Center for Individualized Education was the only one, according to the Penn State Center for the Study of Higher Education, to reach national prominence. In its three-and-a-half years of existence the Center created a consortium of over twenty institutions, sponsored a conference with 275 participating institutions, and, in one year alone, conducted workshops, by invitation, at 52 institutions. The Center's five-year plan never reached fruition, however. Funding was cut off at the end of the third year but there remained enough in the budget to continue the program another six months.[176]

The Center's accomplishments within Empire State College were equally remarkable. Clark brought newly hired mentors to week-long seminars where they worked with seasoned mentors and were introduced to contract learning and assessment through role play and other techniques:

A lot of this was new stuff for a lot of people: "What do you mean criteria?" someone would say. "I'll know an A paper when I see one." "Well fine," [Clark] would counter. "Let's start talking about that, and let's put some criteria out there." So, often those were twelve-hour days and you'd go through the lounge—we did a lot of these at Rensselaerville—at midnight, 1, or 2 o'clock in the morning, seeing people that had never met each other really going at these issues. They were very, very rich, academically challenging, faculty development activities.

My goal was, at the end of the week [new] mentors would feel comfortable when they went back to their centers, sitting down with students and having a sense of self-confidence engaging in that dialog. . . . By the time they left at the end of the week, they had been members of portfolio review and assessment committee; they had negotiated at least three different contracts, albeit in role play; they had met actual Empire State College students; and they had met the president, vice presidents and some of the deans. So they got a sense of the administration. It's very different. That's what faculty orientation should be. I also felt that what we were doing, perhaps idealistically, welcoming people to a special community of scholars, to a special kind of college—a very unique and important institution that had to make it, had to prove itself not simply as an organization, but had to say that this is an important and viable way to serve people, who very often don't have other options. That was a very real prime force. So, they were exhausting times, but they were full, good times.[177]

For those seasoned faculty, whom Clark used on a rotating basis from centers around the College, the seminars were significant developmental activities as well but in ways that created a College-wide perspective on practices and their derivative issues. Clark would not approach centers on an individual basis. When he was asked, for example, to conduct workshops on assessment at specific centers, he replied:

Absolutely not. Part of what I see, right now, is that we've got seven little orthodoxies developing here [referring to seven centers]; we don't have, and what we need, is a College approach, not a Long Island [Learning Center] way of assessing, and an Albany [Learning

Dean F. Thomas Clark (right) of the Albany Regional Learning Center meets with prospective students at an orientaion session held at Draper Hall, part of the downtown campus of the State University at Albany which housed the Albany Center headquarters. In1974, Dr. Clark became the director of the Center for Individualized Education. Subsequently, he served as the vice president for academic affairs at Rockland Community College and succeeded Seymour Eskow as president.

Center] way of assessing; that's going to be dangerous in terms of the institution's development. . . . I think the way to do this is to be very intentional about bringing faculty into the College. And since we had the money to be able to do it, we were able to do it.[178]

Clark then held a highly acclaimed College-wide workshop on assessment in Syracuse.

The effort to bring the College together in a dialog about academic issues included a series of seminars on contract learning. Mentors received a casebook of sample learning contracts. It was particularly valuable to new mentors because it had an excellent sample of contracts for each area of study. Clark was particularly concerned—as was the NYSED accreditation team—about methods of evaluation and about the relationship of credit to the amount and quality of work:

Some people will say, "Well, if there is a kind of quantity, it must be valid"—whether or not there's any evidence of complexity in thinking; this is kind of a moot point. So we had these quantity and quality issues: "Well if you read enough books that's got to be worth X number of credits in some formula." And other people were saying, "Well, it doesn't really matter, if you are reading only one book, but the way you work to analyze and apply, and so forth, does matter"—the whole issue around books and the application of learning skills. So there were real differences around those issues of quantity and quality that I really thought needed to be addressed.[179]

While Clark was instrumental in breaking down the "seven little orthodoxies," he was just as steadfast against creating a College orthodoxy. What he wanted, and what he succeeded doing through the Center for Individualized Learning, was creating a College-wide dialog among the faculty. When the Danforth Foundation prematurely withdrew its support from the five national centers, the administration, unfortunately, decided not to continue the program.

To John Jacobson, the Center came at a critical point in the maturing of the academic program. In the first few years, the College went through a period of "furious policy making," followed by the Middle States and New York State Education Department visits, and then a second period of refining policies. But that was not enough.[180] "The way that you get better academically is not just rewriting the policies but learning how to do what the policies call for. And that was where Clark made such a strong contribution."[181]

At the Roaring Brook faculty development workshop in 1990, one of the senior faculty who lamented the loss of the Center for Individualized Learning, praised its many accomplishments, and recommended bringing it back into existence. Jane Altes, who succeeded John Jacobson as academic vice president in 1987, enthusiastically supported the recommendation. Planning for a formal way to sustain faculty development activities, to be known as the Mentoring Institute, began shortly afterwards. A less ambitious version of the Center for Individualized Education, the Mentoring Institute was planned and is administered by faculty. Thus, the concept and purpose of the Center for Individualized Education emerged Phoenixlike from its ashes but this time held aloft on faculty wings.

Retrospect

The years from 1971 to 1975 were critical for a college on the cutting edge. A heady forty-eight months of building programs and serving students, preceded by twelve months of rigorous planning, resulted in the creation of a viable institution. Empire State College, called by some an honors program for adult students, was at the end of this period vigorous and admirable. By 1975, the College was serving an incredibly diverse population of students in terms of location, age, social origin, ethnicity, race, occupation, and personal accomplishment. The College had reached out to the communities of New York State—as it did on a smaller scale in England—for tutors, libraries, internships, and office space. It was able, therefore, to create programs of study that were outstanding for their uniqueness and for their creative use of resources. There was nothing to compare to the diversity of Empire State College's academic programs in all of American public higher education. Remarkably, this vigorous development occurred during a period when the State University was on a downward fiscal spiral. One might have expected a more conservative approach to institutional development in such circumstances, but just the opposite happened. The national recognition of the College through a number of grants helped to sustain confidence during fiscally difficult times in its mission. It also assisted in the consolidation of a host of accomplishments.

As remarkable as Empire State College's accomplishments were, including successful reviews by Middle States and the State Education Department, there was still much to do. The Learning Resources Center, for example, though producing many praiseworthy learning modules, remained peripheral to the academic program. The College learned from experience. In the coming years it approached the important question of providing structured learning resources to mentors and students from an entirely different and extremely successful direction.

By 1975, we had a good sense of what was academically sound and what constituted effective institutional support necessary to sustain highly diverse academic programs. We had profound trust—and experience to back it up—in the ability of students working with their mentors to plan and execute sound and meaningful programs of study. Most important, as diverse as our programs were, we shared values and practices. We had a college culture.

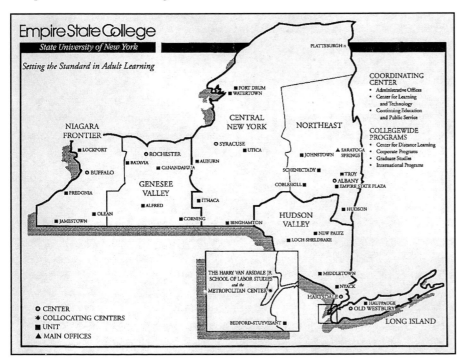

Endnotes Chapter 2

1. "Call to the College," Northeast Regional Center, 12 December 1971, Memorandum, Empire State College Archives, Saratoga Springs, New York, p. 1.

2. Ibid., 1–2.

3. Ibid., 2–3.

4. Ibid., 3.

5. Arthur Chickering to the Inaugural Workshop Participants, 4 October 1971, Memorandum, Empire State College Archives, Saratoga Springs, New York, p. 2.

6. Arthur Chickering to the Empire State College Faculty, 13 March 1972, Memorandum, Empire State College Archives, Saratoga Springs, New York, p. 1.

7. Ibid., 2.

8. Ibid., attachment A, 2.

9. Arthur Chickering, 13 March 1972, Memorandum, p. 3.

10. Ibid.

11. Ibid., 4.

12. Ernest Palola and Paul Bradley, *Ten Out of Thirty; Studies of the First Graduates of Empire State College* (Saratoga Springs, New York: Empire State College, Office of Research and Evaluation, 1973), 53.

13. Ibid., 53–54.

14. Arthur Chickering to the Task Force on Assessing Prior Experience, 17 February 1972, Memorandum, Empire State College Archives, Saratoga Springs, New York, p. 1.

15. Ibid., 2.

16. Arthur Chickering, Interview by Richard Bonnabeau, 16 August 1990, transcript, Empire State College Archives, Saratoga Springs, New York, p. 22.

17. Ibid., 22–23.

18. Chickering, 17 February 1972, pp. 2–3.

19. Ibid., 2.

20. Palola and Bradley, p. 28.

21. Ibid.

22. Chickering, 17 February 1972, p. 6.

23. *Seeking Alternatives I: Empire State College Annual Report (1972)* (Empire State College: Saratoga Springs, New York, 1972), 27.

24. "Office of Admissions. Student Records, and Financial Aids: Status Report and Future Directions" (Saratoga Springs, New York: Empire State College, Office of Research and Evaluation, 29 December 1972), 3.

25. Ibid., 16.

26. Ibid., 17.

27. Ibid.

28. Ibid., 18.

29. Ibid.

30. Ibid.

31. Loren Baritz, Interview by Richard Bonnabeau, 20 March 1990, transcript, Empire State College Archives, Saratoga Springs, New York, p. 8.

32. Ibid., 8–17.

33. Ibid., 17.

34. Baritz, p. 8.

35. Ibid., 8.

36. *Seeking Alternatives I*, p. 28.

37. *Access, Innovation and the Quest for Excellence: Empire State College in 1979*, Self-Study Prepared for the Commission on Higher Education, Middle State Association of Colleges and Schools (Empire State College, Saratoga Springs, New York, September 1979), 16.

38. "Office of Admissions," p. 10.

39. Ibid. 19.

40. *Seeking Alternatives I*, p. 28; *Seeking Alternatives VIII: Empire State College Annual Report* (July 1979–June 1980) (Empire State College, Saratoga Springs, New York, 1980), 5; *Retrospect and Prospect: Strengthening Learning at Empire State College,* Self-Study Prepared for the Commission on Higher Education, Middle States Association of Colleges and Schools (Empire State College, Saratoga Springs, New York, September 1989), 31.

41. Palola and Bradley, p. 5.

42. Ibid., 19.

43. Ibid., 45.

44. Jeanne Brockmann, "A Study of the Impact of Mission on Selected Aspects of College Administration" (Ph.D. diss, University of Massachusetts, Amherst, 1980,) 52.

45. Ibid., 53.

46. *Seeking Alternatives II: Empire State College Annual Report (1973)* (Empire State College: Saratoga Springs, New York, 1973), 8–10; *Seeking Alternatives III: Empire State College Annual Report (1974)* (Empire State College: Saratoga Springs, New York, 1974), 15.

47. Brockmann, p. 55.

48. *Seeking Alternatives IV: Empire State College Annual Report (1975)* (Empire State College: Saratoga Springs, New York, 1975), 13.

49. *Seeking Alternatives II*, p. 12; Brockmann, p. 55.

50. *Seeking Alternatives IV*, pp. 5–7.

51. *Bedford-Stuyvesant Unit Evaluation* (Saratoga Springs, New York: Empire State College, Office of Research and Evaluation, 1977), 21–23.

52. *Master Plan 1972: Empire State College Master of the State University of New York* (Saratoga Springs, New York: Empire State College, 1 July 1973), 63; *Seeking Alternatives: IV*, pp. 24–25; Robert Carey to Richard Bonnabeau, September 11, 1995, Memorandum, Empire State College Archives, Saratoga Springs, New York.

53. Master Plan 1972, pp. 62–63.

54. George McClancy to Richard Bonnabeau, 8 September 1995, Empire State College Archives, Saratoga Springs, New York, p. 1.

55. Ibid.

56. *Seeking Alternatives IV*, p. 13; Kenneth Abrams,

Interview by Richard Bonnabeau, 9 September 1995, transcript, Empire State College Archives, Saratoga Springs, New York.

57. William Dodge, Interview by Richard Bonnabeau, 2 February 1991, transcript, Empire State College Archives, Saratoga Springs, New York, p. 33.

58. *Seeking Alternatives II*, pp. 13–14.

59. Master Plan 1972, p. 65.

60. Ibid.

61. *Seeking Alternatives II*, p. 17.

62. *New Models for Career Education: An Assessment* (Saratoga Springs, New York: Empire State College, Office of Research and Evaluation, April 1976).

63. Ibid.

64. "New Deans for Lower Hudson, Albany Centers," *ESC News,* September 1975, vol. 1, no. 11, p. 1.

65. E. K. Fretwell to Ernest L. Boyer, 10 November 1971, Letter, Empire State College Archives, Saratoga Springs, New York.

66. Ernest L. Boyer to E.K. Fretwell, 10 December 1971, Letter, Empire State College Archives, Saratoga Springs, New York.

67. James W. Hall to Henry Bridges, 6 March 1973, Letter, Empire State College Archives, Saratoga Springs, New York.

68. Paul Bradley, *The Empire State College Mentor: The Emerging Role* (Saratoga Springs, New York: Empire State College, Office of Research and Evaluation, September 1975), 3.

69. Ibid.

70. Ibid.

71. Ibid.

72. Ibid.

73. Ibid., 6.

74. Ibid.

75. Ibid.

76. George Drury, Interview by Richard Bonnabeau, 24 July 1991, transcript, Empire State College Archives, Saratoga Springs, New York, p. 32.

77. Bradley, p. 18.

78. Ibid., 24.

79. Ibid.

80. Ibid.

81. Drury, 24 July 1991, p. 31.

82. Joseph Goldberg, "Address to the College Assembly," 1 November 1973, Empire State College Archives, Saratoga Springs, New York, pp. 1–2.

83. Joseph Goldberg, Interview by Richard Bonnabeau, 30 May 1991, transcript, Empire State College Archives, Saratoga Springs, New York, p. 15.

84. Baritz, p. 3.

85. Baritz, p. 10.

86. Chickering, August 16, 1990, p. 41.

87. Ibid.

88. John Jacobson, Interview by Richard Bonnabeau, 8 April 1993, transcript, Empire State College Archives, Saratoga Springs, New York, p. 13.

89. Chickering, 16 August 1990, p. 42.

90. "Mentors' File: Genessee Valley Learning Center," pp. 1–2, Office of Research and Evaluation, Saratoga Springs, 1973.

91. George Drury, "Prince Street Dialogues," vol. xxix, (Rochester, New York: Empire State College, 1973), 2.

92. Bradley, p. 20.

93. Goldberg, May 30, 1991, p. 14.

94. See: Judson Jerome, *Culture Out of Anarchy: The Reconstruction of American Higher Learning* (New York: Herder and Herder, 1970).

95. T. Coraghessan Boyle, *The Road to Wellville* (New York: Viking, 1993), p. 6.

96. Jacobson, p. 18.

97. Ibid.

98. Ibid., 18–19.

99. Chickering, August 16, 1990, p. 28.

100. Ibid., 26.

101. James W. Hall, Interview by Richard Bonnabeau, 13 June 1990,transcript, Empire State College Archives, Saratoga Springs, New York, p. 11.

102. Timothy Lehmann, Interview by Richard Bonnabeau, 14 January 1991, transcript, Empire State College Archives, Saratoga Springs, New York, pp. 41–42.

103. *Seeking Alternatives I*, p. 32.

104. Ibid., p. 33

105. Ibid.

106. Ibid.

107. Robert Barylski, Interview by Richard Bonnabeau, 25 March, 1993, transcript, Empire State College Archives, Saratoga Springs, New York, p. 8.

108. Robert Pascuillo to John Jacobson, 4 May 1976, Memorandum, Empire State College Archives, Saratoga Springs, New York, p. 2, and p. 16.

109. Chickering, August 16, 1990, p. 27.

110. Ibid., 26.

111. Ibid., 35–36.

112. F. Thomas Clark, Interview by Richard Bonnabeau, 16 March 1990, transcript, Empire State College Archives, Saratoga Springs, New York, pp. 7–8.

113. Pascuillo to Jacobson, p. 3.

114. Ibid., 4.

115. Albert Serling, Interview by Richard Bonnabeau, 7 May 1990, transcript, Empire State College Archives, Saratoga Springs, New York, p. 6.

116. Ibid., 10–11.

117. Ibid., 8.

118. Ibid., 9.

119. Ibid., 10.

120. Ibid., 11.

121. Ibid., 26.

122. Ibid., 16.

123. Ibid., 23.

124. Ibid., 24.

125. Ibid., 45.

126. Ibid., 45.

127. Chickering, August 16, 1990, p. 22.

128. Albert Serling to Richard Bonnabeau, 9 September 1995, Memorandum, Empire State College Archives, Saratoga Springs, New York.

129. James W. Hall, Interview by Richard Bonnabeau, 6 September 1995, transcript, Empire State College Archives, Saratoga Springs, New York, p. 15.

130. Ronald Corwin, Interview by Richard Bonnabeau, 21 June 1990, transcript, Empire State College Archives, Saratoga Springs, New York, p. 16.

131. Ibid., 9.

132. Jacobson, 8 April 1993, p. 9.

133. John Jacobson and Fernand Brunschwig to the Self Study Steering Committee, 9 October 1973, Memorandum, Empire State College Archives, Saratoga Springs, New York, pp. 1–2.

134. "Empire State College Self Study" (Saratoga Springs, New York: Empire State College, 1974), 8.

135. "Report to the Faculty, Administration, Trustees, Students of Empire State College," Prepared by an Evaluating Team Representing the Commission on Higher Education of the Middle States Association, 1974, Empire State College Archives, Saratoga Springs, New York, p. 1.

136. Ibid., 3.

137. Ibid.

138. Ibid.

139. Ibid., 4.

140. Ibid.

141. Ibid., 5.

142. Ibid., 8.

143. Ibid.

144. Ibid., 6.

145. Ibid., 7.

146. Ibid.

147. Ibid.

148. Ibid., 8.

149. Ibid., 8–11.

150. Lee Hornbake to James W. Hall, 13 December 1974, Letter, Empire State College Archives, Saratoga Springs, New York.

151. Alvin Lierheimer to James W. Hall, 14 April 1975, Memorandum, Empire State College Archives, Saratoga Springs, New York.

152. Edward Carr to James W. Hall, 24 March 1975, Memorandum: Report of the New York State Education Department (NYSED) Evaluation Team, Empire State College Archives, Saratoga Springs, New York, p. 2.

153. Ibid., 3.

154. Ibid.

155. Ibid., 4–6.

156. Ibid., 6.

157. Ibid., 7.

158. Ibid., 6.

159. Ibid., 7–8.

160. Ibid., 8.

161. Ibid.

162. Ibid.

163. Ibid., 11.

164. Ibid.

165. Ibid.

166. Ibid., 12–13.

167. Ibid., 13.

168. Ibid., 12.

169. James W. Hall to Ernest L Boyer, 21 March 1974, Letter, Empire State College Archives, Saratoga Springs, New York, pp. 1–2.

170. Ibid.

171. Ernest L. Boyer to James W. Hall, 3 April 1974, Letter, Empire State College Archives, Saratoga Springs, New York.

172. Arthur Chickering to Ernest Palola, 16 May 1974, Memorandum: Proposal: Center for Individualized Education, Empire State College Archives, Saratoga Springs, New York, pp. 3–4.

173. Clark, p. 12.

174. Ibid.

175. Ibid., 13.

176. Ibid.

177. Ibid., 16–17.

178. Ibid., 17.

179. Ibid., 18.

180. Jacobson, 8 April 1993, p. 17.

181. Ibid.

3

NEW
DIRECTIONS

Vice Chancellor of the British Open University, Lord Perry of Walton (center), received an honorary doctorate in humane letters from Empire State College May 2, 1982. Vice President for Academic Affairs John Jacobson (left) praised Lord Perry for his remarkable leadership in making the British Open University—the United Kingdom's alternative to traditional higher education—such a great success and noted the importance of the British Open University to the College's efforts to develop a distance learning program. Lower Hudson Valley Dean Mary Ann Biller (right) accompanies Lord Perry and Dr. Jacobson after the ceremony. Lord Perry, in his response, described Empire State College as "the most ambitious programme ever devised in idealism."

By 1975, Empire State College could point to a significant number of accomplishments: Its successful experiments in contract learning and assessment, the formation of a statewide college composed of regional centers and their satellites, the creation of specialized programs for an extraordinary array of students, the development of a new faculty role in public higher education, and successful reviews by Middle States Association of Colleges and Schools and the New York State Education Department. In the best of times, all of these would have positioned the College for a period of sustained growth. But contracting state revenues dashed all hopes for a statewide college serving the ten thousand students that Boyer's planning task force had anticipated. The lack of state support, however, did not prevent the College moving forward, even in visionary ways. Among new initiatives undertaken from 1975 to 1980 were the creation of the Empire State College Student/Alumni Association, the Empire State College Foundation, a new satellite program in Israel, and two new centers—the Center for Distance Learning and the Public Affairs Center. The College also took major steps toward developing a graduate program and prepared for a second round of reviews by Middle States and the New York State Education Department.

Reaching New Populations: "A Housewife, a Prisoner, a Blue-Collar Shiftworker, a Serviceman in Guam"

The *Prospectus* anticipated that the Learning Resources Center would have a central role in the academic program. It would acquire, develop, and distribute learning resources. In fact, the first staff hired by the College was for the Center. They began preparing learning modules before the first students enrolled. By 1974, the learning modules program, where most of the energy of the Center had been invested, had not taken hold in the fundamental ways the planners had desired. The highly innovative nature of modules, the use of first-rate scholars to create them, the general recognition of the intellectual excellence of the modules, and efforts to facilitate their use had all failed to move faculty to use them in more intensive ways. President Hall began to seek alternatives, both in the kinds of resources developed by the College and in their delivery.

Hall did not want to displace individualized contract learning but wanted to enrich the resources available to all students. At the same time, he wished to offer alternatives for those students who needed more direction and structure in their learning to have alternatives. In fact, Hall greatly admired individualized learning contracts. Yet even Goddard had been reluctant to set incoming students loose to pursue independent learning; they had to wait until their sophomore year. Empire State College students, one might argue, were older and intellectually mature and therefore more prepared to undertake individualized contract learning. Supposedly, they knew what they wanted to learn. Nevertheless, adult students tended to be largely driven by the practical needs of having a degree to survive in the hurly-burly world of work; they were generally less interested in intellectual fulfillment. For these students, especially passive learners or the intellectually insecure, a prepared curriculum was comforting and perhaps necessary. They could earn degrees without having to go through the exercise of planning each learning contract. There could be "a modest amount of individualization as the student proceeded into the study. Thus the program would be reasonably structured though not wholly prescriptive."[1]

This had momentous programmatic implications. In Hall's thinking, a program based on structured learning resources would position the College to serve student populations out of the reach of existing programs such as "handicapped persons, prison inmates, out-of-state personnel, out-of-state students, and those located at considerable distance from our existing centers, students whose occupation or other responsibilities make a home study pattern most convenient."[2] These were students who could not be easily served by individualized contract learning. The College could thus justify serving bypassed groups with a structured learning approach, one whose tutors and courseware could unobtrusively supplement the resources of regional learning center mentors, especially mentors located in remote areas of the state. In other words, rather than base the entire existence and survival of a new learning resources program on the good will of mentors, the administration could launch a new initiative to serve new populations hitherto unserved by the regional learning centers. At the same time, resources from this initiative would be available to mentors. Most important, unlike the learning module effort there would be no expectation that mentors use them. But the resources, tutors included, would be there for the asking to help mentors grapple with their workloads. It was a clever solution. The problem facing Hall was how to create an operational program for what he called "the alternative instructional plan."[3]

Hall began reconceptualizing the organization of the Learning Resources Center as an alternative to individualized contract learning. Though he used the terms "extended learning" and "directed studies" to define it, the new paradigm was distance learning. Hall established a task force of two separate committees to formulate proposals, one on academic offerings, the other on administrative systems.[4] Though given separate tasks, the two subcommittees locked horns on pedagogy. One group recommended that students attend residencies at the learning centers, a position favored by John Jacobson. But this option sharply limited student access. The other group proposed a system based on self-contained resources for distance learning. This would give students the virtually unlimited access favored by Hall. Students could be anywhere in the world.

Hal Roeth, the director of the Learning Resources Center, championed distance learning and opposed Jacobson's position. Roeth brought his thinking directly to the Administrative Council: "To put it . . . simply—even bluntly—we need a program that permits a prisoner, a housewife, a blue-collar shift worker, or a serviceman in Guam to 'take a course' in Psychology now and a course in Sociology six months from now, with the assurance that if the individual selects these 'courses' from an ESC preplanned program of study, he can be working toward a degree at Empire State College."[5]

What Roeth desired was an untrammeled version of distance learning. It would have no group studies, and student and mentor connections would be limited to telephone and mail. Jacobson's view was closer to the British Open University. BOU students, using independent study materials, have periodic group meetings with tutors at study centers and attend summer residencies. One might conclude that Jacobson wanted directed studies residencies operating side by side with the individualized learning contract system at the regional learning centers. The residencies would be available to all students. It was a way of promoting a degree of curricular consistency and quality throughout the College.

Despite their differences, the task force members agreed that the directed studies program would be a free-standing center. The task force called for a new use of the Learning Resources Center faculty. They would work with students as study directors and as occasional tutors in addition to being resource developers. Jacobson's final words in his memo of August 1, 1974, to the administrative cabinet were, "Let's get

Tom Wicker (right), *New York Times* columnist, visited the Learning Resources Center faculty in Saratoga Springs in April 1974. He discussed Watergate and other issues.

going!"[6] More than a year would pass, however, before the administration launched the new program, and it was decidedly not the one sketched out by the task force.

Extended Programs: "Threads of Gold"

The ambitious center conceived by Hall's task force, which was to have been equal to regional learning centers in size and academic standing, had within a year's time dissolved into a weakly funded pilot program operated by two faculty attached to the Center for Statewide Programs. This meager start was a consequence of the State's contracting economy and falling tax revenues. "The days of wine and roses are over," as Governor Hugh Carey put it in his address to the state legislature in 1975. George Bragle, coordinator of the Utica satellite of Statewide Programs, and Richard Bonnabeau, a mentor recruited from the Niagara Frontier Center, came to Saratoga Springs to start Extended Programs. As one of them said, because of the scarcity of resources, it would be like trying "to spin threads of gold from straw."

The administration's decision to isolate Extended Programs from the Learning Resources Center was just the opposite of what might have been expected given the primacy of the Learning Resources Center in planning the directed studies program. A stone's throw apart, the two, Extended Program and the Learning Resources Center, were isolated from each other, with the exception of a flurry of meetings in the fall of 1975. It made some sense to place the program within Statewide Programs, however. William Dodge, the dean, had been the former dean of the SUNY Independent Study Program, and Extended Programs could eventually channel structured learning materials to Statewide Programs' satellites, especially those in remote areas that had much less access to learning resources than the regional learning centers. Also, the program would not be derailed by priorities established by the Learning Resources Center.

Extended Programs began much like the College had, just four years before, with a good deal of latitude to experiment and invent a program using existing learning resources, but specifically to serve students needing structured learning and to reach new populations. Unlike the Learning Resources Center faculty, Bragle and Bonnabeau carried the same full-time equivalent students as faculty in other programs, which put them on the same level as regional center mentors. But their missionary role as proponents of structured learning—provided in a distance learning mode of delivery—though muted, did not initially make many friends for them around the College among advocates of individualized contract learning. Students began to enroll by mid-November 1975, just five weeks after beginning the program. This was purposeful, for the program was to be in direct interaction with students.

Within a year Extended Programs had enrolled fifty students who used a combination of learning modules, SUNY Independent Study courses, and individualized learning contracts. A number of these students were in correctional facilities all over New York State.[7] While the program was not the first in the College to serve incarcerated students, it was the first to do so without the need to send mentors and tutors into the prisons. Moreover, incarcerated students were now able to move from one facility to another—a common occurrence—without interrupting their studies or giving up college altogether. The program served other students in the state, including disabled persons, and those whose work schedules or location made it very difficult, if not impossible, to travel to a regional learning center or satellite. Other students were in California, Connecticut, Louisiana, Maryland, Massachusetts, Minnesota, and Washington, D.C., and overseas in Israel, Japan, Singapore, and the

United Kingdom. Among the students were the chief executive officer of a major federal agency and a documents examiner who gave expert testimony—while enrolled in Extended Programs—at the trial determining the authenticity of the Howard Hughes Mormon will.

Extended Programs had removed the final barrier, distance, from student access. Tutors were now able to work with students at a distance, even huge distances. Through Extended Programs, the College reinvented itself. Empire State College could be more than a college confined by state borders—albeit one in reach of people in every city, town, and hamlet. It could become a college providing access to students throughout the United States and beyond, to anyone accessible by telephone and mail. This low-tech access provided a viable alternative to face-to-face mentoring and tutoring.

The British Open University: In Pursuit of Legitimacy

While Extended Programs moved quickly in its first months of existence to enroll students by using individualized learning contracts to fill in the gaps left between modules and SUNY Independent Study courses, President Hall and John Jacobson investigated the possibility of using British Open University (BOU) course materials. Each BOU course cost millions of dollars to produce. Along with handsomely produced course guides, which featured tutorials in print, the course materials included video and audio components to pace learning. The BOU courses were comparable to courses taught at Oxford or Cambridge, and therefore they could easily allay the concerns of skeptics about the academic legitimacy of distance learning. BOU courses were mostly on large topics in the humanities and the social sciences. They engaged students for a year of study, and were roughly equivalent to sixteen to eighteen credit hours. So the courses needed to be broken down into more digestible units of four, six, or eight credits, a time-consuming effort which required the work of faculty teams.

In February 1977, John Jacobson appointed Robert Hassenger, then acting dean for the Niagara Frontier Learning Center, to take charge of adapting the BOU materials for College-wide use. At the same time, Jacobson had the Office of Research and Evaluation (ORE) coordinate a faculty review of BOU humanities and social science courses. The ORE issued a massive report in the fall of 1977, recommending BOU materials for use by Empire State College for structured learning. By the fall of 1978, Hassenger, who had moved to Saratoga Springs as the director of the Independent Study Program, had prepared three courses with the help of Vincent Worth, a British Open University consultant. The courses were offered as group studies, but students anywhere in the state could study at a distance. They were made available as well to Extended Programs students.[8]

Center for Independent Study: "The Shotgun Wedding"

By the fall of 1977, the College had two distance-learning programs operating in Saratoga Springs: Extended Programs, offering degrees based on independent study materials and individualized learning contracts, and the SUNY Independent Study Program, offering modified British Open University materials to students scattered around the College and to students at other SUNY campuses. In February 1978, the faculty of both programs were called to a meeting by the administration and informed of the decision to marry the two programs to create a distance-learning program offering entire degree programs based on prepackaged courses. The faculty, although bristled by the lack of consultation and viewing the union of the programs more a shotgun wedding than a match made in heaven, worked at making the new entity a success.

The union of the two programs, which became the Center for Independent Study, later known as the Center for Distance Learning, made perfect sense. The key to the Center's survival, which separated it from the Learning Resources Center, was that it would enroll its own students. It did not depend on the good will of mentors in other centers—the same politically astute principle of Extended Programs. Through the late winter and early spring, the faculty planned a center which wedded the best of the two former programs: the degree program thrust of Extended Programs with its statewide, national, and international vision and the Independent Study Program's high-quality British Open University courses, ready-made for distance-learning, though decidedly difficult and foreign.

John Jacobson advised the faculty: "Do not be overly concerned about whether there will be a market for your program. There will be. . . . Your job is to invent and establish a separate and distinct alternative—a new alternative that is distinct from the mentor program and also from the traditional residential program."[9] In addition to adapting BOU courses, the Center would, Jacobson further advised, "stake out" a claim in the effective use of television by selecting a television series to be offered for the fall 1978.[10]

Jacobson's counsel nicely suited the growing national interest by public television stations to broadcast college-level programming with general audience appeal. In 1978, there were over 160,000 telecourse enrollments in the United States.[11] New York State public television stations such as WNET/Channel 13 and the capital district's WMHT/Channel 17 were looking for creative ways to market public television, and serving as a vehicle to offer college credit for telecourses caught their attention. The television components had been designed to have general audience appeal, far removed from the talking-head variety of the 1950s and 1960s. In addition, cable television systems were hungry for programming that would fulfill the public service requirements of their franchises.

Center for Distance Learning: "A Muscular Version of the Center for Independent Study"

By February 1979, the administration was ready to commit additional resources to the Center for Independent Study. President Hall did so, even against a firestorm of protest from those deans who wanted funds for their own centers. The success enjoyed by the University of Maryland's Open University, a program established in 1972 and based primarily on BOU courses, provided overwhelming evidence of a market for distance learning courses. Maryland had over two thousand students in its BOU courses.[12] Hall provided additional faculty and staff lines, and, to align the Center with national and international developments in distance learning, changed the name to the Center for Distance Learning (CDL).

The use of faculty was unlike the regional learning center model, which had been organized to serve students face-to-face. In the regional centers and their satellites, mentors worked with a specific number of students to whom they were oftentimes assigned randomly as advisers, facilitators, and tutors. Although the faculty at the Center for Distance Learning, and before that the Center for Independent Study, had their own students to advise in degree program planning and course selection, they were primarily responsible for the acquisition and design of course materials for a

Harriet Bell, 1979 graduate of the Center for Distance Learning, began her studies in 1977 with Extended Programs. Paralyzed by polio in 1954, Harriet, a young mother of three children, spent twenty-five years at the Goldwater Memorial Hospital on Roosevelt Island, New York, and then moved to a nearby apartment. Because of her disability Harriet had been rejected by many colleges in Metropolitan New York before she found out about Empire State College. An excellent student, in 1983 Harriet won the Wonder Woman Foundation Award. The award honored Harriet's efforts to win rights for hospital patients and her personal struggle against polio. Harriet went on to earn a master's in health advocacy at Goddard and then completed a Ph.D. She also established the Polio Information Center with her friend and author Florence Weiner. Ms. Bell became a leading expert on post-polio patients. Photograph by Seth Harrison.

specific part of the Center's curricular offerings. In addition, CDL faculty hired, supervised, and evaluated tutors. They were much like department chairs in traditional colleges.

Scheffel Pierce, coordinator of the Plattsburgh satellite, was appointed director of CDL. The Center served two types of students with high-demand business and human services courses: Its own students and students from other learning centers. Providing courses to students from the other learning centers was part of a workload reduction effort. With courses made readily available for their students, mentors could invest less energy in identifying and training tutors, and mentors could do less tutoring themselves. The workload reduction program paved the way for CDL to become an integral part of the College's academic program. The effort began immediately. In fact, the announcement for the Fall 1979 term, CDL's first, was boldly inscribed as the *Mentor Workload Reduction Program.*[13] This "handmaiden function for the rest of the College," as Vincent Worth called it, had forerunners in the Learning Resources Center's learning modules program as well as Robert Hassenger's initial offering of BOU courses, and Center for Independent Study's fall of 1978 statewide telecourse project.[14]

In March 1980, an assessment of the Center for Distance Learning conducted by the Office of Research and Evaluation, just as the second term was underway, and most likely commissioned by an administration anxious to see early results from its investments in capital and faith, produced impressive findings. Student evaluations of the courses were overwhelmingly positive: "They speak of having learned a lot, liking the texts and associated materials, being impressed and very much helped by the tutors. Many of the cross-registered ESC students seemed to like the structure offered by CDL courses."[15] The report observed that the Center was "filling a real need in higher education."[16]

The report, however, did point to the labor intensive nature of distance tutoring. Tutors often had as many as forty students in a course. Other distance-learning programs such as California's Coastline Community College, using telecourses with self-assessment print-materials and computer-based examinations, had tutor-student ratios in the hundreds. The Center for Distance Learning's commitment to the centrality of tutors—deeply rooted in the College's individualized contract-learning program—resulted in much higher student completion rates, more than seventy percent.

The Center's efforts at course development over the years, limited as they have been by insufficient funds, lacked the sophistication of the lockstep, multimedia extravaganzas of the British Open University and the more modestly produced multimedia courses of the International University Consortium and other consortia. What CDL has offered students is more individualized course assignments, active advisement and tutorial support, and the ability to do a limited number of individualized learning contracts. This flexibility has captured the attention and praise of distance learning programs throughout the world, including the British Open University.

The growth of the Center for Distance Learning, a muscular version of the Center for Independent Study, was remarkable. By the fall of 1981, the Center had over four hundred students and many students were on course waiting lists. Today, CDL has more than two thousand registrations a term. Although this explosive growth, consisting of CDL's own matriculants and students from other centers, has secured the Center's future, CDL has had a history of being chronically short of resources, which continues in the 1990s. Despite the infusion of more faculty and staff lines, there were never quite enough resources to satisfy the constant demands placed on CDL by other centers and its own potential for growth.

Distance learning at first rankled mentors who championed individualized contract learning, and therefore questioned the CDL's pedagogical merits and demand on College resources. Nevertheless, the rapid advances in technology during the 1980s and 1990s—video cassette recorders, fax, electronic mail, computer conferencing—

and the growing international stature of distance learning eventually began turning suspicion to acceptance.

Dr. Daniel Granger became director after Scheffel Pierce died in 1981. A former associate for academic affairs in the Office of the Academic Vice President, Granger has guided CDL to programmatic maturity.

The Graduate Program: A Bold New Direction

Of the initiatives the College pursued in the 1970s, the attempt to launch a graduate program was perhaps the boldest. President Hall proposed a graduate program, sketched out by Loren Baritz, to Chancellor Boyer on November, 27, 1972. Hall and Baritz, responding to Boyer's call on September 29, 1972, for the State University to achieve more with less, envisioned a statewide program coordinated by Empire State College that would draw from the talents of faculty throughout the State University as well as from the faculty of private and public colleges and universities from around the state. This core of graduate faculty, to include Empire State College mentors appointed to the graduate program, would be headed by the Learning Resources Center faculty.[17]

The program would "free graduate instruction from the constraints of usually required residence on a single campus" by offering rotating seminars around the state and, not surprisingly, engaging students in learning modules especially designed for graduate-level work.[18] Hall proposed three areas in cultural studies—comparative cultural analysis, urban studies, and environmental studies—as well as in the administration of large organizations, the allied health professions, social services, and education.

There was already faculty interest in a graduate program. Irving Kriesberg, an accomplished artist and mentor at the Long Island Regional Learning Center, prepared a proposal for the arts the very day that Hall sent his proposal to Chancellor Boyer:

The Empire Graduate Program will be neither large, nor monolithic nor conspicuous in the New York landscape, but it can help young professionals who are capable of independent action make the very best use of the welter of institutions, facilities, agencies, expertise and evaluations that exist in New York. . . . I believe that in the field of the arts we can offer a rigorous, demanding program with all the safeguards and articulation that exist in the more traditional schools and I believe that when it comes to faculty we can offer our students an unsurpassed array of distinguished experts.[19]

Offering a master's program in the arts, or, for that matter, in any number of fields, including those proposed by Hall, made perfect sense. The undergraduate program, itself, had many of the aspects of a graduate program: mature students, heavy emphasis on independent study, one-to-one relationships with teachers, research-oriented activities, and the development of critical thinking, research, and writing skills. In fact, many faculty would be hard pressed to demonstrate how the work of their better and more advanced-level students differed from work done by students at the master's level. It was not unusual to hear from our graduates who had moved on to graduate school about the decided ease of transition and how much better they were doing than their counterparts. Some even complained about being bored for lack of a challenge. The creation of a graduate program, therefore, one that would serve its own graduates and graduates from traditional colleges, seemed to be a logical next step in the College's evolution.

The youth of Empire State College worked against early implementation of the graduate program. The need "to gain full accreditation for [the undergraduate] program required that we defer development of a master's program during the early years."[20] Also, it was politically brazen to launch a graduate program while the undergraduate program was still in its formative years. In reality, Empire State College was part of a large and politically charged network of campuses. Being innovative, successful, and the most junior member of SUNY made it vulnerable, even if this upstart institution enjoyed Chancellor Boyer's favor.

Kenneth Abrams, Empire State College's London satellite chief, informed Loren Baritz about the negative reaction his former colleagues at the State University at Stony Brook had about the possibility of students doing graduate work through the London program: "Empire State College was overstepping its mandate, and if it stuck to its own undergraduate problems for awhile, they might listen to a graduate argument later. They predicted, and this, too, was last September [1973], that it would be political suicide for ESC to push for a graduate program now."[21]

The College additionally faced opposition, if not hurdles, from the State Education Department and the Division of the Budget. The Education Department's visiting team for registration recommended that a graduate program "be put off until the undergraduate operation . . . realized maximum improvement and . . . [has] earned the respect of the academic community."[22] In addition, the Division of the Budget stood ready to challenge the fiscal efficacy of launching a program in a period of contracting revenues. Associate Provost for Graduate Education Vernon Ozarow wrote: "[The] coordination of graduate offerings and efficient use of resources on a University-wide basis are the current watchwords. We are reminded of this almost daily through increasingly stringent review, regulation, and questioning by the Division of the Budget and by the Education Department."[23]

President Hall persisted. In the latter part of 1975, after carefully discussing another attempt at launching a master's program with Chancellor Boyer, Hall established a committee to design a master of arts program. He dropped his plan, however, for a statewide program. Hall took his cue from the SUNY Commission on University Purposes and Priorities. The Commission, headed by Loren Baritz who left Empire State College in 1975, supported a nonresidential independent study master's program but with regional sponsorship. Hall had already received positive reactions about a regionally sponsored program from the presidents of State University at Stony Brook and State University College at Old Westbury, both Long Island campuses. He therefore requested Acting Dean George Dawson of the Long Island Learning Center to join Mentor Fernand Brunschwig in heading the committee.[24]

In advising Dawson and Brunschwig on what had to be done next, Hall noted that Chancellor Boyer had urged him not to develop the initially proposed programs with a professional orientation. They competed with programs offered by public and private campuses and "would unnecessarily complicate the process of approval." In their stead, Boyer recommended programs based on "broad social issues in the humanistic vein."[25] Hall observed, "We felt that the more specific vocational content could be followed under those larger rubrics, not only placing the more narrow study in a broad perspective but making a unique and broad gauge program at the same time."[26]

By May 26, 1976, Chancellor Boyer submitted a University Master Plan Amendment to the SUNY Board of Trustees, authorizing Empire State College to grant master of arts degrees in liberal studies. The master of arts would have three concentrations: labor studies, business and management, and cultural studies, each governed by a social policy framework. Significantly, Boyer proposed a small pilot in the New York City region, where there were no competing SUNY campuses. This would draw upon faculty from local colleges and universities as well as from Empire State College. He proposed an initial program of no more than fifteen students for each concentration; each student would be guided by a three-member degree panel.[27]

The SUNY Master Plan Amendment was bold, if not impertinent, for the ink had scarcely dried on the State Education Department's registration report, dated March 24, 1975, which clearly advised the College to delay proposed plans for graduate studies and to focus its energies on the undergraduate program. So, despite the support of Governor Hugh L. Carey, Chancellor Ernest Boyer, and the SUNY Board of Trustees, the Regents, not surprisingly, refused to approve the University's Master Plan Amendment. In rejecting the amendment, the Regents repeated the advice that the College focus on the undergraduate program and then dismissed Empire State College as a possible host for an experimental graduate program: "Nontraditional graduate education, still in its experimental stages, should be undertaken only by graduate institutions with established records of excellence."[28]

Hall would not give up, however. He spent the next six years working with a new chancellor, Clifton R. Wharton Jr., refining the plan with faculty advisers and building in the process a wide base of support. A second attempt for approval followed the momentum of an extremely successful Middle-States review.

International Programs: Israel

Sometimes a new direction is an old direction. In 1974, a fiscally difficult year, the College agreed to eliminate the London satellite. This was the result of actions taken by the New York State Division of the Budget. The London program had been enormously successful. "By 1974 . . . it was the largest and most successful program of twenty-six programs of the State University of New York in the United Kingdom."[29] Loren Baritz, who had evaluated it the year before, observed, "Abrams has done a superb job (under the most difficult and isolated circumstances). He has opened resources for students in over one hundred institutions—the most important academic institutions being the City University and Middlesex Polytechnic—with additional individual persons in scores of additional schools, universities, libraries, museums, and social service agencies."[30] The work of two and half years had been eliminated by the stroke of a pen. An angry Abrams returned to New York, joining the Urban Studies Center in Manhattan, a program of the Center for Statewide Programs, where he coordinated "Communications and Media in the City."

Empire State College's retreat from international programs was short-lived. In 1976, Rockland County Community College President Seymour Eskow proposed a collaborative venture which would provide opportunities for Rockland students in its successful program in Israel to pursue baccalaureate degrees through Empire State College.[31] Eskow with Abrams had designed the London satellite at the 1971 Inaugural Workshop. Eskow wanted Empire State College, either jointly or by itself, to establish a cooperative service learning program with Mate'eh Yehudah, a regional council representing Jewish agricultural villages, kibbutzim and Arab villages near Jerusalem, which, in effect, would create a "regional community college."[32]

President Hall was deeply interested. He included in the preliminary College budget a request for a faculty line to place a mentor in Israel to work with approximately forty students. He believed, nevertheless, that this request would not succeed unless it were part of a larger State University initiative in Israel and that the mentor would have to "relate closely to program officers from other State University campuses."[33]

Rockland Community College already had paved the way for the beginnings of a SUNY-wide collaboration. Hall looked to other SUNY programs as well as CUNY (City University of New York) for such linkages. He discussed with Chancellor Boyer and Loren Baritz, who became SUNY provost, a "long range concept for a coordinated approach to international programs in a single country."[34] Israel appeared to them to be an ideal country for a pilot program, because of the manageable number of SUNY programs in Israel and the abundance of learning resources. In 1977, Hall then appointed Kenneth Abrams to coordinate the program, "primarily to serve upper division American students and a limited number of Israeli students who wish to pursue baccalaureate degrees."[35]

By late October, Abrams was in Israel with Hall. They joined other SUNY and CUNY officials to meet administrative and faculty leaders from major Israeli universities and post-secondary institutions, the United States Ambassador, the Chairman of the Israeli Council for Higher Education, and the Minister of Foreign Affairs. Hall and Abrams had initiated the first successful steps for a program that would begin in January and establish cooperative linkages with SUNY and CUNY units in Israel. Hall made it clear, however, that the program, though a cooperative entity, was independent. He identified Abrams at every opportunity as "its agent in Israel."[36] The Israel venture was off to a good start. Being a cooperative venture, one of just a handful of SUNY programs—far fewer than the twenty-six SUNY programs that had existed in England—it was much less vulnerable to arbitrary budget cutting. Abrams remained with the program until 1979, when he was succeeded by Dr. Amnon Orent. Abrams shared his experience and the experience of students in Israel with the readers of the *ESC News:*

Despite the Palestine Liberation Organization, and despite land seizures and national bankruptcy and refugees of all persuasions, an American faculty member could walk his panting dog and eat his yogurt and go off to meet with his students and know that at the end of the day, if they all survived, and they all did, that those students would have spoken Hebrew, met with a tutor, taken a course, read a chapter, looked at a newspaper, taught English to some tired Israeli children and their exhausted parents in an isolated mountain village outside of Jerusalem that was inhabited by an older generation that had come by donkey from Yemen or by plane from Morocco to spawn children who could see that walled city and know that the blood, like this history, that was fresh and visible went centuries deep into the earth, and that the richness of history and politics and ethnicity and religious study and language and the agony of humanness would have rubbed against each of us before we had gone to sleep that night, and that the stars would appear brighter than we had remembered them and the sky bluer when we awoke than we had any right to expect.[37]

Shortly after returning to New York, Abrams was appointed dean of the Metropolitan Regional Learning Center. Today, the Israel program, because of agreements with the Israeli Council of Education, serves only American students and students from other countries.

Empire State College Foundation: Private Funds for Public Goals

In June of 1972, less than a year after the College's founding, President Hall had attempted to establish the Empire State College Foundation to provide the legal means to solicit and administer gifts and grants, but Chancellor Boyer deferred approval because SUNY had no official position on foundations. Hall was required to wait until the larger question of the relations between the State University and existing foundations could be studied and a policy established. Nevertheless, Boyer had not yet established a committee, so the wait would be a long one.[38] This made the receipt and

disbursement of funds more and more difficult, especially for programs such as the Fine Arts Workshop in Manhattan, which depended on a significant amount of private funding.[39] A year after Hall had forwarded the Empire State College Foundation charter to SUNY for review, Boyer's committee submitted its endorsement of college foundations.[40]

Another year went by, however, before the Empire State College Foundation filed its certificate of incorporation with the New York Department of State. This was on July 17, 1974. Once established, the Foundation could aggressively seek funds. On September 15, 1975, it launched the first annual drive with a target at $30,000, modest in comparison to the $250,000 goal for 1996 but still ambitious for a new college. Hall urged students, staff, alumni, and friends of the College to lend their financial support "during these difficult times of state budget restrictions and priority reordering . . . when public, like private colleges, are feeling the effect of economic recession."[41]

The Foundation was important to the College. By 1975, the College had grown tremendously. From the first batch of students admitted in the waning months of 1971, the student population had grown to forty-two hundred; there were already fifteen hundred graduates. The growing number of students created needs that state subvention could not meet nor anticipate. Hall outlined four programs that were vital to ESC's continued growth and success: special support to minorities, women, and

Dr. Jeanne Brockmann (foreground, right), then director of alumni affairs, sits next to Marjorie Meinhardt, associate for alumni affairs, at a March 1978 Board of Governors meeting of the Empire State College Federation of Alumni/Student Associations. Behind Brockmann and to the right is Ruth Decker, the first president of the Federation and graduate of the Long Island Center. In 1978 Brockmann was among the first thirty State University of New York professional staff to receive the Chancellor's Award for Excellence in Administration.

others needing financial assistance to complete their studies; special tutorial and counseling services for students; learning resources identification and acquisition, especially in audio-visual and learning media equipment for centers, units, and satellites; and the establishment of a general fund to "support unanticipated events or expenses that would arise during the year and need timely action."[42] The fund drive proved to be a bit ambitious and missed its goal by slightly more than $3,500. Students from the Labor College had donated almost $15,000, which was placed in a trust fund to generate annual interest for scholarships. Gifts for the identification and acquisition of learning resources barely exceeded $100, but funding for the other programs received generous support.[43]

Though the first annual fund drive fell short of its target, it was in other ways a remarkable success. From the outset, it was impossible to predict what kind of support there would be for a public institution funded by tax dollars. Because Empire State College is, in effect, more a virtual college than a bricks-and-mortar reality, it is invented anew for each student. There were other concerns. Empire State College was so young, still forging an identity; it had nontraditional students, many of whom were sending their own children to college; and it had none of the trappings and fanfare of other campuses which fixed them in place and time. Empire State College had no sports teams, no stadium, no marching band, no sororities, no fraternities, no student union, no classrooms—with the exception of the Labor College—no semesters, no College song, and not even a College-wide graduation ceremony. Students rarely gathered, except for the occasional group study. Also, the College was spread about the state in over thirty locations, nearly all of them leased. In launching the first annual fund drive, the Foundation was faced with a question that only the drive could answer: Had Empire State College in its brief existence created a sense in its students, and its faculty and staff, of being part of, and wanting to support an entity that was larger than their regional learning center or satellite? The first annual fund drive answered that question for all time. It had.

Under four directors, Gretchen Marcell (1974–1977), Zimri Smith (1977–1981), E. Thomas Ezell (1981–1988), and Jamie Sidgemore (1989–1995), the Foundation's assets and importance to the College have grown enormously through the financial support of thousands of students, alumni, and friends, including businesses and corporations. In 1984, ten years after its founding, the Empire State College Foundation's assets had grown to over $600,000, much of it permanent funding for scholarships and funding for student financial aid, faculty research, staff development and awards for excellence in College service. By 1996, twenty-one years after its founding, Foundation assets approached $6 million.

The Foundation also provided a vehicle to honor College pioneers such as Jeanne Brockmann, Scheffel Pierce, and Sig Synnesvedt through the creation of scholarships as well as through funds for special programs. In 1994 the Foundation established a bequest society in honor of Ernest L. Boyer and his spouse, Kathryn Boyer, an early ESC graduate and longtime member of the Empire State College Foundation Board.

Alumni/Student Federation: "Seeking an Identity"

From the outset, Empire State College encouraged the creation of student and alumni organizations at the regional learning centers and their units. These organizations enjoyed a good deal of success. There were student-alumni publications and a host of local activities sponsored by students and alumni who, often mature in years and experience as managers, were exceptionally good at organizing, and expert— as were the Labor College students and alumni especially—at exerting political pressure to serve the interests of the College. What was lacking, however, was a College-wide association. Students and alumni related quite well to their local units, if not their centers, but could they appreciate the importance of a statewide organization to promote the interests of the College? In 1973, the College surveyed alumni to find out and received a 95 percent mandate to establish an alumni association. Topics of interests included tutorial services for students, recruitment, job placement, private employment of students, alumni development activities, and an alumni advisory board.[44] The creation of a College-wide association, however, took three years.

Patricia Bartlett, executive assistant to President Hall, working with Jeanne Brockmann, director of alumni affairs, initiated planning in 1976. They began with an Alumni Convocation Task Force that prepared the ground for alumni to begin planning a statewide confederation the following July at a workshop in Saratoga Springs.[45] By early fall, a planning group selected from the alumni at the July workshop had prepared a constitution for the Federation of Empire State College Alumni/Student Associations. The alumni had wisely decided to include students in the Federation. With the exception of the Labor College, which had separate student and alumni associations, the local alumni/student associations always had worked in concert as single entities. It was inconceivable, therefore, for a College-wide alumni association to leave out students and, even more, to have a College-wide student association in addition to a separate alumni association, each representing a constituency indivisibly composed of alumni and students. In reality, Empire State College students, unlike their counterparts in traditional colleges, were much older and more accomplished. They did not remain students for long, on average, less than four years. Their maturity made it difficult to separate them from graduates in any practical way. In fact, just the opposite had to happen. The Federation, therefore, wisely recognized the need to continue on a statewide basis what existed locally. The Federation elected Ruth Decker, alumna of the Long Island Regional Learning Center, as its first president.

The creation of this College-wide alumni/student federation reflected an institutional angst, manifested in many fora in those early days, to establish an identity at a time when Empire State College underwent extraordinary growth and programmatic diversity. Not surprisingly, the preamble of the Federation's constitution begins with the following statement, "Whereas there is a recognized need to generate within our graduates and students a sense of identity with Empire State College as an entity."[46]

Marge Meinhardt, one of the alumna who helped organize the Alumni Convocation Task Force meeting in Saratoga Springs and who later became associate for alumni affairs, observed:

Those who came didn't know each other at all. But by the end of the first evening, I heard many of them say, "Now I feel part of the College. . . ." They all arrived thinking "I don't know if I really want to go to Saratoga, because I don't know anybody." I'm an alumna of Empire State, and I felt that way. I was registering participants, and I didn't know anybody. I thought I was really going to be nervous; but terrific people came, and by Sunday afternoon we all were sad to have the meeting concluded and to be saying good-bye to one another.[47]

By September 1979, the Alumni/Student Federation was thriving. It drew its strength from fourteen local alumni/student associations—another three were being organized—which included among their active membership almost 10 percent of the College's alumni, an extraordinary accomplishment.[48]

Mentor Evelyn Wells, Long Island Center faculty member, chats during a break at an All-College Meeting.

The Union: Political Firings?

The period of remarkable programmatic growth was a period of discord as well. In 1976, the faculty union accused the administration of "political firings."[49] The ESC chapter of the United University Professionals charged that "nearly 10 percent of approximately 120 full-time faculty . . . had been fired." Many were union activists and officers.[50] The union viewed the wave of firings (technically nonrenewal of contracts) in the context of productivity. As the union saw it, the New York State fiscal crisis required Empire State College, which "received special mention in the Governor's budget as the SUNY unit with the lowest per student cost . . . [to continue to press] this comparative advantage to its utmost limits."[51] The union identified Loren Baritz, executive director of the State University Commission of Purposes and Priorities, as "head of a SUNY-wide effort . . . to get the rest of the university up to [ESC] standards of productivity and managerial control. . . . The ax has fallen most heavily on the loudest of the administration's critics, on those who have most publicly resisted the speed-ups [in productivity] . . . while decreasing the quality of education."[52]

The controversy attracted national attention. A countrywide defense committee marshaled over a hundred faculty, including Noam Chomsky, from colleges and universities throughout the United States. And the American Federation of Teachers/AFL-CIO issued a resolution condemning union busting at SUNY Empire State College.[53]

How the administration viewed its own actions was another matter. For example, Ronald Corwin, dean of the Long Island Center, had been singled out by the union for firing "nine mentors critical of administrative designs. . . ."[54] Corwin had not participated in the hiring of the Long Island faculty and, in fact, was the last one hired at the Center in 1972. He had concerns about the calibre of some of the faculty:

When I first met the faculty. . . . I said to myself, "Oh, brother! We are in deep trouble. Because this group isn't going to be able to build anything, and we are going to have to make some changes. . . . We would have had, if we kept that original Long Island crew, a place in significant risk. We were a critical center because we were a big new on-line center. . . . I think that we came on line at a very critical time for the institution. As a practical matter, accreditation was more or less just around the corner. . . . It was coming.[55]

Hall saw the union imbroglio as the most difficult time of his presidency. He perceived no basis in the accusations and feared that because of the apparent merits of the case a political solution might circumvent the legal process. Hall observed:

As William Faulkner once said about the ability of literary critics to find patterns in his writing, if I objectively looked at these 12 cases, I could say, "Well it's true. Virtually each of them had become a union officer and so on and so forth." Eventually that case was won wholly by the College. . . . But once that was settled, that political dimension of the College stopped, and I think the people who were basically moderates in the faculty, then rallied together and we went forward.[56]

Over the years, the union has remained an important vehicle to express faculty viewpoints about the fundamental issues shaping the evolution of the College.

The Public Affairs Center: "Dramatically Redefined the Northeast Center's Mission"

Empire State College was able to maintain its commitment to growth despite the vagaries of the state's fiscal climate. But it was enormously frustrating for an innovative institution on the cutting edge—one that was cited by *Change* magazine in 1978 as a national leader in nontraditional education and lifelong learning—to be held back.

The Office of Research and Evaluation (ORE) staff at a 1975 meeting. Left to right are Dr. Timothy Lehmann, then director of program evaluation and now the director of the National Council on Adult Learning, Dr. Ernest Palola, assistant vice president for evaluation, Laura Montague, research assistant, and Richard Debus, director of costs. The ORE produced over two hundred studies for the College.

The potential was enormous: the population of adult learners in New York State was huge; the programmatic possibilities, as witnessed by regional learning centers, satellites, specialized programs, distance learning, overseas programs, were vast. Most of all, the faculty and administration were energized with a pioneering spirit.

It was not difficult to imagine, as the College approached its tenth anniversary, that it should have had thirty-five thousand FTE enrollments instead of thirty-five hundred. What the College needed was freedom from the fiscal constraints placed on it by the State University, yet Empire State College drew sustenance from the same state support as did other equally aggressive SUNY campuses. To grow could be only at the expense of other campuses. Each campus guarded its apportionment; each had vigilant State Assembly representatives and a State Senator sensitive to its interests. The College grew only as much as SUNY System administration permitted: the enrollment was limited by the number of faculty; the tuition collected by the College went directly into State coffers and not for new faculty; and nothing, neither in the State's economic growth nor the College's standing in the confederation of SUNY campuses, signaled that better times lay ahead.

Indeed, Empire State College had to do more with less. In March 1979, for example, the administration created the Public Affairs Center from an existing program, the Northeast Regional Learning Center (popularly known as the Albany Center) to serve State agency employees. In 1978, a memorandum from the President's Committee on College Development noted the following:

Service to State agencies has become an area of high interest throughout SUNY, in large part because of Chancellor Wharton's focus on public service. Empire State College is in a very good position to move forward in this area because of its Statewide presence and flexible educational approach and because of its established relationships with the Department of Taxation and Finance, the Department of Labor, and the Department of Correctional Services.'57

Jane Shipton, Long Island Center assessment specialist, worked with Mentor Elizabeth Steltenpohl in the pioneering of assessment materials, including a handbook for students which was used throughout the College.

The administration dramatically redefined the Northeast Center's mission. Since its founding in 1971, the Albany Center had served students from every walk of life, and was located in the midst of New York State government. Reconfigured as the Public Affairs Center, it could focus its marketing energies on thousands of state employees, including mid-level managers and ambitious clerical workers. It also could serve federal and municipal government employees as well as people involved in civic affairs. The Center would be well-positioned to negotiate contracts with government agencies interested in promoting the career interests of their employees, not only in the capital district but throughout New York State. In fact, the Albany Center already had demonstrated the feasibility of having formal links with state agencies. What remained was to do this on a grand scale with state subvention and to turn the old Northeast Regional Learning Center, which had been lagging in enrollments, into a state, if not a national, showcase.

There was a bit of alchemy in this plan, however. The Public Affairs Center gained some new personnel. But it was mostly the Albany Center reconstituted, with additional faculty and staff drawn from elsewhere in the College. Within the first year of operation it became clear that the Center still had difficulties. A study conducted by the Office of Research and Evaluation identified a number of problems: The Center had to meet its commitment to existing students; new personnel needed time to acclimate to the mission as well as to their colleagues; enrollment targets had to be met at the same time that agency relationships were to be cultivated; and new assessment procedures and records systems had to be put into operation. All these operational commitments interfered with "developmental . . . priorities." They fragmented tasks, diminished energy, and diffused purpose. They were compounded by an understaffed administrative core which had to market the program aggressively and to provide leadership. The ORE report pointed to difficulties stemming from philosophical differences between faculty committed to an individualized approach and the mission of the Public Affairs Center: "There is a concern that the emphasis on academic programming for groups of students with common backgrounds may mean, in practice, little more than prescribing a fixed curriculum."[58]

Although the Public Affairs Center met its enrollment targets by 1981 and successfully negotiated contracts with the Department of Labor, Office of General Services, Department of Social Services, and Department of Taxation and Finance, the Center did not experience the robust growth its architects had anticipated. In 1982, consequently, the Albany organization was incorporated into the Center for Statewide Programs. This experiment defined the limits of our organizational flexibility.

The 1979 Self-study and the Middle States Review: "A Fresh New Breeze Blowing in Higher Education"

The Empire State College that prepared itself for the Middle States review in 1979 had made remarkable progress since its first review five years earlier. The 1979 self-study lacked the diffident undercurrent of the 1974 report. In 1974 the College was still going through an explosive period of experimentation and growth. There were stumbles and trips, but through it all the institution was heading in the right direction. Scarcely three years old in 1974, the College proudly pointed to accomplishments built on a trial-and-error pragmatism. How different was the tone of 1979 self-study. It reflected a college that had come through its *rite de passage*. The institution stood now at the threshold of maturity and brimmed with confidence. It boldly announced an institutional "quest for excellence." The Middle States team captured the spirit of the College's achievements, energy, and promise in a single sentence: "Empire State College is a fresh new breeze blowing in higher education."[59]

The self-study focused on how the College tried mightily to insure the academic quality of its programs. The role of the Office of Program Review and Assessment (OPRA), for example, had become highly focused, providing "a quality control review on assessment decisions made at Centers" and fostering a College-wide "consistency" in practices.[60] OPRA was assisted in the latter by faculty task force committees. Created by the Academic Planning and Learning Programs Committee, these faculty groups examined assessment practices and made recommendations for credit limits in such areas as secretarial science and physical education. In addition, OPRA had issued a handbook for mentors, *Resources and Criteria for Assessment and Program Review*, to provide credit recommendations for noncollegiate programs. There were other efforts, such as faculty workshops by the Center for Individualized Education and the distribution of all kinds of assessment materials. These efforts reflected tensions in a college that was at once committed to the concept of individualized assessment while struggling to create a system that was fair, efficient, and respected.[61]

New York City labor leader Harry Van Arsdale Jr. (standing) applauds Labor Center graduates at a 1976 ceremony. He is joined (right to left) by President James W. Hall, Empire State College Council member Kitty Carlisle Hart, and Dean Bill Goode.

Most important, the College was moving toward the assessment of prior learning as seen in the context of degree program design, and away from assessment as amassing credit for a quick degree, a trend first noted in the 1974 report. The self-study observed: "Clearly, the College has moved significantly in assessment from a piecemeal approach to a holistic Degree Program perspective. The emphasis now is on students' educational goals and on requests for advanced standing in the context of these goals."[62] It was about this time that a few Empire State College students who had earned degrees in a mad rush during the early 1970s returned for degrees more suited to their goals.

By 1979, the College was located in thirty-six sites and had enrolled 3,330 students from all but a few of New York State's sixty-two counties. The College continued to attract an enormous range of students, mostly mature adults, average age of thirty-seven; 54 percent of the students were women, 81 percent employed—65 percent full time, 9 percent African-American, 2 percent Hispanic, 2 percent other, and 87 percent Caucasian; 10 percent were homemakers, 10 percent were blue-collar workers, 10 percent clerical, 20 percent were mid-level supervisors, 33 percent were in semiprofessional and professional employment, and 91 percent had formal education beyond the post-secondary level. Empire State College was as nontraditional in the populations it served as in the programs it offered. The large number of recent high school graduates it anticipated serving never appeared. The majority of students in 1979 were older; they were women, married, employed, and white.[63]

The self-study apologized for the College's relatively low level of racial and ethnic diversity but noted the higher percentages of African-Americans, Hispanics, and other minorities served by the centers in Manhattan—Metropolitan and Labor—and by special programs at Bedford-Stuyvesant, the South Bronx, and the Lower East Side. The self-study raised fears, however, that funds for grant-based minority programs would be expiring. In a steady-state budget environment, a way had to be found to make such programs a permanent part of the College, not just short-lived if well-intentioned forays into diversity.[64] Empire State College students were ambitious, self-disciplined, upwardly mobile and responding to a society that increasingly demanded academic credentials for social and economic advancement. Students had clear educational objectives. Some simply wished to expand their intellectual horizons or become more active citizens; most wanted new careers, specific job skills, or increased professional status; while others prepared for graduate school. The bulk of the students, 56 percent, pursued concentrations in business, community and human services, human development, and the arts.[65]

The College was finding that while students had clear goals, ones that fused education and self-interest, motivation was simply not enough for academic success. More and more students were less prepared to undertake college study. A survey conducted in 1978, for example, showed that 30 to 50 percent of those tested needed to improve their writing. In the initial years, the College viewed itself as serving bypassed students who were prepared for independent study.[66] With time, as the College began to attract more applicants deficient in skills, it began to recognize that preparing students to do independent study had to be an institutional goal and could no longer distance itself from student failure, dismissing it as a "self-selection" process.[67] Starting in 1977, the College made efforts to address what would become known as "basic skills needs" of enrolled students.[68] That year, a College-wide panel on writing skills produced a handbook to assist faculty with their students, both as a diagnostic instrument and as an instructional resource.[69] The 1979 self-study was quick to note, however, that much remained to be accomplished in developing "diagnostic and prescriptive services in the areas of reading, writing, research methodology and computational skills. . . ."[70]

Addressing student deficiencies in academic skills was important to the future of the College. Empire State College had a worrisome attrition rate. Although the College had devised a flexible system that allowed students to withdraw and reenroll, almost at a moment's notice, attrition could not be fully explained by the personal and professional contingencies faced by adult students. One Office of Research and Evaluation study tracked a cohort of students who had enrolled in 1974. It showed an attrition rate of 43 percent over a four-year period; these were students who had been withdrawn for more than eight consecutive months.[71]

Mentors had to enroll more students to compensate for this attrition. Students needed to be oriented, degree programs designed, contracts negotiated, tutors located—most of it up-front and exhausting work. Mentors found that the greater the rate of attrition, the greater the workload, especially when full-time students were replaced by half-time students. It was not difficult to imagine that a high attrition rate had an inherent capacity to feed on itself as currently enrolled students were served less well by overworked faculty and were, therefore, more likely to drop out, only to be replaced by a quickening, if not maddening, pace of new students. Attrition caused collateral problems. Students who had dropped out, especially those badly served by frazzled mentors, were more likely to speak poorly of the College. This had the potential to cause marketing problems for a college that depended on word-of-mouth advertising to attract new students. Though the loss rate for students at Empire State College was about the same as traditional colleges, the self-study was right, therefore, to flag attrition as a concern. The workload—and not just for faculty—as well as the marketing implications were staggering. Attrition was Empire State College's Achilles' heel.

For Empire State College students who made it to graduation, and by 1979 over fifty-five hundred had earned degrees, the findings of various surveys were remarkable. A 1975 survey showed that 44 percent of the graduates sought additional professional training and graduate education. Almost three-quarters of those applying for graduate school had been admitted and 21 percent had applications pending approval. Only 5 percent had been denied admission. In regard to changes in work status, about half of the graduates had found new employment; 50 percent had experienced such benefits as increases in pay, heightened professional status, or improved satisfaction. Many graduates, almost half, credited the College for their "improved self-confidence, increased independence, clarified goals, and developed self-discipline."[72]

Another study, sponsored by the New York State Legislative Commission on Expenditure Review, provided comparison with traditional institutions. Almost 80% of Empire State College graduates responding to the survey gave a positive assessment of their undergraduate experience, compared to about 52 percent of the graduates of traditional institutions. The graduates gave higher ratings to the quality of such service as career counseling, and academic advisement and support. Notably, Empire State College graduates, by about twofold, saw their major fields of study as more relevant to preparing for full-time employment, graduate school, and activities beyond the scope of work.[73]

The self-study highlighted mentoring. A college that gave access to education in extraordinary ways had to create an extraordinary, cutting-edge faculty to facilitate that access. Mentors served in a role that they had not been trained for in graduate school. Mentoring meant subordinating one's disciplinary interests to facilitate student objectives and goals, oftentimes in fields of study as unfamiliar as the plains of Venus. Mentoring demanded long hours of taxing work. In the midst of all of their responsibilities to students and colleagues, mentors labored to find time to tutor contracts in their disciplines, to keep up with their reading, to give presentations at conferences, and to write scholarly articles or books. Working in the absence of departmental structure put mentors in isolation from their own disciplinary colleagues. Successful mentoring, then, was sometimes achieved at the expense of exhausting, as Baritz observed, one's intellectual capital. As the self-study noted, echoing several College reports, "several aspects of mentoring continue to require attention so that the role can allow faculty to work, grow, and develop without feeling either that they must neglect some part of themselves professionally or that by remaining mentors they have consigned themselves to the academic hinterlands."[74] One could rightly worry about the long-term viability of the role.

A study of mentoring undertaken by Mentor Carolyn Broadaway, and supported by the Center for Individualized Education, noted mentors' concern about the heavy workload and the tension between the fragmented nature of the role and the demands of their disciplines.[75] The self-study noted the measures the College had taken to sustain the personal and intellectual vitality of the faculty, including an annual professional development month and professional reassignment opportunities.[76] Soon after, the College instituted a calendar of no-appointment weeks when faculty were not required to meet with students. These could be devoted to catching up on paperwork or research. The self-study noted the heavy and fragmented workload of administrators and the difficulties they faced "in planning professional development and career development" as well as the difficulties faced by professional personnel and support staff who found themselves in roles defined by the unique mission and needs of an evolving institution.[77]

The Middle States team's praise for the College was effusive, so much so that the College printed the entire report in two issues of the *ESC News*:

The outstanding quality of your administrators, faculty, and staff and their willingness to search for new approaches to teaching and learning have brought national recognition to the College. The President of Empire State College was cited in Change *magazine (October 1978) as one of the 100 "most respected emerging leaders in higher education," and Empire State College was noted to be "nationally recognized as a leader in non-traditional education and life-long learning. . . ." Your strengths are many and we will comment on many of these throughout the report. You have a right to be proud of your accomplishments.*[78]

Empire State College has implemented a set of provocative assumptions about student learning largely through the stunning unselfishness of mentors. . . . So impressed and stimulated were we by hearing the highly individual narratives told by alumni and current students . . . that we recommend the College find more occasions to give state leaders the same opportunity. . . . ESC . . . is nationally and internationally known and highly respected; it has set a national standard and in many ways has been a model for non-traditional learning in the United States. . . . The College has been able to reach its high level of achievement in large measure as a result of what appears to be extraordinary effort on the part of the professional and clerical staff. . . . Although the college enrollment is technically listed at 3,300, it functions administratively as a college more than twice as large. From this perspective we view the College as considerably understaffed.[79]

The accomplishments of the College were so meritorious that the Middle States Association awarded a ten-year reaccreditation, the maximum allowable period.

A ten-year reaccreditation was a crowning achievement for such a young college. It occurred at the end of a robust decade of experimentation and growth which had begun with Chancellor Boyer's planning group in 1970. The period had been defined sharply by New York State's fiscal distress. One could easily imagine what might have been had the College come forth in better times. The Middle States team observed:

You are facing a serious problem with a virtually stationary budget in trying to meet your three main institutional objectives: access, innovation, and excellence. We commend you for placing requests for new monies in your budget in the area of excellence. However, the attainment of your other two goals, access and innovation, also requires additional finances if your are to meet the demands of the mature learner for access to Empire State College and if you are to continue your efforts to experiment with alternatives in higher education.[80]

Empire State College welcomed this endorsement from Middle States. Yet the fiscal climate of New York State offered little promise for a significant infusion of expanded resources. As Empire State College entered the decade of the 1980s, the prospect of getting fewer resources was greater than that of having more because of a contracting state economy. Early in the decade, moreover, the state would face a major fiscal crisis.

Endnotes Chapter 3

1. James W. Hall to the Administrative Council, 29 March 1974, Memorandum, Empire State College Archives, Saratoga Springs, New York.

2. Ibid., 1.

3. Ibid.

4. James W. Hall to D. Bolef, J. Brockmann, M. Huber, R. Rader, H. Roeth, A. Schwartz, A. Serling, 3 September 1974, Memorandum, Empire State College Archives, Saratoga Springs, New York, pp. 1–2.

5. Hal Roeth to John Jacobson and the Administrative Council, 31 October 1974, Memorandum, Empire State College Archives, Saratoga Springs, New York, pp. 1–2.

6. Hall to the Administrative Council, pp. 6–7; John Jacobson to James W. Hall, Loren Baritz, Arthur Chickering, and Al Schwartz, 1 August 1974, Memorandum, Empire State College Archives, Saratoga Springs, New York, pp. 1–2.

7. "Extended Programs Update," 6 October 1976, Memorandum, Empire State College Archives, Saratoga Springs, New York, p. 1.

8. Robert Hassenger to Empire State College Colleagues, 23 September 1977, Memorandum, Empire State College Archives, Saratoga Springs, New York, p. 1.

9. John Jacobson to the Center for Independent Study Faculty, 5 May 1978, Memorandum, Empire State College Archives, Saratoga Springs, New York, pp. 1–2.

10. Ibid., 2.

11. Richard Bonnabeau to Scheffel Pierce, 19 September 1979, Memorandum, Empire State College Archives, Saratoga Springs, New York, p. 1.

12. Mark Gelber to James Hall, 27 March 1979, Memorandum, Empire State College Archives, Saratoga Springs, New York, p. 1.

13. "CDL Fall 1979 Term Announcement," August 1979, Empire State College Archives, Saratoga Springs, New York.

14. Vincent Worth and Richard Bonnabeau to John Jacobson, W. Ferrero, C. Johnstone, R. Orrill, and CDL Faculty, 24 September 1981, Memorandum, Empire State College Archives, Saratoga Springs, New York, p. 1.

15. "Center for Distance Learning: Research Findings" (Saratoga Springs, New York: Empire State College, Office of Research and Evaluation, February 26, 1980), p 1.

16. Ibid.

17. James W. Hall to Ernest L. Boyer, 27 November 1972, Letter, Empire State College Archives, Saratoga Springs, New York, p. 1.

18. Ibid.

19. Irving Kriesberg to James W. Hall, 27 November 1972, Memorandum, Empire State College Archives, Saratoga Springs, New York, pp. 1–2.

20. James W. Hall to George Dawson and Fernand Brunschwig, 15 December 1974, Letter, Empire State College Archives, Saratoga Springs, New York, p. 1.

21. Kenneth Abrams to Loren Baritz, 15 May 1974, Memorandum, Empire State College Archives, Saratoga Springs, New York.

22. Edward Carr to James W. Hall, 24 March 1975, Memorandum: Report of the New York State Education Department (NYSED) Evaluation Team, Empire State College Archives, Saratoga Springs, New York, p. 23.

23. Vernon Ozarow to James W. Hall, 20 December 1974, Letter, Empire State College Archives, Saratoga Springs, New York, p. 1.

24. Hall to Dawson and Brunschwig, p. 1.

25. Ibid., 2.

26. Ibid.

27. Ernest L. Boyer to the SUNY Board of Trustees, 26 May 1976, Memorandum, Empire State College Archives, Saratoga Springs, New York, pp. 1–2.

28. Regents of the University of the State of New York, "Minutes," 1976, Albany, New York, p. 137.

29. Kenneth Abrams, Interview by Richard Bonnabeau, 17 May 1990, transcript, Empire State College Archives, Saratoga Springs, New York, p. 31.

30. Loren Baritz to James Hall, 2 March 1973, Memorandum, Saratoga Springs, New York. Empire State College Archives, Saratoga Springs, New York.

31. Mary Ann Biller to Margaret Traxlor, 11 May 1976, Letter, Empire State College Archives, Saratoga Springs, New York.

32. Seymour Eskow to Loren Baritz, 18 May 1976, Letter, Empire State College Archives, Saratoga Springs, New York.

33. James W. Hall to Loren Baritz, 22 July 1976, Memorandum, Empire State College Archives, Saratoga Springs, New York.

34. James W. Hall to Ronald Corwin, John Jacobson, and Jeanne Brockmann, 17 November 1977, Memorandum, Empire State College Archives, Saratoga Springs, New York.

35. Ibid.

36. Kenneth Abrams, "A Report on my Trip to Israel: October 26–November 9, 1977," 1977?, Memorandum, Empire State College Archives, Saratoga Springs, New York, p. 7.

37. Kenneth Abrams, "The Challenge of ESC Study in Israel," ESC News, March 1980, p. 3.

38. Ernest L. Boyer to James W. Hall, 23 June 1972, Letter, Empire State College Archives, Saratoga Springs, New York.

39. James W. Hall to Walter Relihan, 11 April 1973, Letter, Empire State College Archives, Saratoga Springs, New York.

40. Committee on Campus Foundations to Ernest L. Boyer, 11 May 1973, Letter, Empire State College Archives, Saratoga Springs, New York.

41. "College Launching First Annual Fund Appeal This Month," ESC News, September 1975, vol. 1, no. 11, p. 1.

42. ESC News, September 1975, p. 1

43. "First Annual Appeal Ends; Contributions to Climb Near Goal, ESC News, June–July 1976, vol. 2, no. 2, p. 1.

44. "Grads Cast Overwhelming Vote of Confidence in '73 Alumni ESC News, February–March 1974, vol. 1, no. 1, p. 1.

45. John Hall to James W. Hall, 3 August 1976, Memorandum, Empire State College Archives, Saratoga Springs, New York, pp. 1–3.

46. "Constitution of the Federation of Empire State College Alumni/Student Associations," 16 October 1976, Empire State College Archives, Saratoga Springs, New York, p. 1.

47. "Conversation with the Alumni Office Staff," ESC News, September 1979, p. 4.

48. ESC News, September 1979, p. 4.

49. The Faculty Action Committee of SUNY/Empire State College, Letter and Attachments, 4 October 1976, Empire State College Archives, Saratoga Springs, New York, p. 1

50. Ibid., 8.

51. Ibid., 12.

52. Ibid., 13.

53. "Union Busting-Empire State College, State University of New York," Resolution, The American Federation of Teachers, AFL-CIO, 20 August 1976, p. 1.

54. Faculty Action Committee, p. 13.

55. Ronald Corwin, Interview by Richard Bonnabeau, 21 June 1990, transcript, Empire State College Archives, Saratoga Springs, New York, p. 29.

56. James W. Hall, Interview by Richard Bonnabeau, 6 September 1990, transcript, Empire State College Archives, Saratoga Springs, New York, pp. 10–11.

57. President's Committee on College Development, 6 September 1978, Memorandum, Empire State College Archives, Saratoga Springs, New York, p. 3.

58. "Status Report and First Year Evaluation, Public Affairs Center" (Saratoga Springs, New York: Empire State College, Office of Research and Evaluation, July 1980), 8–10.

59. "Middle States Report," ESC News, March 1980, p. 2.

60. *Access, Innovation and the Quest for Excellence: Empire State College in 1979*, Self-study Prepared for the Commission on Higher Education, Middle States Association of Colleges and Schools (Empire State College, Saratoga Springs, New York, September 1979), 18.

61. Ibid.

62. Ibid.

63. Ibid., 23.

64. Ibid., 25.

65. Ibid., 24.

66. Ibid. 14.

67. Ibid., 14 and 25.

68. Ibid. 14.

69. Ibid.

70. Ibid., 26.

71. Ibid., 27.

72. Ibid., 26–27.

73. Ibid., 27.

74. Ibid., 35.

75. Ibid., 35–36.

76. Ibid., 36.

77. Ibid., 38.

78. "Middle States Report," ESC News, March, 1980, p. 2.

79. Ibid., 2–3.

80. "Middle States Report," ESC News, June, 1980, p. 2.

Georgianna Johnson is a 1976 graduate of the Harry Van Arsdale Jr. School of Labor Studies.

1981–1996

4

CONNECTIONS

Signs at the NYNEX corporate headquarters, 1095
Avenue of the Americas, Manhattan, signal the
College's connection to the corporate world.
Photograph by Miller Photography, New Hyde Park,
New York.

n 1981, Empire State College celebrated its tenth anniversary. By that time, Middle States had reviewed the College twice. The second review granted a much esteemed ten-year reaccreditation, the best measure possible of what the institution had accomplished in a decade. The Middle States report had resounded with praise for Empire State College. There was much to celebrate, and President Hall asked Ernest Boyer, founder of Empire State College, to join in the celebration. Boyer had resigned from his post as chancellor of the State University in January 1977 to serve as United States Commissioner of Education in the Carter Administration. Boyer assumed the presidency of the Carnegie Foundation for the Advancement of Teaching in July 1979. Hall invited Boyer to be the keynote speaker at the College's tenth anniversary convocation, held July 10, 1981, in Albany. Almost the entire College—support staff, faculty, administrators, and some students—had assembled at Albany's Convention Hall in the Empire State Plaza, the locus of state government offices. Dominick Del Ra, a gifted musician and 1980 graduate of the Public Affairs Center, conducted a small orchestra, which played an instrumental piece he had composed and dedicated especially for the anniversary. It was called "Fanfare for a Festive Occasion." President Hall had asked Boyer to focus on the College's future. Boyer beamed with pride as he stood at the dais to give his keynote address:

Ten years ago, I dreamed a dream. My dream was a college of great excellence. A college where the focus was not on buildings or bureaucracy or on rigid schedules—not on mindless regulations but on students and education. . . . My dream was a college located all across the state geared to serve the student, not the institution or the process. And one of my first moves as Chancellor of the State University of New York was to propose a new, radical, non-campus institution called Empire State College. Today, ten years later I am filled with tremendous pride. . . . Empire State College has a reputation for excellence all around the world.[1]

Boyer then shared his vision of the future Empire State College, "The College with Connections." Among the connections Boyer identified, two, the coming Information Revolution and the need to reach out to American businesses and corporations, would consume much of the energy of the College for the coming years. Of the Information Revolution, Boyer rightly predicted its explosive force and the importance of the personal computer. Of the outreach to business and corporate America, Boyer spoke of the opportunity for a liberal arts apostolate but warned the College "not to imitate or be consumed by business."[2] He cautioned Empire State College as well to recognize "the enormous impact" the Information Revolution would have on American education.[3] It was more a warning of the dangers of not harnessing its power rather than about fears of marching into the mouth of the technology dragon.

The Information Revolution: "Serpent in the Pristine Garden of Academe"

In the fifteen years since the Convocation, the Information Revolution and the technology that drives it, have more and more defined what the College is and will become. The interest in technology originated with the planning of the College. Boyer's task force had embraced technology. In fact, the outline for the College that Hall drafted on All Hallows' Eve, in 1970, had a significant technological component, and the *Prospectus*, drafted in February 1971, identified a whole range of technologically based resources to buoy student learning. The task force recommended the creation of a media development staff, which became the Learning Resources Center, "to plan the integration and development of the various media forms for delivery systems serving the program objectives and curricula."[4]

In his 1971 inaugural address, President Hall warned his colleagues and guests of pedagogical Jeremiahs "who proclaim that the computer and technology is the most recent, if electronic, serpent in the pristine garden of Academe."[5] He affirmed the College's commitment to technology to support independent learning. But Hall did not want technology to become "the tail wagging the dog."[6] He was particularly concerned about not repeating the mistakes of the defunct SUNY of the Air, which wagered everything on one use of television and the delivery of talking-head lectures. Hall promoted learning enhanced by technologically based resources through the Learning Resources Center, many of whose staff came from SUNY of the Air and the SUNY Independent Study Program. Learning Resources Center personnel devoted the bulk of their energy to producing learning modules, which occasionally included various kinds of media such as audio cassettes and films. The Center produced some televised colloquia, featuring Loren Baritz debating other scholars, which were broadcast by the New York Network, and spearheaded the first effort to offer telecourses on a statewide basis. These efforts did not have a major impact on the academic program, however. As we have seen, mentors relied mostly on print-based resources and face-to-face tutorials.

Nevertheless, Hall believed that educational technology, especially communications technology, could make a significant contribution to the academic program. In January of 1974, exactly one year before the first personal computer, known as the Altair, became available to anyone who had $400 dollars and a soldering iron, Hall distributed a "highly speculative" plan with the Administrative Council and the Academic and Learning Programs Committee: "We should direct major effort to implementing fully the use of communications technology. Such development . . . would rest upon a solid framework for study, and could be invaluable in extending the College outreach. The Instructional Resources Faculty should increasingly devote time and resources in this direction."[7]

Technology came of age at Empire State College in 1978 with the creation of the Center for Independent Study, which a year later became the Center for Distance Learning. The Center was the first of the College's programs to employ technology-based learning as an integral component of the curriculum. Using materials developed by the British Open University as well as the Maryland Open University, and various national consortia, the Center offered a whole range of courses with television and audio components; and its tutorials were based on one of the oldest of telecommunication technologies, invented almost a century before the College came into existence, the telephone.

By the early 1980s, the revolution in personal computer technology captured the College's imagination. The significance of the technology, as both an educational tool and administrative device, was manifestly obvious. Mentors could use computers as word processors for learning contracts and evaluations; as tracking devices to record the progress of students; as a means to communicate with colleagues and students via electronic mail; and as a way to tutor students, either through a one-to-one format or through computer conferencing. Beyond these capacities, the marriage of the personal computer to compact-disk technology promised low-cost interactive and multimedia based learning. Now, at the threshold of the twenty-first century, students can summon virtual warehouses of information in words, sounds, and pictures, either in separate or combined formats, through software packages, compact disks, and through the Internet. Furthermore, the new technologies accommodate a variety of learning styles.

Dominick Del Ra, a 1980 graduate of the Public Affairs Center, now part of the Northeast Center, conducts the tenth anniversary convocation symphonic band. He composed "Fanfare for a Festive Occasion" for the event. The convocation was held July 10, 1981, at Albany's Convention Hall at the Empire State Plaza. Ernest L. Boyer was the keynote speaker.

Just as Gutenberg's printing press had revolutionized learning five centuries ago by bringing the printed word to the masses, the computer, the compact disk, and the Internet are redefining the ways knowledge is gathered, communicated, received, and used. Paper-and-ink based learning is being replaced by silicon wafers, disks of polished aluminum, and electronic packets of digitized data rushing through uplinks and downlinks, networks and nodes. This revolution is happening on a scale and at speeds that are yet difficult to comprehend: It conjures up images of classrooms in cyberspace, of the student no longer as a passive learner but in command of phenomenal learning resources and finally free of the medieval time-bound, place-bound, lecture-bound transmission of knowledge.

Computer Technology: "Transcends Space, Place, and Time"

If ever a college were suited to an emerging technology, it is Empire State College. The first words uttered in the *Prospectus,* describing Empire State College's purposes and goals, seemed to prophesy a college for the coming Information Revolution: "an institution which transcends constraints of space, place and time."[8] Empire State College purchased its first microcomputer (personal computer) in 1980, and in the early 1980s aggressively sought out opportunities to make the microcomputer part of its academic program. The computer was changing the landscape of American work, and a significant percentage of Empire State College applicants for admission, 33 percent wanted to learn how to use the technology, up from 10 percent just five years before. This need to become knowledgeable about computers matched student employment-related objectives for earning a degree. Most students, 87 percent, pursued degrees in professional fields: business (35 percent), human services (30 percent), and science and technology (12 percent).[9]

The challenges facing the College were great, however. In 1981, Empire State College lacked a mainframe, and the financial plight of New York State made such a future acquisition a remote possibility. The College also lacked a computer science faculty. The faculty's knowledge of computers was "minimal to non-existent."[10] What the College did not possess in trained faculty it compensated for with a widespread interest among mentors to become computer literate. As an early report noted, "the availability of relatively low-cost microcomputers . . . sparked our imagination as to how we can provide instructional computing for our students."[11]

Faculty Computer Literacy Project: "Teach Mentors to Teach Other Mentors to Teach Students"

Teach mentors to teach other mentors to teach students. This is how the College planned, in a pilot project, to begin reaching its students. Mentors had already acquired a great deal of expertise in teaching adults. They could easily teach adult students computer skills, because they had approached the task of becoming computer literate as adults themselves.[12] "The chief beneficiaries of competent and enthusiastic teachers will be our students. Faculty who can say to students, 'I knew nothing about computers a year ago and now look what I can do,' can go a long way in helping students who are their peers in age overcome their hesitation and anxiety in approaching the study of computers."[13]

In January 1982, the College began a faculty reassignment program, coordinated by Carol Twigg, assistant vice president for academic affairs. Vice President for Academic Affairs John Jacobson offered a number of one-month mini-sabbaticals to interested faculty. The participants met as a group and then worked independently on projects in their own fields of study. The group activities included programming in BASIC, reviewing recommended readings for students, and discussing instructional strategies. By the end of the sabbatical, faculty were ready to work with students on introductory level contracts.[14]

One of the participants, Barbara Marantz, recalled her experience and its impact on her mentoring:

I had learned what a computer could do, and a bit about how it did "it." I was intrigued and motivated to explore its potential as a work-saving tool. At that time I had no sense of what telecommunications was about or how the computer might be used educationally. . . . Several years passed before I came to recognize the power of the medium as an educational tool. . . . I have done two computer-based studies with students. The first was an individual learning contract done with a CDL student who lived in Colorado. I had "met" Richard . . . in one of the CAUCUS [computer-based seminar] discussion groups running on the VAX [computer mainframe], became interested in his ideas about the medium's educational potential, e-mailed him privately, and out of our communication, developed a study on the history of educational media for him that I tutored (a study in which I learned as least as much as he did). It was doing this study that helped me learn how to use the medium, the VAX, CAUCUS discussion "space," and uploading and downloading capabilities to support work with a student at a distance. (Richard and I published an article about our experience and learning about the medium's potential in a reviewed electronic journal). . . .

About a year or two later, I developed and implemented a small study group in psychology for several Hudson Valley students who could not meet with me face-to-face. The entire "seminar" was run on-line. Students "met" regularly in a CAUCUS to discuss readings and issues they raised, or to respond to those I provided for discussion. They uploaded papers to me and shared them with one another; I downloaded responses and papers as they learned to upload them to me via e-mail as well as in hard-copy; they communicated with me and with each other privately via e-mail; and I was able to share

articles and other material which I kept in open VAX files, accessible to them, in much the
way a library might use "RESERVE" capability. I believe the students enjoyed this
asynchronous way of learning; I found it possible to work as closely as I ever had, and often
in ways that were much more convenient and responsive than would have been possible in
real time. However, I found that this way of learning is incredibly time-consuming; students
are ALWAYS there and expect that you will be too.[15]

At the same time the faculty computer literacy project was initiated, the College began to purchase more personal computers. Deans were invited to request additional computers for instructional purposes over a two-year period. At that time each center had one Apple II. Over a two-year period the College purchased fifty additional Apple computers.[16]

The faculty literacy project continued for the next several years. In time, however, the growing popularity of personal computers made the project unnecessary. This was a consequence of the rapid fall in the price of personal computers, the phenomenal growth of their power, and the proliferation of inexpensive software to run them. Mentors as well as students joined the millions purchasing personal computers. The College invested money instead in the purchase of computer hardware and software, and did so, wisely, because mentors began to purchase personal computers for home use. What the College had to do was to invest available funds in providing desktop computers for every member of the faculty.

Annenberg/CPB Project: "Luddites in Wonderland"

At the time the College was beginning to make headway in its faculty computer literacy project, the Annenberg/Corporation for Public Broadcasting Project caught the attention of the College. In 1981, Ambassador Walter Annenberg, founder of *TV GUIDE* and the Annenberg School of Communications, announced a project offering $150 million in grants—$10 million per year—for a fifteen-year period to American colleges and universities to "advance higher education through telecommunications."[17] The College saw an opportunity to greatly accelerate the integration of computers in the academic program. Two proposals were submitted to the Annenberg/CPB Project in 1983. The first proposal, a cooperative venture with Skidmore College, planned to create a telecommunications network, consisting of "hierarchically linked computers . . . to form eighty statewide 'Advanced Education Stations' and demonstrate the impact of a combination of telecommunications and information processing technologies on mode of delivery, cost and quality of college-level programs serving students at a distance."[18]

The proposal for the $2,749,000 project nicely fit the Annenberg guidelines. However, it offered very little in the way of developing computer software materials and was more of a computer technology demonstration project to be underwritten by Annenberg/CPB Project funds. The reviewers rejected the proposal. Of the reasons given, including a lack of focus and the absence of software development and application, perhaps the most curious, which evoked shades of Luddites in Wonderland, was that the system was too powerful: "Some of the panelists feared a strong negative impact on faculty workload. . . . This system would eliminate some of the natural barriers protecting teachers from student questions, requests, etc. . . ."[19]

With encouragement from the Annenberg people who wanted to "continue the relationship" with Empire State College, a second proposal was quickly submitted in December.[20] The proposal had a well defined subject-matter orientation—reentry-level study in writing, mathematics, and computer studies—using a computer network

Dr. Angela Li-Scholz, a physicist, joined the Albany faculty in 1972. She was one of the first faculty to recognize the importance of the microcomputer to mentoring. Photograph by Tony Tassaratti.

to deliver instruction in "a highly decentralized educational environment."[21] Unlike the previous proposal, which required tremendous outlays for the purchase of personal computers and a VAX, this modest proposal focused on the development of instructional software packages as well as on the creation of a "networking and support system . . . to facilitate work, communication, and record-keeping between faculty-mentors and students"—today, known as MENTORNET and MENTORPAK.[22] Upon receiving word of the second proposal, Chancellor Clifton R. Wharton Jr., Boyer's successor, sent Hall encouraging words: "Whatever the outcome of the grant, your commitment to move ahead with work on new forms of communication and instruction seems most appropriate for Empire State College. I regret that state support of the entire project is not possible under a University budget which allots so little for innovation and experimentation."[23]

The reviewers turned down the second proposal. This time the reviewers failed to understand Empire State College. They were concerned that a demonstration project would be of limited value because of the unique nature of the College and that the project might not be "sufficiently different" from activities at other colleges.[24] Instead, Annenberg funded three course development proposals from other colleges as well as funded a microwave project.

There is no question that the failure to secure funding from the Annenberg/CPB Project in 1983 delayed the College's efforts to be at the vanguard of the Information Revolution. The great effort invested in preparing the proposals, nevertheless, created a forum for faculty and administrators to consider the importance of computer technology to the future of the College. Faculty began to consider how the computer could redefine Empire State College. As years go, 1983 might have been our worst for securing major grants, but the Annenberg/CPB proposals enhanced the vision of what the College could become and increased the resolve to make the computer an integral part of the academic fabric of Empire State College, not just a technology to make our business operations run smoothly.

By 1984, therefore, in the midst of a decade which might be remembered as the decade of the personal computer, both for America and for Empire State College, the College drafted a five-year plan for "computer independence." The plan detailed the creation of a computer system connecting all the centers and the units through electronic mail. Students would be connected by electronic mail to the College's computer network through their own personal computers or computers made available through work or community organizations. Students, using electronic mail, could access information from libraries and databases, participate in computer-based seminars, forward completed assignments to their mentors, communicate with other students, and contact College offices regarding such matters as tuition payments and financial aid. Mentors would use personal computers to check their student records; prepare and transmit learning contracts, evaluations, and other documents; have access to hundreds of illustrative degree programs; communicate with faculty and administrators; advise and tutor students; do research; and communicate with colleagues in nearby colleges and elsewhere.[25]

The implications for workload reduction were staggering. Up until this time, the only tools available to mentors were the typewriter—electric for the fortunate few—paper, and pen. In addition to word processing, the personal computer had the capacity to organize work. This included the record-keeping functions essential to good mentoring and the professional dimensions of working with one's colleagues within and beyond the College.

In the Wake of Annenberg: "The Electronic University of the Future"

Despite the second Annenberg rejection, which must have piqued tempers particularly after the Annenberg entreaty to try again, the College continued to push the computer technology initiative forward. In September 1984, Hall submitted a proposal to the Alfred P. Sloan Foundation to fund an international colloquy to plan, as he called it, "the electronic university of the future." The proposed list of distinguished educators and leaders in telecommunications included, among others, Ernest Boyer, then president of the Carnegie Foundation for the Advancement of Teaching; Donald McNeill, provost of the American Open University; David Hargreaves, head of continuing education for the BBC; K. Patricia Cross, chair of administration, planning, and social policy of the Harvard University Graduate School; Edwin F. Taylor, senior research scientist at Massachusetts Institute of Technology; Dustin Heuston, chairman of the board, WICAT systems; and representatives from IBM, Bell Laboratories, and Exxon.

Hall observed in the proposal:

Planning the electronic university of the future probably does not begin with the iconoclastic notion that the university of the present is outmoded, irrelevant and ineffective. Rather, it begins with an assumption that the university, with its great strengths and enduring values, can be adjusted structurally, so that the qualitative essentials of a great university—faculty, scholarly and research capacities, and pedagogy—can be extended to reach students not now well served. In short, the electronic university will transform and fulfill the older notions of university extension and outreach. As a result, the quality of education in university extension will approach the established quality of traditional campus instruction. This will be possible because, for the first time, the faculty and resources of the university will be practically available to the off-campus student.[26]

Of particular interest was the appendix, part of the alluvium from ESC's Annenberg efforts which, unfortunately, did not make its way into the proposals. (The Annenberg reviewers had difficulty understanding the College and, therefore, did not fully appreciate the significance of the proposals.) The appendix, drafted by Douglas Johnstone, dean for Collegewide Programs, provided a context for visualizing how Empire State College, through the lives of three students—each representing a different phase of development—reaches its technological apotheosis in the year 1990.

By 1990 the student is fully immersed in technology; she has her own microcomputer and her own video phone—as do almost all ESC students. Notably, her mentors do as well, and they work mostly from their homes. She has access to a series of computer-assisted courses with all sorts of branching for individualized study, and, most important, she has access, as do her tutors and mentors, to the electronic resource bonanza of the Internet. All her work is submitted to her mentor and tutors and evaluated via electronic mail, "all of her records are computerized, and her contracts and evaluations are recorded with a rapidity not dreamed of seven years earlier. Then associate deans gnashed their teeth if evaluations were a few months overdue. Now they gnash them after a few days."[27] In fact, the student becomes so physically removed from her mentor and tutors, knowing them only as disembodied words, voices and images of virtual reality, that flesh-and-blood meetings are held more for human comfort than for learning.

Sloan funded the proposal, and the College held the planning colloquy the following spring, in Saratoga Springs, May 16–17, 1985. Ernest Boyer gave the keynote address. His views were summarized by one of the colloquy rapporteurs:

In the past . . . many of the much heralded technologies for education have neither succeeded nor lasted. The overhead projector is the one exception. The reasons for this lack of adaptation by the educational community include the fact that the hardware has been better than the software, faculty have been largely uninvolved in using technology, and there has been minimal user control of the technology—i.e., the technology has been user passive. Now, however, with the new computer technologies, the software is improving, the faculty is becoming involved, and the user can be active. Boyer predicted that this new technology will succeed.[28]

The colloquy, which had all of higher education in its scope, further clarified the College's vision about students: increasing access; about faculty: retraining; about the use of technologies and their support systems: adapting them to fit particular needs; about curriculum: keeping individual learning styles in mind; about costs and resources: keeping software costs in line; and about issues of quality, access and control: adding system supports to ease the transition to the new technologies.[29] Both the colloquy and the Sloan grant, though modest, brought some national attention to a college still smarting from the two Annenberg/CPB rebuffs.

Rushworth Kidder, senior columnist for the *Christian Science Monitor*, punctuated his closing remarks at the colloquy with some chilling caveats—especially for Empire State College—which recall the titanic clashes between Baritz and Chickering that yet tug at the institutional fabric. Kidder asked: "Is there a danger that the Electronic University will monopolize and overcentralize the curriculum?" Further, "If there is a quality of education that is dramatic, how can a student have a dramatic interaction with a computer?. . . Expert systems have techniques of teaching creativity, but creative learners do not follow the techniques. Are we, through the use of electronic systems, stifling the leap which is basic to creativity?"[30]

These are questions that the College confronts as it enters a century that most assuredly will revolutionize student access to and use of information: Will students learn in prescribed, programmatic ways, or will they become fully autonomous, liberated learners? Computer technology may answer affirmatively to both questions,

Dr. Fernand Brunschwig, a physicist and founding mentor of the Long Island Center faculty, spearheaded the faculty use of microcomputers. Mentor Brunschwig was co-chair of the 1974 self-study for the Middle States accreditation visit. In 1991 he became founding director of the NYNEX/Corporate College program. Photograph by Mel Rosenthal.

and in ways which may, surprisingly, harmonize discordant voices by creating the basis for a system of learning that will serve all types of learners equally well. Part of the answer may be found in the incredible strides made in the technology of disk storage systems. Today's personal computers hold almost one billion bytes of data for each square inch of memory—500,000 times more than storage systems of the mid-1950s. Carnegie Mellon computer scientist Mark H. Kryder estimates a storage range perhaps as much as 50 billion, possibly by the year 2005. These magnetic disk drives "Will be the parking lots for the information superhighway."[31] And not long to follow will be "intelligent" highly interactive computers that might explode the boundaries between traditional and nontraditional education.

The Computer and Management Systems: "Information Processing Crisis"

The application of computer technology to the academic program was enhanced by the College's efforts in the 1970s to computerize its record keeping system. In fact, because of the rapid growth of the student population, from a handful of students in the fall of 1971 to twelve hundred in January 1973, the College found itself in an information processing crisis. "The manual systems that had been employed to that point had become exceedingly time consuming and inaccurate."[32] At Empire State College—a college that lacked semesters—students studying at their own pace enrolled and disenrolled willy-nilly. This wrought havoc with manually based systems for tracking tuition collections, disbursing financial aid, and calculating FTE. In fact, the College's dispersion from Long Island to Buffalo compounded the crisis because each learning center had its own manual system of recordkeeping. No other college in the United States faced a similar problem.[33]

In 1974, the College began to implement a computer-based system for billing and record-keeping procedures but without state support. Funds for computer operations came from external grants.[34] This first effort, which focused on the creation of a student-system database for the Admissions Office and the Business Office, was a "resounding success." It eliminated "a tremendous amount of manual effort . . . from the clerical staffs in both these offices while at the same time providing management with some meaningful information."[35] There was much left to be accomplished, although "after the people at ESC had seen and experienced a real live computer system, their desire for additional data bases was fueled."[36]

By 1975, data systems had been created for personnel, inventory, academic information, and the Business Office accounting system. Nevertheless, these systems operated in isolation from one another. Information from one system was transmitted manually to another. The data generated by the accounting system, for example, could not be automatically shared with the personnel database. The accuracy of the data, therefore, became more compromised as they were fed manually from one system to the other and back again, and the data were rarely up-to-date. The College needed an overarching management information system to integrate its disparate databases, but that was in 1975, and perfectly reliable management information systems were "elusive."[37] As Al Rickard of the Computer Services Office noted at that time, "People have been talking about them for many years with very few success stories to date." Rickard was confident, however: "I *firmly believe* ESC is in the position to become a model within the SUNY system, and maybe even in the entire higher education system in the United States!"[38]

Dr. Bernard Flynn (foreground) Metropolitan Regional Learning Center philosopher and mentor with Paul Bradley (background), then director of institutional research for Office of Research and Evaluation, at an All-College Meeting in the 1970s.

Rickard pointed to the remarkable progress that had been made as evidence of the College's ability to implement a management information system. He believed the computer would "shrink the distance between and among our Learning Centers and the Coordinating Center."[39] Rickard recognized also the academic potential of an integrated system. He wanted the system to be a resource for students and for faculty. Through terminals located at each center, students could access the system for "problem solving" activities and for information on resources available through the Learning Resources Center and to support learning activities.[40] The shortage of adequate state funding, however, continued to frustrate efforts to have a first-rate computer-based record-keeping system. In a note to Harry K. Spindler, SUNY vice chancellor for finance and business, Ronald Corwin, who as executive vice president was overseeing the effort to modernize the information system, complained: "We have had gradual, grudging, support for computer services from the state. For the most part, monies available permitted minimal hiring (but only at the trainee level) yet ironically, no monies were also available for training. The result is that our computer programs are inadequate, in most cases incompatible and nonintegratable, and in many cases written in the wrong "language."[41]

The College began the shift to an integrated database system for accounting, billing, financial aid, and academic records in 1977. It was a gradual move, compounded by the lack of resources, which took years to complete. In 1977 an Empire State College tradition, "Computer Wednesdays," was born to plan and implement the changeover. The College assembled a task force lead by Ronald Corwin, and then, after Corwin resigned to take a prestigious post with Citibank, by William Ferrero, vice president for administration, to supervise the transition. The task force was composed of staff from the offices of admissions, business, personnel, and the alumni office as well as the Empire State College Foundation, and included representatives from the regional learning centers. They met on Wednesdays for a number of years until the system was fully operational.[42] By 1982, a new student accounting system was brought on-line and only one piece remained, academic records. It was earmarked for completion in 1983. Besides accuracy, the computer systems made it possible for the regional learning centers, through their own terminals, to have immediate access to up-to-date information. "Questions which could be answered only by a phone call to Saratoga Springs can now be handled directly by the Centers, which will mean better and faster service to students."[43] The College was particularly proud of this accomplishment because it had gained "external recognition as the first of its kind in completeness and full integration."[44]

A Crowded Mainframe at SUNY

What the College needed, however, was its own computer mainframe. A VAX would allow the College to have a statewide system completely responsive to its growing needs. An Empire State College controlled VAX would free the College of the vagaries and whimsy of SUNY System's crowded mainframe. A VAX was also a necessary precondition for creating a statewide computer network to support the academic program. In 1986, Empire State College installed a VAX 11/750; it became the technological headwaters for a college that saw its academic future more and more a part of the sea change in American higher education created by the revolution in telecommunications. Within a few years the impact of the VAX on the management of the College and the academic program was remarkable. The VAX was creating a virtual community—once loosely held together by phone, mail, and meetings—with

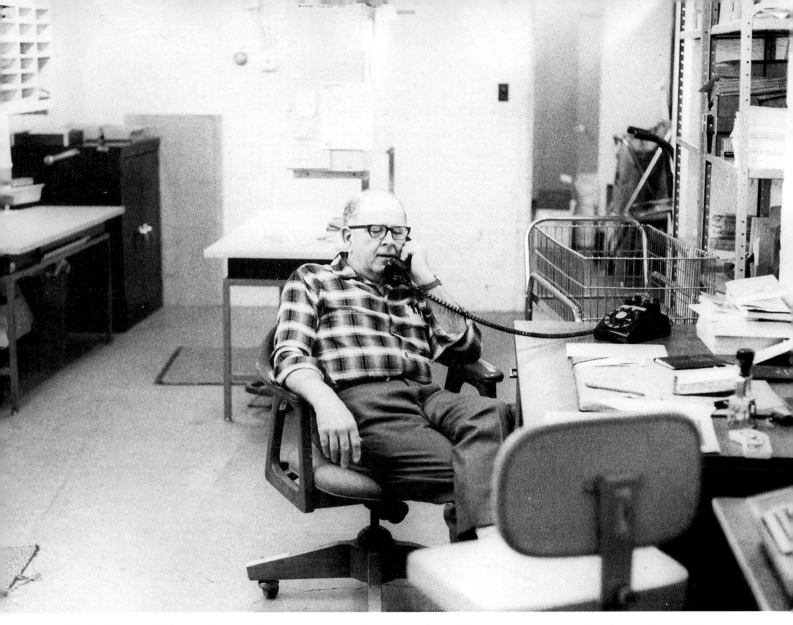

a remarkable plenum of electronic connections: computer conferencing, electronic mail, electronic bulletin boards, and Internet access. For mentors and students, for managers and staff, distance was becoming threshold, isolation connectivity.

For Vice President for Administration William Ferrero, the VAX meant that Empire State College centers, units, and programs—more than forty spread over the state—could finally be connected in an electronic web that insured the fast transmission of data and information to keep "administrative operations running smoothly."[45] Eventually, the VAX gave electronic mail access to Empire State College satellite programs overseas—Jerusalem in the late winter of 1993 and Athens in the fall of 1994.

In 1989, over one hundred students had VAX accounts; by 1996, the number was almost two thousand. Students began using the VAX "to communicate with their mentors, to transfer academic work back and forth, and to contact other students."[46] One student, Lewis, a computer science major, who held two degrees in biology before he enrolled at Empire State College, created a computer caucus called STUDENTS. It enabled students with VAX accounts to communicate with one another on a number of formal topics as well as the opportunity to converse informally, creating what might be called a "campus club" for students.[47]

To match the student interest, the College worked aggressively to complete its program of buying personal computers with modems for all its mentors. At the Center for Distance Learning, Mentor Lowell Roberts directed the Center's use of the computer-conferencing capacity of the VAX for distance-learning courses, an effort which he had begun in 1986. At other centers, mentors began tutoring via electronic mail—individualized learning contracts for the students of colleagues at other centers—and began offering computer conference courses through the computer network. By 1989, the Center for Distance Learning was using electronic mail and computer conferencing to solicit statewide suggestions from ESC mentors for new courses, to discuss curriculum, and to evaluate course guides. The VAX made it possible for mentors at different learning centers to undertake collaborative efforts. For example, Xenia Coulter of the Ithaca Unit of the Genesee Valley Regional Learning Center, Elizabeth Lawrence at the Rochester headquarters of that center, and Louvan Wood at the Niagara Frontier Learning Center in Buffalo used the VAX network to prepare a paper on numerical skills. Drafts and comments were sent back and forth across the state by electronic mail.[48]

To support faculty in computer applications to mentoring, the College established a faculty conference on the VAX, called "ACOMPUTE." By 1989, the conference became so congested that separate discussion groups had to be created to handle the traffic. Among the groups created was the user support conference for faculty, using specific computers and software packages and "CSOURCES" that helped mentors identify a host of computer resources, including software, texts, and organizations.[49] The VAX created new opportunities for professional development. Fernand Brunschwig, a physicist and a pioneer in applying microcomputer technology to mentoring, began using the VAX to stay abreast of developments in his field. In 1990, he observed, "Because of BITNET I've been in touch with my old college roommate for the first time regularly in many years. . . . He's a chemist at UCLA now and spending two years at the National Science Foundation. I got firsthand news about cold fusion research from him immediately after he had been at a conference on the subject."[50]

In addition to the computer networking made possible by the VAX, by 1989 the faculty had begun to employ software packages such as Microsoft and Enable for "student database information and word processing capabilities to create the contract text in a common format."[51] That year, Brunschwig researched computer access to electronic card catalogs at libraries in Metropolitan New York and Long Island.[52] Looking back on the impact the personal computer has had on her work as a mentor, Carolyn Broadaway, another participant in the faculty literacy project, observed:

The computer has had major impact on my work at the center. Most of it has been in terms of record-keeping and paperwork. The computer marked a major switch from documents being produced by support staff to documents being produced by mentors— learning contracts, contract evaluations, letters, memos, schedules, etc. In terms of advising, it allows me better access to past records. . . . And in the last few years, the access to library catalogues and periodical literature searches has helped quite a bit in finding resources for students and in showing them how to do searches by computer. And communicating with students via e-mail has alleviated phone tag.[53]

Center for Learning and Technology: Leading SUNY

By 1989, the College's accomplishments in telecommunications had attracted the attention of Chancellor Bruce Johnstone. He recognized Empire State College's

Dr. Carolyn Jarmon and Dr. Otolorin Jones, business faculty of the Center for Distance Learning, are seen discussing administrative matters before the start of a new term in September 1990. Jarmon succeeded Dean Theodore DiPadova as director of the graduate program in 1993 when he became academic vice president for New England University. Jarman and Jones served as directors of the SUNY by Satellite program.

potential to provide leadership for the rest of SUNY. With this in mind and with the intention to support Empire State College's own efforts, Chancellor Johnstone provided funds to move Empire State College from a jerry-built program in telecommunications to a full-fledged center called the Center for Learning and Technology. It would serve as a laboratory to test and evaluate educational technologies for the College and the rest of SUNY. Director Twigg and other staff, Lawrence Greenberg, training coordinator, Robert Perilli, PC-/VAX user support coordinator, and Loralee Montague, learning resources coordinator, moved the College into a high-gear effort to apply technology, especially computer technology, to the academic program.[54] To support faculty forays into computer technology and other areas of educational technology, the Center created the Venture Fund. The Center, in its first year of operations, completed a College-wide project to make bibliographic resources available to mentors and students. The Center also conducted workshops to train faculty in computer conferencing as well as to provide managerial and technical support.[55] In 1993, Lowell Roberts, on loan from the Center for Distance Learning, became acting director of the Center as well as acting vice president for educational technology. He replaced Carol Twigg who joined Educom.

By 1992, the Center had a major role in creating SUNY by Satellite (S.B.S.), a statewide interactive technology project that provided baccalaureate degrees in business to SUNY community college graduates. Under the leadership of Carolyn Jarmon and, later, Otolorin Jones, both loaned from the Center for Distance Learning, SUNY by Satellite featured Empire State College and State University faculty who lectured at the New York Network studios in Albany. The Network transmitted the lectures by satellite to students at remote locations across the state, including Fort

Drum. Students supplemented their studies through courses developed by the Center for Distance Learning and through cross-registration at SUNY campuses and private colleges. In 1994, SUNY by Satellite moved from a live-interactive to an asynchronous format of video-taped lectures because of insufficient enrollments to support the costs of operating twelve sites. The SUNY by Satellite program is an example of a complex and collaborative project within the College and within the State University to bring technology to the forefront of higher education.[56]

In 1993, Chancellor Johnstone recognized Hall's leadership in educational technology, both within Empire State College and within the SUNY system, by appointing him to a two-year term as vice chancellor for educational technology. Hall was already chair of the SUNY Presidents' Task Force on Educational Technology and had served as chair of the SUNY Council on Educational Technology. Johnstone instructed Hall to "infuse the uses of technology into SUNY's educational programs in order to improve student access, strengthen the quality of teaching and learning, assist faculty research and scholarship, and enhance system productivity and effectiveness."[57]

M.H.R.L.N., short for the Mid-Hudson Regional Learning Network, is an excellent example of a path-setting SUNY-wide effort that Chancellor Johnstone had in mind. Coordinated by the Center for Learning and Technology, M.H.R.L.N. utilizes the resources of Empire State College and State University College at New Paltz as well as Dutchess, Orange, and Ulster Community Colleges, makes it possible for students to earn degrees in business administration through a hypermedia network. The program began enrolling students in September 1995, to test the concept of "on demand" multimedia education that makes it possible for students "to get an education at their own pace, whenever they want and wherever they may be."[58] A grant from the Alfred P. Sloan Foundation, and SUNY infrastructure funds set aside for technology initiatives, made it possible for the Center for Learning and Technology to construct the hypermedia network: Students and faculty have common access to an electronic storehouse of documents, videos, graphs, and illustrations in addition to the abundant resources of the Internet. The network also enables faculty teams from the collaborating campuses to "redesign" their classroom-based courses for use in an electronic format.[59] Merlin the Magician, the project's logo, is quite suited for this innovative project.

Of the efforts spearheaded by the Center for Learning and Technology, perhaps the most important, and one that is not without controversy, has been its technology plan for the College, *Prelude to the 21st Century*. It is important because it carefully details how to keep the College on the cutting edge of technology and controversial because it challenges traditional mentoring.

Prelude, now in its third draft, calls for the implementation of a highly advanced College-wide data communications network; an advanced groupware for processing and transmitting documents, including graphics; multimedia computers with graphical interface for students at the learning centers and units, including appropriate instructional software; a technological service for distance-learning students; automatic VAX accounts for all students; Internet access through Gopher and World Wide Web servers for students, faculty and staff; a software/CD-ROM technical library; a video production studio; and a training program for faculty and staff.[60]

The most important part of the plan, technology-mediated mentoring, remains blank, awaiting input from faculty and administration. *Prelude* points to a complete break with the past, a reengineering of the academic program, a mentoring metamorphosis. Computer technology will eliminate physical space as a factor in

Dr. Victor Montana, dean of the Genesee Valley Center from 1978 to 1988, stands in front of the Center's Prince Street headquarters in Rochester. He is dean of the University of New Hampshire School of New Learning. Photograph by Reed Hoffman.

student access. The face-to-face meetings of students with mentors and tutors will become archaic forms of pedagogy, just as will classroom-based instruction. But there is more: the elimination of "presumptively wasteful" practices such as "a hundred ESC students studying essentially the same thing with twenty-five different mentors."[61] For mentors who subscribe to the Chickering credo of individualized—albeit labor-intensive approaches to mentoring and tutoring—and who do not recognize the enormous potential of computer technology for individualized learning, will *Prelude* stir opposition and divide the faculty? For mentors who have successfully adapted computer technology to their world of work, mostly as an auxiliary technology to make traditional mentoring more efficient and who espouse facilitating student access as the ideological core of mentoring, will they be ready for the next step—virtual mentoring?

Prelude notes the following:

We could simply ignore the efficacies of technology and continue our primary instructional modalities unchanged. We could take the position that we will neither adapt technology to our pedagogy nor our pedagogy to our technology. . . . To not change is to remain labor intensive and relatively unproductive (in terms of both learning and cost), largely mismatching faculty expertise and student need, denying access to the resources students and faculty should have to learn and conduct research, and accommodating to a minority of learners (in terms of both access and compatibility with learning and cognitive styles). It also means that ESC will become more and more marginalized in higher education.[62]

The word *reengineering* is not used lightly. It is the new ethos of corporate America—an effort to be more competitive in a changing environment, more efficient, more profitable, but achieved at great cost to employees snared in the global meshwork of technological and economic change. The blank page in *Prelude* will be viewed by some, therefore, as a threat to traditional mentoring; to others it might be the new *Prospectus for a University College,* an opportunity to imagine a future that would have been inconceivable just twenty-five years ago.

In the June issue of the Empire State College-United University Professions Chapter newsletter, faculty urged the administration not to be overcome by the "dazzle" of technology. "The big problem with going blindly with the dazzle is that programs based primarily on dazzle become continuously and voraciously demanding of resources to run and maintain them. . . . And the beast becomes the biggest priority, and then the only priority. . . ."[63] The newsletter recommended cautious steps in developing technology-based programs: accurately assessing needs, devising a pedagogy appropriate for adult students, assessing the competition, learning from the experience of others, and being careful not to waste scarce resources. All this is wise advice in an era of contracting revenues that values technology as much for cutting costs as for creating new avenues for learning.

Corporate and Business Connections: A New Paradigm

Ernest Boyer's view about the College connecting to the business and corporate world was as astute his vision about technology. Since its inception the College has had connections with many major businesses and corporations in New York State. With few exceptions, including the New Models for Career Education Program, launched in 1973 with a FIPSE grant, these had been informal. Business executives with advanced degrees had served as tutors and participated on advisory boards, while hundreds of uncredentialed executives flocked to centers and units to pursue associate and baccalaureate degrees. The College worked with corporate and business managers, whether as tutors or students, as individuals and not in a relationship defined by a company contract or agreement.

What the College had achieved, and remarkably so in its first ten years of existence, was to establish connections with labor, especially through the Harry Van Arsdale Jr. Center for Labor Studies; connections with a wide array of human services agencies; and connections with a host of community organizations throughout the state. The failure to establish strong institutional linkages to business, especially corporations, in those first ten years is explained perhaps by the fallout of the Vietnam War.

By the early 1980s the passions excited by the Vietnam War had subsided and the College made a number of forays into the business community. In June 1981, under Dean Kenneth Abrams' guidance, the Metropolitan Center established a satellite program coordinated by Mentor Mary Folliet at IBM's Bedford-Stuyvesant plant. The plant served minority students. Within a year, thirty-three students had enrolled in the program.[64] In 1982, Dean Douglas Johnstone established on-site satellite programs with the Crouse-Hinds Corporation and with Bristol Laboratories, both in Syracuse.[65] In 1983, the Niagara Frontier and Genessee Valley Centers initiated a joint Empire State College-American Institute of Banking (AIB) pilot project. It provided an avenue for bank employees to earn degrees through Empire State College by applying experiential credits from AIB courses to Empire State College degree programs; and in 1983, the Genesee Valley Center received a major grant to initiate a

Dr. Mary Ann Biller was associate dean of the New Models program, which the College launched in 1973 with a three-year grant from the Kellogg Foundation. In 1975 Biller became dean of the Lower Hudson Center when the College joined New Models, headquartered in Suffern, with three satellite programs. She stands next to then Mentor Alan Mandell (right) who is now associate dean and director of the Metropolitan Center and Hudson Valley Center.

nationwide management program for circulation managers, mostly from the Gannett Corporation, in the newspaper industry.

Toward Privatization: A New Funding Mechanism

The connections that we began to make in the early 1980s began to accelerate later in the decade as a more liberal use of IFRs (Income Fund Reimbursables), special accounts authorized by SUNY, allowed us to charge higher tuition for specialized programs while keeping the income from such programs to cover the additional costs of running them. These specialized programs have expanded so much that Empire State College has reduced its dependence on State support to 40 percent of its budget. It is a process that is privatizing the College.

Residency Program for Independent Learners

The Center for Statewide Programs became the North Central Regional Learning Center in the early 1980s, and then the Center for Collegewide Programs in the early 1990s. Under Dean Johnstone's leadership the Center developed a unique residency program which created a major vehicle for corporate outreach in the mid-1980s. Johnstone had been the Adult Degree Program dean at Goddard. The program, which Goddard had launched in 1963, was a predecessor of the College Without Walls movement in the United States. Adult students came to Goddard for eleven-day residencies every six months. There they worked intensely in group settings with faculty, who evaluated the previous six months of independent study and helped students prepare for the next six months. These individualized plans of study were integrated fifteen-credit blocks rather than three or five credit pieces.[66]

Empire State College had nothing like Goddard's residency program. Centers had held occasional workshops and seminars, and some College-wide residencies were coordinated by the Office of Residencies in Saratoga Springs, but these group-based activities were not separate avenues for earning degrees. They were decidedly the exception to the norm of students working separately from other students on individualized learning contracts, a position which Arthur Chickering, another Goddard émigré, championed. Johnstone joined the College in the summer of 1979, succeeding William R. Dodge after he took a post at World University. Johnstone argued that "many students want more peer support in their studies, more opportunity to develop a shared sense of experience. Many students would manifestly benefit from the stimulation of short-term residencies, both in the preparation of their learning contracts and in their accountability for work produced in those contracts."[67]

Johnstone's Residency Program for Independent Learners (RPIL), administered by Mentor Frederick Mayo and then Mentor Wayne Ouderkirk, got underway in 1981. Much like Goddard's Adult Degree Program, RPIL did not target specific markets for its interdisciplinary degree programs; the outreach to corporations would come later. There were two residencies a year, each followed by twenty-two weeks of guided independent study. At the nine-day residencies, one held in January and one in June, students worked individually as well as in small-group settings with mentors. Mentors evaluated the work for the old contracts, helped plan new sixteen-credit contracts for the twenty-two weeks between residencies, and assisted students in preparing individualized degree programs and portfolios. Returning students gave oral presentations, and special seminars were offered on a number of topics geared to the specific needs of new and returning students as well as to topics of general interest such as the impact of computers on the workplace, conflict, networking, and the crisis in Central America. Topics varied from residency to residency and sometimes served as springboards for new contracts.

RPIL was a hybrid. It captured "the benefits of peer support through the residencies, and the benefits of individualized independent study during the extended non-residential periods."[68] RPIL, however, did not attract many students, even at a time when the Center for Statewide Programs had hundreds of prospective students on its waiting list. A *New York Times* advertisement in 1981 drew just a handful of inquiries and presaged difficult times for this interdisciplinary baccalaureate program. In fact, recruiting efforts garnered more interest in the College than in the residency program.[69] Though averaging just sixteen students per term from 1981 to 1984, RPIL showed promise for its contribution to the academic vitality of the College and for "its potential contribution to the design of . . . graduate studies." It was "too good to lose."[70]

RPIL with a Professional Focus: Colloquium

RPIL continued to be plagued by low enrollments. Even a cosmetic name change to Colloquium in 1985, which eliminated the confusion about it being solely a residency program, did not help. Johnstone terminated the program in 1986 but not before giving Wayne Ouderkirk, hired in 1985, a chance to try innovative approaches at marketing the program. Academically, it was a success. What Colloquium had lacked was a successful marketing strategy. Ouderkirk had started to target specific groups aggressively: child-care workers, BOCES secretaries, and airline employees. Also, he moved away from the interdisciplinary focus that had been prominent in previous recruitment efforts and offered the program to students pursuing disciplinary

Students meet with faculty at a 1985 Colloquium residency. The director of Colloquium, Wayne Ouderkirk (left, background) leads a discussion with the Associate Dean Christopher Rounds (center, background), and Mentor Darrell Leavitt (right, background).

degrees, including business. Ouderkirk advertised the program within the College. RPIL and Colloquium alumni and students joined in the recruiting effort. And to remove a possible last barrier to recruiting working adults, he and Christopher Rounds, the associate dean, shortened the residency to four days. These efforts, which doubled the number of new students from four to eight by the time of the January 1986 residency, were not enough to sustain a tuition-based program. Clearly, the effort had been on the right track, but time and resources had run their course.[71]

Ouderkirk, however, was instrumental in establishing an important precedent for working with adult students in a different format. The academic and organizational principles he established were sound and praiseworthy. Other programs, following the Colloquium model, soon emerged and successfully followed his lead in targeting specific groups.

Circulation Management: A Nationwide Program

RPIL and the Colloquium had demonstrated to the rest of the College the feasibility of establishing a degree-based program that combined elements of group studies and distance learning. In 1983, for example, the Genesee Valley Regional Center launched the nation's first program combining these elements in a journalism program for circulation management. The program offered baccalaureate degrees in circulation and marketing, and was coordinated by Mentor Scott Chisholm who worked closely with Victor Montana, Genesee's dean. The circulation management program was negotiated with the International Circulation Managers Association and designed to address a serious need to upgrade the professionalism of circulation departments. A $125,000 grant from the newspaper industry got the program off the ground. Much like RPIL and Colloquium, the program was based on two terms a year, each term twenty-four weeks in length; students from all over the United States attended short seminars at the Circulation Management Institute in Rochester to fulfill the residency component. Before and after seminars, they worked independently, using study guides designed by College faculty and professionals from the industry. In announcing the program, the *ESC News* quoted Ronald T. Farrar, professor of journalism at the University of Kentucky, who said that the problems confronting circulators "were nothing short of staggering."[72]

FORUM: The Corporate Connection

In 1986, the North Central Regional Learning Center, formerly the Center for Statewide Programs, launched a new residency program that became immensely successful. In the spring of 1985, the Center hired Philip Reagan to coordinate the Center satellite program established by Mentor Jane Small three years before at Bristol Laboratories in Syracuse. In June 1985, Johnstone received word that the Bristol division sponsoring the program planned to leave Syracuse in a few months. Johnstone and North Central's associate dean, Christopher Rounds, as well as Philip Reagan, and representatives from Bristol quickly reconceptualized the Center's connections to the business community. From that effort emerged FORUM, a program consisting of three weekend residencies a term (beginning, middle, and end) made available not just to the managers of one company, which had been the Achilles' heel of the Bristol program, but to any business and public sector organizations in Syracuse and its environs.[73]

FORUM came into existence just as Colloquium faded, and it was immensely successful. Reagan, now in charge of FORUM, held its first residency in September 1986. Within four years, the program had enrolled two hundred managers from sixty major corporations in the central region of New York State. Students came from Bristol Myers, Squibb, General Electric, Empire Blue Cross & Blue Shield, Niagara Mohawk, and others, and the retention rate was high.[74]

FORUM was more highly focused than RPIL and Colloquium. The new residency program offered primarily business degrees to corporate and business managers, though some students came from the nonprofit sector. Admission to the program required employer sponsorship and substantial financial support. Students tended to be male, about forty years of age, almost half had about two years of prior college study, and many had employers who were willing to underwrite their tuition. FORUM terms were twenty-four weeks in length but three two-day residencies broke up the long, isolated stretches between the mega residencies that had existed in RPIL and Colloquium. Students still gathered for group studies as well as to meet individually with their mentors. FORUM students supplemented group studies through individualized learning contracts, courses through the Center for Distance Learning, and cross-registration at local colleges.[75]

FORUM/West: Niagara Frontier Center

The success of FORUM attracted the interest of Thomas Rocco, the dean of the Niagara Frontier Center, headquartered in Buffalo, New York. In the fall of 1990, the Center launched FORUM/West for western New York with Mentor Penn Wettlaufer serving as its director.[76] Although initially the business faculty supported the proposal, other Niagara faculty were skeptical. Nevertheless, by electing a curriculum committee, representing the full faculty; by having students go through the same assessment and degree program planning process; by having Niagara faculty, full and part-time mentors, advising and instructing students; and by having FORUM students participate in regular graduation recognition ceremonies, the program became an integral part of the Niagara Center.[77] FORUM/West began with just sixteen students and three corporate sponsors, but a year later there were fifteen corporate sponsors and forty-five students. Among the corporate sponsors were New

Robert Thrasher, retired NYNEX executive vice president for operations, supported Empire State College's role in providing programs for the diverse educational needs of NYNEX employees.

York Telephone, now NYNEX, Sierra Research, Motorola, and General Motors. The program also recruited students from southern Ontario, Canada.[78]

FORUM/East: Center for College-Wide Programs

FORUM/East followed FORUM/Syracuse and FORUM/West. Launched by Dean Johnstone in the fall of 1991 and administered by Michael Fortunato, a business mentor who transferred from the Saratoga Springs satellite, FORUM/East completed Empire State College's network of business and corporate outreach in upstate New York. FORUM/East followed a similar model established by the others: three intensive weekend residencies on selected themes, during a twenty-four-week term, followed by guided independent study; individualized degree program planning; and individualized contract learning to supplement the residency-based group studies in the liberal arts and business. A striking difference between FORUM/East and its siblings is the format of the group studies: "In FORUM/East, the theme study is organized in a debate format, through assigned topics and positions. Though facilitated by a faculty member, each group is responsible for organizing its own project, assigning tasks to its several members and reporting out its findings to the other groups during the residency."[79]

Initially, though a number of corporations in the capital district worked closely with FORUM/East—including General Electric Plastics and Continental Telephone—NYNEX "flooded" the program with students.[80] NYNEX, under intense competitive pressure to restructure its operations and to reduce its workforce, needed a program for managers that would both augment their value to the company and, at the same time, make it possible for those who might lose their positions through retrenchment to find new employment. FORUM/East answered both needs. In fact, the program became so popular that NYNEX managers from Metropolitan New York soon joined the ranks of managers from the capital district. This influx of students from the Metropolitan region and the lower Hudson Valley generated interest in a logical next step, FORUM/South, which awaits further planning and approval.[81]

NYNEX/Corporate College: A College within a Corporation

The FORUM programs, Syracuse, West and East, are brilliant examples of how flexible Empire State College is in responding to the workforce needs of New York State. But of all the corporate connections the NYNEX/Corporate College, established in 1991, was perhaps the most daring and inventive. It was a bold move. Not only because the College established its headquarters and classrooms within the confines of a major corporation, but because of the uniqueness of the students. They were recent high school graduates, predominantly minorities, and recruited to begin working as NYNEX customer service representatives at the same time that they began college studies.

The idea for Corporate College and the idea for developing continuing education programs for NYNEX, emerged in 1989 from a discussion Hugh Hammett, Empire State College vice president for external affairs, had with James King, Pamela McFadden, and Raymond Buccharia of NYNEX's Personnel Development Division. Despite NYNEX's generous tuition reimbursement policy, they felt that colleges and universities had been unresponsive in meeting the required education needs of employees. In fact, the group had been "actively exploring whether to undertake the ambitious effort of creating and seeking accreditation for its own in-house university."[82] Hammett suggested developing a partnership with Empire State College because the College had a well-established record serving adult students. These discussions took place over a three-year period—interrupted by a long New York Telephone strike—and resulted in a proposal being submitted to New York Telephone President's Policy Council. There it received "a rocky reception. . . . There was already a growing apprehension over storm clouds of competitiveness and downsizing in the telecommunications industry. Finally, when Robert Thrasher, then vice president for operations, championed the proposal, the Corporate/College idea was given a chance at life."[83]

Empire State College had no practical experience working with young minority students in group settings, though at times mentors had worked face-to-face with individual students. Many seasoned mentors doubted a successful outcome. Nevertheless, the College's commitment to serving the economic and social needs of the state as well as a long history of successful innovation kept the optimists resolute. In the late winter of 1991, Johnstone recruited a faculty advisory committee. The committee planned the program and hired a talented faculty, many of whom had both high school and college teaching backgrounds. In the spring, Empire State College, NYNEX, and New York City high schools began a unique partnership—each with specific roles—of identifying, testing, and admitting promising individuals to the program. The first students, seventy-eight recent high school graduates and forty-eight long-term NYNEX employees, enrolled in September 1991. In the first semester, students worked in group-study settings, beginning with a required collegiate seminar to introduce them to college-level work, at NYNEX locations near their job sites. In subsequent semesters, students had a range of group studies to select from as well as opportunities to do independent contract learning, when appropriate to their level of intellectual maturity. Fernand Brunschwig, Long Island Regional Center mentor and advisory board member, served as the NYNEX/Corporate College's first director.[84]

In its fourth year of operation, Corporate College, directed by Rhoda Miller, formerly a Hudson Valley Regional Center mentor and also a member of the faculty planning group, has 218 students in the program, including long-term NYNEX employees. Of this number, 78 percent of the students are female, 57 percent are

The NYNEX Corporate/College Program of SUNY Empire State College began enrolling students in September 1991. From left to right are Mentor Rhoda Miller, a member of the Corporate/College planning group, Director Fernand Brunschwig, and Mentors Evelyn Ting, James Wunsch, Antonia Pena, and Cathy Copley-Woods. Photograph by Miller Photography, New Hyde Park, New York.

African-Americans, 18 percent Hispanic, 2 percent Asian, and 2 percent other.[85] There are six Corporate College locations in NYNEX facilities in New York City and Long Island, including the administrative headquarters at the NYNEX Metro-Tech Center in Brooklyn, New York. Some locations are satellites administered by a mentor and others are simply places for mentors and students to meet. Corporate College has the potential to expand to upstate New York, if the program is opened to other job titles.[86]

The College connection to NYNEX is further strengthened by the representation of NYNEX executives on the Empire State College Foundation Board. They include NYNEX manager Mary Ellen McGory, a Hudson Valley Center graduate who first brought Empire State College's unique ability to serve NYNEX to the attention of Robert Thrasher; Philip Thompson, former general manager and vice president for NYNEX Upstate; Richard Amadon, upstate director for community relations; and Bailey Geeshin, former NYNEX vice president for regulatory matters. Duane Albro, NYNEX vice president for the New York State region, now serves on the Foundation's Executive Board.

Empire State College's connection to the corporate world continues as it develops programs with AT&T and other corporations. The connections that Empire State College is making with businesses and corporations come at a time when state subvention is shrinking. For the College to survive it must make corporate and other connections, but in ways that are true to its mission. This is probably the most significant challenge Empire State College will face in the coming years, because of the inherent dangers of becoming a market-driven institution.

Endnotes Chapter 4

1. "Convocation Address by Ernest L. Boyer," *ESC News,* September 1981, p. 6.

2. Ibid., 7–8.

3. Ibid., 7.

4. *Prospectus for a New University College: Objectives, Process, Structure, and Establishment,* State University of New New York, Albany, 8 February 1971, p. 34.

5. James W. Hall, "Investiture Address," *ESC Newsletter. Special Edition,* September 1972, p. 3.

6. "Opening Session: Learning Resources Center and Materials Development," Inaugural Workshop, 18 September 1971, Rensselaerville, Empire State College Archives, Saratoga Springs, New York, p. 1.

7. James W. Hall to the Administrative Council and the 1974, Memorandum, Empire State College Archives, Saratoga Springs, New York, p. 4.

8. *Prospectus*, p. 4.

9. Untitled Draft, 1981?, Empire State College Archives, Saratoga Springs, New York, pp. 1–2.

10. Ibid., 2.

11. Ibid.

12. Ibid. 3.

13. Ibid., 4.

14. Carol Twigg to the Empire State College Faculty, 2 December 1981, Memorandum, Empire State College Archives, Saratoga Springs, New York.

15. Barbara Marantz to Richard Bonnabeau, 27 February 1995, E-mail, Empire State College Archives, Saratoga Springs, New York, pp. 1–2.

16. Carol Twigg to the Administrative Council, 15 December 1981, Memorandum, Empire State College Archives, Saratoga Springs, New York, pp. 1–2; "Middle States Association Periodic Review Report," Presented by Empire State College, 1 November 1984, p. 18.

17. "CPB/Annenberg Project Announces Procedures and Criteria for Submitting Proposals," News Release, Corporation for Public Broadcasting 1981, p. 1.

18. "A Proposal to CPB/Annenberg School of Communications Project," 25 July 1983, Empire State College, Saratoga Springs, New York.

19. John Jacobson to James W. Hall, Thomas Ezell, William Ferrero, Carol Twigg, and Kay Katzer, Memorandum, 4 October 1983, Empire State College Archives, Saratoga Springs, New York, p. 1.

20. Ibid.

21. "A Proposal to the CPB/Annenberg School of Communications Project," December 1983, Empire State College, Saratoga Springs, New York.

22. Ibid.

23. Clifton R. Wharton Jr. to James Hall, 27 January 1984, Letter, Empire State College Archives, Saratoga Springs, New York.

24. James W. Hall to Clifton R. Wharton Jr., 23 April 1984, Empire State College Archives, Saratoga Springs, New York, p. 2.

25. "Middle States Association Periodic Review Report," 1 November 1984, p. 18.

26. James W. Hall, "Planning the Electronic University of the Future," A Proposal Submitted to the Sloan Foundation. Empire State College, 13 September 1984, Empire State College Archives, Saratoga Springs, New York,

27. Ibid., p. 3, Appendix C, p. 3.

28. "A Report on the Electronic University of the Future: A Planning Colloquy," Presented by Empire State College, 16–17 May 1985, Saratoga Springs, New York, p. 2.

29. Ibid., 33–34.

30. Ibid., 31–32.

31. R. Lipkin, "Strong Vast Amounts of Data in Tiny Spots," *Science News,* April 1992, vol. 147, no. 16, p. 245.

32. Al Rickard to Roger Trumbore, 5 November 1975, Memorandum: Data Processing at Empire State College, Empire State College Archives, Saratoga Springs, New York, p. 1.

33. Ibid.

34. Ronald Corwin to Harry Spindler, 20 September 1977, Letter, Empire State College Archives, Saratoga Springs, New York, p. 1–2.

35. Rickard to Trumbore, p. 2; *Seeking Alternatives III: Empire State College Annual Report (1974)* (Empire State College: Saratoga Springs, New York), 7.

36. Rickard to Trumbore, p. 2.

37. Ibid.

38. Ibid.

39. Ibid.

40. Ibid., 3.

41. Corwin to Spindler, pp. 1–2.

42. *Seeking Alternatives VIII: Empire State College Annual Report (July 1979–June 1980)* (Empire State College: Saratoga Springs, New York), pp. 8–9.

43. "Systems Development Milestone," *Bits & Pieces from the Office of Computer Services News,* Fall 1982, Empire State College, p. 1.

44. *Seeking Alternatives VIII,* pp. 8–9.

45. "The Inside Look: Linking the Administration," *News: Empire State College State University of New York,* 1990, vol. 18, no. 1, p. 2.

46. Carol Twigg, "The College Computer Network," *Empire State College Exchange,* February/March 1989, p. 1.

47. "Adult Education Gets a Technological Boost," *News: Empire State College State University of New York,* 1990, vol. 18, no. 1, p. 4.

48. "The College Computer Network," p. 1.

49. "The College Computer Network," p. 4.

50. "Bitnet," *News: Empire State College State University of New York,* 1990, vol. 18, no. 1, p. 9.

51. "The College Computer Network," p. 4.

52. Fernand Brunschwig, "Accessing Library Databases," *Empire State College Exchange,* February/March 1989, pp. 8–9.

53. Carolyn Broadaway to Richard Bonnabeau, 22 February 1995, E-mail, Empire State College Archives, Saratoga Springs, New York, p. 1.

54. "Adult Education Gets a Technological Boost," *News: Empire State College State University of New York,* 1990, vol. 18, no. 1, p. 5.

55. *Annual Report: 1990–1991,* Empire State College, Saratoga Springs, New York, p. 24.

56. Jane Altes, SUNY by Satellite: The Experiment at Empire State College. May 1995, Empire State College, Saratoga Springs, New York, Saratoga Springs, New York, pp. 1–7.

57. "Hall Appointed Vice Chancellor for Educational Technology," *Exchange,* 1 February 1993, Empire State College, p. 1.

58. "SUNY/Sloan Project-MHRLN," *Center for Learning and Technology News,* Empire State College, Spring 1995, vol. 1, no. 1., p. 8.

59. Ibid.

60. Robert Perilli and Lowell Roberts, "Prelude to the 21st Century: SUNY Empire State College's Technology Plan 1994–1999," November 1994, Memorandum, Draft #3, Empire State College Office of Educational Technology, Saratoga Springs, New York.

61. Ibid., 5.

62. Ibid., 3.

63. *Newsletter,* Empire State College-United University Professionals, June 1995, p. 5.

64. *Seeking Alternatives X:* Empire State College Annual Report (1 July 1981–30 June 1982) (Empire State College: Saratoga Springs, New York), 11; Mary Folliet to Richard Bonnabeau, 3 July 1995, Letter, Empire State College Archives, Saratoga Springs, New York.

65. *Seeking Alternatives XI:* Empire State College Annual Report (1July 1982–30 June 1983) (Empire State College: Saratoga Springs, New York).

66. Ann Benson and Frank Adams, *To Know for Real: Royce S. Pitkin and Goddard College* (Adamant, Vermont: Adamant Press, 1987), 231–232; Douglas Johnstone to Richard Bonnabeau, 27 March 1995, E-mail, Empire State College Archives, Saratoga Springs, New York, p. 1.

67. Douglas Johnstone, "Proposal: Residency Program for Independent Learners," 1980?, Center for Statewide Programs Archives, Empire State College, Saratoga Springs, New York, p. 2.

68. William Ferrero to Harry Spindler, 3 September 1981, Letter, Empire State College Archives, Saratoga Springs, New York.

69. Mary Mooney, "Residency Program for Independent Learners Report," 7 January 1982, Memorandum, Center for Statewide Programs Archives, Saratoga Springs, New York, p. 1.

70. "Residency Program for Independent Learners Enrollment Data, 1981–1984," 1984?, Memorandum, Center for Statewide Programs Archives, Saratoga Springs, New York, p. 1; Douglas Johnstone to James W. Hall, 30 November 1982, Memorandum, Center for Statewide Programs Archives, Saratoga Springs, New York, p. 1.

71. Wayne Ouderkirk, "Colloquium Report," 1986? Memorandum, Center for Statewide Programs Archives, Saratoga Springs, New York, pp. 1–7.

72. "Ten Students Begin Circulation Management Program," ESC News, Fall 1983, p. 1.

73. Douglas Johnstone, Interview, 12 April 1995, Notes, Empire State College Archives, Saratoga Springs, New York, p. 2.

74. Robert Tolsma, "A Glimpse at FORUM," *Empire State College Exchange,* October 1990, p. 6; Johnstone, Interview, 12 April 1995, p. 2.

75. Ibid.

76. Joyce Haines, "Niagara Frontier Begins Forum Program," *Empire State College Exchange,* September 1990, p. 4.

77. Thomas Rocco to Richard Bonnabeau, 3 April 1995, E-mail, Empire State College Archives, Saratoga Springs, New York.

78. Michael Kanaly, "The Buffalo FORUM Program," *Empire State College Exchange,* October 1991, p. 4.

79. Carolyn Shadle, Michael Kiskis, and Anne Bertholf, "FORUM Faculty Handbook," 1994?, Empire State College, p. 2.

80. Johnstone, Interview, 12 April 1995, p. 3.

81. Ibid., 2.

82. Hugh Hammett to Richard Bonnabeau, 17 September

1995, Memorandum, Empire State College Archives,
Saratoga Springs, New York, p. 1.

83. Hammett, pp. 1–2.

84. Annual Report: 1990–1991, p. 18; Michael Kanaly,
"Education and Business Joining Forces: The
Corporate/College Program," *Empire State College Exchange,*
November 1991, pp. 1–2.

85 Antonia Pena, "Affirmative Action Data: Corporate
College," 5 April 1995, Memorandum, Empire State College
Archives, Saratoga Springs, New York, p. 6.

86. Rhoda Miller to Richard Bonnabeau, 12 April 1995, E-
mail, Empire State College, Saratoga Springs, New York,
p. 1.

Dean Douglas Johnstone addresses graduates, their families, and friends at the 1988 North
Central Regional Center graduation recognition ceremony held at Assembly Hall in Saratoga
Springs, New York. Photograph by Bruce Squiers.

5

CONNECTIONS,
CROSSINGS,
CELEBRATIONS,
AND CRISES

Dr. Carolyn Broadaway (left), a founding member of
the Albany Center faculty, and former culture and
policy studies chair for the Graduate Program, meets
with Gertrude Lawson, at the time a student at the
Albany Center. Lawson graduated in 1987.
Photograph by Lary Abrams.

While connections to technology and business have greatly inscribed the history of the College since 1981, in these past fifteen years there have been other accomplishments that are testaments to the vision and stamina of a college hammered by Spartan budgets. In 1981, Empire State College negotiated successfully a SUNY-wide student internship program in government agencies; in 1982, the College finally won approval for a graduate program; in 1985, the College created the Office of Continuing Education and Public Service; in 1989, the College established the National Center on Adult Learning to support research in the field of adult pedagogy; and in 1987 and in 1993, the College expanded its programs overseas to include Cyprus and Greece. In addition to these further connections, in 1983, the Center for Distance Learning received from the American Association of State Colleges and Universities the G. Theodore Mitau Competition Award as a model for educational access; in 1985, the College passed muster in a successful five-year periodic review by Middle States; in 1988, the College won the CAEL Institutional Service Award for its path-setting accomplishments in the assessment of experiential learning; in 1990, the College received a second ten-year reaccreditation from Middles States, confirming the crossing over to institutional maturity; and in 1995, Empire State College launched a program for students of World University, headquartered in Madrid, Spain, to complete their baccalaureate degrees with Empire State College through a series of summer residencies held in New York State.

The Fiscal Crisis of 1982–1983

To appreciate these accomplishments, however, they must be seen in the context of contracting state revenues. In fact, in the winter of 1982 the College found itself in the midst of a severe fiscal crisis, just at the time when it had won a long struggle to offer a master's program. The College was forced to eliminate 44 positions by April 1, 1983—a 13 percent reduction in staff, from 321 to 277 lines. Though retrenching a number of lines across the College, the administration targeted the Metropolitan Learning Center for deep cuts. All the faculty, mostly senior mentors, at 300 Park Avenue South, the location of the Center's headquarters, were let go.[1] Other Metro programs such as the Bedford/Stuyvesant satellite, serving African-Americans, and the Solidaridad Humana satellite, serving Hispanic-Americans, were left untouched.

With Dean Abrams' support the Center waged a vigorous campaign for its life. Faculty, administrators, students, and alumni expertly harnessed the formidable resources of New York City's media to generate public support. As the *ESC News* reported, not even horrific weather discouraged them: "A torrential rainstorm pelted Manhattan on Friday, March 18. The winds were so fierce you couldn't open an umbrella. But that didn't keep more than 150 students, alumni, faculty and staff from a standing-room only meeting at the Metropolitan Center."[2] The Metropolitan Alumni/Student Association mounted a campaign that included picketing, calls to New York State legislators, and a bus trip to Albany to meet with SUNY system officials, aids to the governor, and members of the state legislature.[3] Supporting legislators postured that they would "put President Hall on the rack" until he changed his mind, but they offered no moderation in the required cuts.

With the Metropolitan Center campaign becoming enmeshed in city and state politics and a sudden surge in state revenues in the spring of 1983, it became possible for the administration to restore the cuts. In the April meeting of the College Senate, President Hall praised the Center, which "demonstrated that it has strong friends and supporters willing to speak very clearly about the importance of the work it is doing in New York City."[4]

Reflecting on the turmoil of those months and the happy outcome, one cannot but wonder—indeed, it has been speculated often—that the administration deliberately chose the Metropolitan Center in anticipation of the public outcry. No other center, save the Labor College, could have marshalled such support. Much of the credit goes to the students. At a party celebrating the Center's successful campaign students were quoted as saying, "I tried sitting in a classroom. This is a last chance for me." "I've been to Berkeley and to Radcliffe, but traditional schools don't offer the kind of education a nontraditional student needs." "Within three weeks of enrolling here, I learned more than I had at my other school in a whole year. The mentors here aren't just my teachers; they're my friends."[5]

Although SUNY had promised Hall full restoration if the retrenchments at the Metropolitan Center were rescinded, these promises were soon voided, and the College was forced by SUNY to reduce the number of lines by the end of the fiscal year. The message was ominous. The fiscal future of the College, because it could not collect revenues from tuition, was chained to the state's economy, which seemed headed more toward contraction than expansion. At best, the future would be slow growth; at worst, a painful, downward spiral; or, ranging in the middle, a bland homeostasis. The only possibility for new initiatives, in the absence of grants or contracts, would be the painful shifting resources from one program to another.

Remaining Innovative

Although the long-term viability of the College to remain innovative seemed to be in jeopardy, the College's commitment remained undaunted. In fact, the achievements of 1982–1983 fiscal year were remarkable. The Center for Labor Studies established a new on-site program for the Service Employees International Union Local 32B-32J. The Niagara Frontier Regional Center opened satellites in Jamestown and Lockport "to meet a strong demand for the program."[6] The Center signed an articulation agreement with Erie Community College to provide office space and other kinds of support for mentors to assist Erie graduates in pursuing baccalaureate degrees through Empire State College. The Center for Distance Learning enrollments grew to sixteen hundred, boasted a course completion rate of 70 percent, and was positioned to grow exponentially, if only the resources could be found. The Public Affairs Center in Albany had made significant progress in developing statewide linkages with various state agencies. The Center for Statewide Programs negotiated articulation agreements with Fulton-Montgomery Community College and the Schenectady Community College, developed outreach programs for local communities in upstate New York, and launched a residency program, based on the Goddard model, for adult learners.

Fulton-Montgomery Community College Satellite: "Full Range of Baccalaureate Studies"

The articulation agreements that the College entered into with community colleges throughout the state are especially important to their local communities. For Fulton-Montgomery Community College (FMCC) graduates seeking a four-year degree, for example, an Empire State College satellite on the FMCC campus means that they do not have to commute long distances to a State University campus. The satellite is especially important to working adults who have no other alternative.

The 1985 agreement with Fulton-Montgomery Community College spelled out special arrangements for maintaining a full-time office at the campus with Michael Andolina as the first mentor coordinator. To provide the appropriate studies for a baccalaureate degree, the coordinator of the satellite uses faculty from Fulton-

In the midst of a serious New York State budget crisis, students, alumni, faculty, and staff gathered March 18, 1983, to protest the proposed retrenchment of Metropolitan Center faculty at the 300 Park Avenue location. Seated in the front row (left to right) are students Jeanne Seelav, David Belmont, and Iris Lozado. The campaign to save the faculty positions became enmeshed in city and state politics. A sudden surge in state revenue in the spring of 1983 made it possible for the Empire State College administration to restore the lost lines. Photograph by Mel Rosenthal.

Montgomery College as tutors, as well as tutors from the community for individualized learning contracts. In addition, the coordinator cross-registers students in appropriate community college courses and Center for Distance Learning courses. In this way, FMCC graduates have the full range of baccalaureate studies available to Empire State College students elsewhere in the state.[7]

Albany Semester Program: Serving State University of New York

Of its many achievements, Empire State College should be remembered for its service to other State University campuses: The Arts in the City program, bringing SUNY and Empire State College students to work with talented artists in New York City; the SUNY community colleges articulation agreements, making it possible for their graduates to pursue baccalaureate degrees with Empire State College; and SUNY by Satellite, an innovative project in telecommunications linking community colleges across the state. All mark Empire State College's commitment to serve the broader interests of the State University of New York.

The Albany Semester Program, administered by the College's center in Albany, currently the Northeast Center, which provides internships for SUNY students, including ESC students, and students from private colleges in state agencies, is yet another program providing service to the rest of the State University. The Albany Semester Program began in 1978 as a consortial program of seven SUNY colleges and was administered by the SUNY system until Empire State College assumed responsibility in 1982. Dennis DeLong, now the dean for the Northeast Center, coordinated the program. In 1984, Arnold Harris succeeded DeLong and administered the program until his untimely death in 1990. Since that time Carolyn Williams has been the coordinator.[8]

From the spring of 1983 to the spring of 1984, over sixty students from eleven SUNY campuses served as interns in ten state agencies. These students, who participated in an Empire State College seminar while in the internship program, had the unique opportunity "to apply their learning, examine career options, and gain an understanding of state government."[9] By 1986, the Albany Semester Program had placed students from twelve SUNY campuses as well as from two private colleges in twenty-two state agencies. This program quickly "gained an outstanding reputation in SUNY and national stature as a model for other states seeking to establish similar programs."[10] From 1978 to the present, the Albany Semester Program has provided placements for over eight hundred students from twenty different SUNY campuses in more than thirty New York State agencies and offices. In 1996, it continues as an exemplar of intercampus cooperation.

The Graduate Program

In 1976, Chancellor Ernest Boyer and Governor Hugh Carey had strongly endorsed Empire State College's request to initiate a master's program. Nevertheless, the Board of Regents of the State of New York, at the urging of the State Education Department, had flatly rejected the State University's request to approve an amendment of the SUNY Master Plan to allow the Empire State College initiative.

The College, supported by new SUNY Chancellor Clifton R. Wharton Jr. and SUNY Provost Loren Baritz, persisted.[11] In 1978, the State University—still prohibited by the Regents' injunction not to amend the SUNY Master Plan—affirmed that Empire State College would be the only vehicle for a nontraditional graduate program.[12] This triggered a series of positive exchanges with the State Education

Department, resulting in a plan that the department was ready to endorse. In 1981, the department "took the initiative to bring . . . the plan before the Regents" for approval.[13] In February 1982, the Regents granted an experimental registration for three years, limiting the number of students and the regions in the state where the program could be offered.

The graduate program was unique to American higher education. It offered three nonresidential degrees, Business and Policy Studies, Labor and Policy Studies, and Cultural and Policy Studies for mature adults working "in settings that involve complex contemporary public issues and decisions."[14] In addition to core policy seminars, students chose among a variety of flexible study options—cross registration, individualized tutorials, and field experience. In addition to these studies, students completed a final project. To emphasize the SUNY-wide spirit of the program, faculty were recruited from across the State University to supplement Empire State College faculty. A graduate council, mostly composed of distinguished SUNY administrators and faculty, was appointed by Chancellor Wharton.

The approval for the pilot program came in the midst of yet another state budget crisis. By the time Governor Carey gave final approval in July 1982, the College had had a number of staff reductions. This left no one available from among the administrative ranks to get the program off and running; and no new funds were allocated for the program. We had to "build upon the already strained resources of the existing College program."[15] The prospects for the new program were bleak, but, fortunately, in the of summer 1983, the Fund for the Improvement of Post Secondary Education (FIPSE) provided a three-year $280,000 grant and, after reviewing the first term of the graduate program, renewed the grant for a second year.[16]

The FIPSE funds had made it possible to move the program into high gear. Graduate faculty were hired, and Empire State College mentors such as John Bennett, Robert Carey, Carolyn Broadaway, Reed Coughlan, Clark Everling, Frederick Mayo, Elana Michelson, Crystal Scriber, Steven Tischler, and Wayne Willis were identified to serve as advisers and mentors, either in full-time or part-time capacities. This also provided another avenue for faculty development. And through a national search, Theodore A. DiPadova, formerly professor and associate dean at Old Dominion College and dean of graduate studies at Russell Sage College, was appointed graduate dean in October 1984. The program grew rapidly, drawing a third of its students from Empire State College graduates.

In 1987, the State Education Department closely reviewed the graduate program. The department praised the graduate program's "residency format and the individualization of the curriculum around common core requirements."[17] In 1988, the department reregistered the program, removing "all limitations as to location, program and enrollment."[18] By August of 1989 there were over two hundred students in the program, which already had graduated twenty-nine, most of whom enrolled in the Business and Policy Studies track. Students were adults, slightly more than three years older than Empire State College undergraduates, whose average age was thirty-seven. In contrast to the undergraduates, however, the majority, approximately two-thirds of the graduate students, were male as opposed to a female undergraduate population of 63 percent, and approximately 90 percent of the students enrolling in the graduate program was Caucasian, as opposed to 85 percent of the undergraduates.[19]

In 1992 the State Education Department approved offering a master's in liberal arts (M.A.L.S.). The degree made it possible for students to pursue individualized

Dr. Roger Keeran is a labor historian and chair of the labor and policy studies section of the Graduate Studies Program. Photograph by Walt Ulbricht.

programs of study with an interdisciplinary focus. It was much more flexible than the policy-oriented degrees. Mentor Elana Michelson, on loan from the Harry Van Arsdale Jr. Center for Labor Studies, got the program underway as the first chair, with an initial enrollment of thirty students. Many were teachers seeking advanced certification. Michael Andolina, coordinator of the satellite at the Fulton-Montgomery Community College, succeeded Elana in 1992.[20] Under Andolina's direction and then Director Carolyn Jarmon's the program continued to grow. Jarmon had replaced Theodore DiPadova in 1993 when he assumed the position of academic vice president at the University of New England. The program enrolled almost two hundred students in 1995, approximately half of them in the Policy Studies cluster. The success of M.A.L.S. resulted in plans to offer the degree in Israel through the cooperation of the Empire State College Office of International Programs. Other developments in the graduate program included plans to offer a master's in Business and Policy Studies in Russia, combining on-site seminars with distance-learning technologies, and New York State Education Department approval for a combined undergraduate-graduate program, permitting talented students to complete their undergraduate degrees in business while beginning work toward master's degrees in business and policy studies.[21]

Continuing Education and Public Service: "Vital Training Needs"

The Office of Continuing Education and Public Service, created in 1985, has for the past decade provided noncredit specialized training for both the public and private sectors. Hugh Hammett, former associate dean at the Genesee Valley Regional Center, was appointed executive director in July of that year. He and Ellen Blake, associate director, formerly with the Office of Program Review and Assessment, along with Julie Smith, launched the program. In less than a year, Continuing Education had served fifty apprentices who worked in state agencies as electricians, stationary engineers, and motor equipment mechanics. The venture demonstrated the College's ability to meet the "vital training needs in far-flung state facilities."[22]

By 1988 Continuing Education had secured major contracts with Civil Service Employees Association (CSEA) and the Adirondack Educational Consortium of Health Organizations (AECHO) and added Joseph Boudreau to its staff. Through the CSEA contract, Continuing Education became a "major statewide provider" for the Joint Apprenticeship Committee, and served apprentices and thousands of supervisors and journey-level state workers. The contract with AECHO provided training to hospital employees in the northern reaches of the state who would have been otherwise unserved.[23] From June 1989 to July 1990, the Office of Continuing Education had sponsored more than three hundred separate technical and career development activities for seven thousand people, mostly from public sector contracts, and had generated $1.2 million in revenues. Among other activities, the Office of Continuing Education, in cooperation with New York State/CSEA Joint Labor Management Program and with the Governor's Office of Employee Relations, provided apprentice training in skilled trades. The Office of Continuing Education became "the major statewide educational provider" for the Joint Apprenticeship Committee, providing college-level technical skills to several thousand apprentices, supervisors, and journeyman-level state employees.[24]

Carolyn Williams (left), then assistant to the dean of the Albany Center, works with alumnus Lee Serino during the 1986 phonothon.

By sponsoring national conferences, serving as a national clearinghouse for adult learner research, funding practitioner research, and shaping public policy regarding adult learning, NCAL, under the leadership of Director Timothy Lehmann, has created a cutting-edge vehicle to shape a dynamic component of American higher education.[28]

1989 Self-study and Middle States Review: "Student Centered Principles"

Empire State College prepared for its third review by Middle States assiduously, as if it were the first time. The dispersed nature of the College—over forty regional centers and units—and the dynamism of an institution reinventing itself through new programmatic developments made the self-study process a pilgrimage of introspection. Empire State College revisited its origins, reassessed purposes, examined failures and successes, and, through it all, confessed its sins, however slight, and bared its collective soul to the Commission's plenipotentiaries when they visited in the fall of 1989. Empire State College did this more than perhaps any traditional college would need to, would care to; it did so because, despite a record of singular academic accomplishments, the College was still unsure about itself, still uncertain about how it was viewed in the world of higher education.

What the team found delighted them, and the Commission commended the self-study for its excellence. Jane Altes, vice president for academic affairs, who replaced John Jacobson in 1987 when he assumed the presidency of Hope College and Marjorie Lavin, assistant vice president for academic affairs, guided and supported mentors and administrators in this two-year effort.

Empire State College had changed since the last review in 1979. A college where individualized contract learning had been a matter of orthodoxy a decade before now stated proudly that all of its regional learning centers had created opportunities for group-based studies and that generic learning contracts—known pejoratively as boilerplates—were appropriate under many circumstances. While change had been noted, there was also remarkable consistency. The student-centered principles that had informed the development of the College since its inception had remained unchanged and were very much a part of the "faculty structure and ethos."[29]

The Middle States team found a college with approximately sixty-four hundred students, whose average age was thirty-seven. Students selected Empire State College because of "the flexibility of time, place, pace and format" that allowed adults to earn a degree while they worked, to earn credit for nonformal experiential learning, and to pursue individualized programs of study.[30] The majority of students, 70 percent, worked full time; 48 percent held professional, semiprofessional, and supervisory positions; 84 percent of the students studied part time; 63 percent were women; 67 percent were married; 8 percent were African-American; 5 percent were Hispanic; 2 percent were other; and the remainder, 85 percent, were white; 4 percent planned to earn associate's degree; 39 percent bachelor's degrees; and 59 percent planned to earn professional or graduate degrees after completing their studies at Empire State College.[31]

Of the students entering the College, 31 percent chose Business, Management, and Economics as an area of study (up 19 percent since 1980); 17 percent chose Community and Human Services; 12 percent chose Science, Math and Technology; and 12 percent chose the Arts. The percentage of students wanting to earn postgraduate degrees had not changed since 1974. In fact, since 1974 entering students had remained "remarkably consistent" in their statement about reasons for entering college.[32] Of these students, 83 percent saw themselves as persistent,

ambitious, and independent individuals with leadership skills, with the ability to handle stress, and with the requisite academic competence. What had changed was the desire to earn more money (up from 43 to 57 percent) and to know more about science and technology (17 to 29 percent). These desires were consistent with the 1980s "greed-is-good" decade of devout materialism and the deification of computer technology.[33]

The 1989 self-study naturally focused on the role of the mentor. It is, after all, Empire State College's unique contribution to American higher education. The term *mentor*, once used sparingly, is now uttered frequently in higher education and in business. The self-study noted that role of mentor—the complex one-to-one relationship between a faculty member and a student—developed as the College evolved, but that the process had not been "painless" and that problems persisted.[34] Mentoring remained, as Lee Herman noted, author of the mentoring section of the report, a fragmented role: mentors still counseled and advised students; assisted students in designing individual degree programs and contracts; provided instruction; assessed prior learning; managed and developed instructional resources; managed the records of their work with students; and some mentors, known as unit coordinators, administered regional learning center satellites while carrying a full load of students; and all of these were jumbled with faculty committee work and the need to keep current in one's discipline.[35]

Workload had remained an issue, even after the College had negotiated lower FTE expectations for its faculty, because the ratio of full-time students to part-time students had flipped over. There were now significantly more half-time than full-time students; and two half-time students did not equal a full-time student in the space-

Empire State College Studio Arts students stand on the roof of the Wesbeth Studio located in lower Manhattan. Students come from Empire State College as well as other State University campuses. They are joined by students from private colleges in New York State and from other states, as well as by students from other countries, to work under the direction of Mentor George McClancy. The program, which began in the early 1970s, takes full advantage of New York's stature as the international center of the contemporary art world. Photograph by Mel Rosenthal.

Alan Luddington (right), a Center for Distance Learning graduate, demonstrates the use of new fire equipment to the members of his Harriman, New York, fire company. The Center for Distance Learning gave Luddington, an executive with the American Broadcasting Company since 1951 and a volunteer firefighter, an opportunity to enhance his technical and managerial skills as a firefighter.

time continuum of mentoring. Further, students who had disenrolled temporarily and who did not, therefore, count as FTE still haunted mentors as a "ghost-load" responsibility.[36] While the self-study spoke of an anxiety that plagued a maturing pioneer faculty who faced, unlike counterparts in traditional colleges, a fragmented professional existence, it noted also a significant increase in the percentage of time faculty devoted to professional development. It increased from 2 percent in 1973 to 19 percent in 1985. Mentors might have been short of breath from their workloads, but they were obviously not consumptive.[37]

Middle States Evaluation:

The College faculty, administration, and support staff impressed the Middle States team with their high level of enthusiasm, dedication, competence, and creativity. The team praised them all for their dedication to students. The team made special note of the Harry Van Arsdale Jr. School of Labor Studies for its unique contributions to the development of New York City's work force , particularly the Center's work with Local 3 of the IBEW (International Brotherhood of Electrical Workers). The team praised the Center for Distance Learning for its accomplishments, ranking it among the top programs in the world. The team commended the Center for adhering to the student-centered mission of the College while avoiding the pitfalls of an industrial model of distance education. The team advised the College to market the Center aggressively. A larger student base would realize economies of scale in course production, but care had to be taken not to lose sight of ESC's student-centered philosophy.[38]

The team had a number of concerns. Faculty workload, the leitmotif of institutional existence, headed the list. The team was particularly concerned about the workload's potential negative impact on the quality of the academic program and recommended additional resources, computer technology, streamlining processes, and the greater use of group studies as possible remedies. The team expressed concern as well about the absence of minorities in the senior administration of the coordinating center in Saratoga. It urged the College to enhance its efforts to recruit minority staff and students.[39] The team noted that the high attrition, while not surprising for an adult population struggling with demands from employment and other demands competing for their limited time and resources, including sending their own children to college, could be addressed through such activities as better orientation and counseling before and after enrollment.[40]

The assessment process struck the team as being much more complicated than it had to be, even taking into account the issue of quality control. Assessment had four levels of quality control. These began with the mentor who supervised the work of evaluators of experiential learning; continued with the assessment professional who provided a second-level check by reviewing the evaluations before they were submitted to the faculty assessment committee; moved to a third-level check by individual members of the committee before the evaluations were examined at the assessment meeting; and culminated in a fourth and final overview of the materials by the Office of Program Review and Assessment. If one considers that evaluators often were used more than once, which resulted in expert testaments time and again, these many levels of review, which applied also to college transcripts and the results of standardized exams, were excessive and wasteful of scarce resources.

This process reflected an institution that felt isolated from the rest of higher education, vulnerable, and possibly defensive. The College had devised, therefore, a process to protect it from critics who could otherwise accuse the College of violating some sacred cannon and thereby tongue-lash Empire State College right out of existence. The Middle States team urged the College to rethink how it did assessment but recommended devising a system that guaranteed uniform results for students.[41]

In March of the following year the chair of the Middle States Association forwarded a letter to President Hall congratulating the College for "the excellence of its Self-study and responses it has made to its ongoing challenges and concerns."[42]

1992–1993 Fiscal Crisis

Since the founding of the College in 1971, fiscal crises came with the regularity of a medieval pestilence. In February 1992, less than two years after the Middle States Association renewed the accreditation for ten years, the College braced itself for yet another crisis. The state faced an estimated $4.8 billion revenue shortfall. To balance the budget, Governor Mario Cuomo, among other measures, cut revenues to state agencies, including the State University of New York, by approximately 15 percent. For the State University this meant a $143 million cut shared by sixty-four campuses. Approximately half of this was met with a tuition increase, $535 per year, per student. The remainder had to be made up with cuts in operating funds. This meant that in February 1992 Empire State College faced a projected $1.2 million budget cut as well as a mandate not to sustain the same FTE target, 4,185.[43]

Since 1975 the once robust State University has been debilitated by budget cuts. Between fiscal years 1975–76 and 1991–92, there were permanent budget losses of $394 million and 4,018 positions lost; and between fiscal years 1988–89 and 1991–92 SUNY sustained an additional $140 million in permanent budget cuts and an

Alice Fulton, 1978 graduate of the Albany Learning Center and student of Mentor Carolyn Broadaway, received the 1991 MacArthur "genius" Award for her poetry. At the time she received the award, Fulton was an assistant professor of English at the University of Michigan. She praised Empire State College for allowing her to "begin life as a thinking person." Photograph by Hank De Leo.

additional loss of 892 positions, despite a significant increase in tuition. The 1992–1993 crisis threatened an additional 1,100 SUNY positions as well as an increase in tuition. Tuition, more and more, had become a major component of State University funding, from 12.6 percent in 1988–89 to 40.6 percent in 1992–93. As a consequence, the State University of New York had become less accessible to lower income families while at the same time the quality of the education diminished as a result of enrollment targets remaining the same despite a significant reduction in faculty and administrative staff.[44]

On April 10, 1992, President Hall announced the budget plan for the coming fiscal year to the College community. He had consulted with the Program Planning and Budget Committee and the Senate, both bodies mostly composed of faculty, and the faculties and staffs of the regional centers, the College administration, and the College Council. He also made the budget a major agenda item for the April All-College Conference, a gathering of almost the entire College. At a late night "open door discussion" with faculty and staff, some faculty demanded that significant cuts come from administrative ranks.

In the preamble of his budget plan, Hall noted the political and economic contexts that shaped this budget:

New York State (and therefore SUNY) will continue to experience a comparably weaker economy than many other regions of the USA. The difficulties devolve upon us from Federal and State policies and priorities that severely damage higher education as well as most other services and human support systems built up over many years. Jobs will continue to flow from the State. New York State's revenues growth will be slow. Maintenance of our remarkable social organizational infrastructure will continue to be challenged. Politicians will continue to know what they should do to change the situation, but they will not do it because of political realities. Specifically, entitlements will not be reduced; taxes will not be raised; users of State services will get less, and they will pay more. In a nation and state of great wealth, the current political reality is a commitment to private gain, and a disinvestment in the public weal.[45]

Hall minimized the pain to Empire State College personnel as much as possible. He reduced OTPS (Other than Personnel Services), which permitted significant delays in layoffs, some stretching out more than a year. He compressed office work weeks in July and August as well as closed the College between Christmas and New Year's, a time when faculty were on vacation or engaged in reading and research. This produced significant savings in utilities and communications. Other savings were made by reducing the rental costs, especially for the Harry Van Arsdale Jr. Center, which accounted for 30 percent of the College's leasing arrangements, and by reducing the number of sabbaticals and promotions. All these generated significant savings. Cuts in personnel still had to be made. At the center level, faculty cuts were based on enrollment performance, but aimed at part-time faculty in centers chronically below target.[46]

Streamlining the administration of centers was another objective. President Hall noted how the original plan for the College, twenty regional learning centers each serving five hundred to one thousand FTE students, had been limited by bad budgets and not by student demand to seven centers. He argued that the administrative core of the regional centers already was lean. Essentially a dean, in effect a quasi-president and department chair, and an associate dean were responsible for the operation of the academic program. Along with an assessment professional, they were linked administratively to the coordinating center and worked with a multidisciplinary faculty team providing direct service to students. Hall noted as well that the coordinating center, comprised of "highly specialized and thinly staffed operations (by any university measure)," had since 1976 lost fifteen lines while lines committed to direct service had been increased by fifty. He, nevertheless, entertained a major restructuring of the regional centers—a paradigm shift—essentially fusing the administration of nearby centers. One dean would be henceforth responsible for the

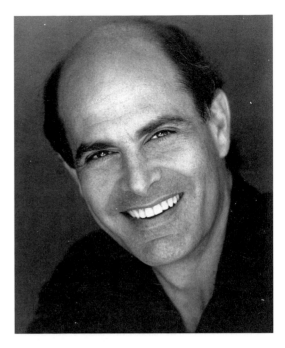

Actor Alan Rachins, a 1974 graduate of the Metropolitan Center and a student of Mentor Joseph Goldberg, became famous for his role as Douglas Brackman on the television series "L.A. Law." Rachins served as chair for the Empire State College Foundation's 1991–1992 Annual Fund. Photograph by Peter Kredenser.

Scott Bucking, a 1992 graduate of the Metropolitan Center, stands next to Mercedes Barry, assistant to the dean. After graduating, Bucking went to Trinity College at Cambridge University. Barry joined the Metropolitan Center in 1972. Photograph by Mel Rosenthal.

Administrators, tutors, and students gathered for the 1994 graduation recognition ceremony at the Zionist Federation Center in Jerusalem. First row, left to right, are graduates Dganit Livne, Rachel Greenhut, Roselyn Feldman, and Martin Greenberger. Second row, left to right, are Israel satellite coordinator Amnon Orent, tutor Eve Menes, tutor Adina Katzoff, tutor Lilly Polliack, Dean Kenneth Abrams, and tutor David Starr-Glass.

centers in a given region with responsibility for planning, budgeting, personnel, and public relations. The day-to-day administration of the centers within a region would be each in the hands of a center director, either a surviving dean or an associate dean. The faculty compensated for the loss of some of the associate deans by electing chairs to assume some of the responsibilities of associate deans.[47] Mentors at the Genesee Valley Center developed a very successful council of elected faculty to assume the responsibilities of the associate dean.

The College was now composed of four regional administrations, their centers, and an entirely new entity called the Center for Collegewide Programs (CWP). The CWP, headed by Douglas Johnstone, the dean for the former North Central Center, merged five formerly independent programs: the Center for Distance Learning, Graduate Studies, Corporate College, FORUM/East, and International Programs. Each was characterized by programmatic elements that made them different from the regional learning centers.[48] The reorganization, especially the administration of the regional learning centers, was a risky venture because there was no guarantee that any of this would work well. But faculty had impressed on President Hall the importance of the administration sharing the pain. He complied in ways that brought faculty into the management of the College to compensate for the loss of management confidential lines. As creative as the response to the fiscal crisis was, the cuts in personnel had to be endured. Of the sixty-four personnel actions taken, mostly terminating part-time lines (and some as little as a one-eighth fraction), three faculty, three support staff, and four management confidential administrators lost their jobs.[49]

After the smoke of the 1992–93 fiscal crisis had cleared, Empire State College emerged as a more streamlined institution and funded more by tuition and Income Fund Reimbursable accounts than by state subvention. This meant that students had to assume more of the costs. This was consistent with an era that celebrated the new ethos of privatization and the retreat of government from the public welfare. For lower-income citizens it meant less access to public education.

Hall was particularly concerned about the morale of the College. In July he addressed the College community through the *ESC Exchange,* asking all to look toward the future and "to put the negativism of the budget behind us."[50] He quoted Governor Cuomo's praise for the College's recent achievements as a national model for innovative education, and observed:

You [the College community] have expanded the College's academic programs and created new sources of revenue. International Programs, Graduate Studies and Continuing Education were the first such efforts. More recently, you launched new corporate initiatives (FORUM and Corporate/College programs) and Department of Social Services programs.

The amazing thing is that these programs currently generate approximately $6 million of revenue, enough to fill the gap between where ESC's state allocated operating budget should have been by 1992 and our present actual state allocation. The mission, then, is moving forward as planned, while we continue to seek new funding sources. Furthermore, in this process, the jobs of many experienced and valued colleagues have been saved.[51]

The College had managed its worst budget crisis well. Still many mentors argued for the need to maintain the instructional quality of the program. They claimed that more management/confidential lines should have been surrendered and less sacrifice asked of faculty. Through it all, however, the institutional morale remained high. The College community would need this to sustain it, yet again, for a budget crisis of even greater magnitude not far off in the future.

This February 1993 photograph shows Saratoga Mentor Mary Nell Morgan (left) assisting her student, Darlene McMorris, to prepare for a five-month internship with the United States Information Agency in Washington, D.C. Photograph by Larry Abrams.

Student Opinion Survey: "The Best News this College Ever Had"

A major boost to morale came in 1994 when the College received the results of the Student Opinion Survey (S.O.S.) conducted by American College Testing. This national survey ranked Empire State College as first among State University campuses, including all of the thirteen university colleges, and first by intoxicating proportions

Raymond Harris (left), Metropolitan Center student and 1991 Leach Fellow, stands next to Mrs. Richard Porter Leach and President Hall. The award honors student achievement in the performing arts.

Dr. Bernard Rosenberg, a graduate of the Labor Center, received his doctorate from Rutgers University in 1989. He served as a member of the Empire State College Board of Directors and the College Council. Photograph by Larry Abrams.

in sixteen of seventeen categories, and second only in one category. In fact, the summary prepared by American College Testing noted that because the College ranked first "for so many items that describing them or listing them would be impractical."[52] Among the categories examined in the S.O.S. were the quality of instruction; faculty respect for students; students' sense of belonging; concern for students as individuals; academic advising service; personal counseling services; availability of student advisers; availability of courses; and extent the College has helped students to appreciate diversity.[53] This was "the best news this College has ever had," according to Academic Vice President Jane Altes who reported the findings at the Winter Retreat of the President's Administrative Council. But it was not the kind of news the College could make much of publicly.[54] To say, for example, that Empire State College is number one in SUNY as part of a marketing strategy would be viewed as chest pounding and be sure to alienate our SUNY sister institutions. "We are a collaborative institution, so we have to be careful about showing off."[55] Empire State College depends on other SUNY campuses for cross-registering students, for tutors, for libraries, and even, oftentimes, for office space. The College owes much of its success these past twenty-five years to SUNY's good will. The College administration chose, therefore, to soft-pedal the sensationally good news in the *ESC Exchange,* third page, under a modest banner. Indeed, the reader must first know the elements of statistics to grasp fully the survey's significance.

The SUNY Fiscal Crisis of 1995: "No Equal in the History of American Public Higher Education"

In the spring of 1995, practically on the heels of the S.O.S findings, the College faced its second fiscal crisis in three years. This time it was the most severe crisis in the annals of the State University and of a magnitude unequaled in the history of American public higher education. Republican electoral victories in the fall of 1994, which produced a Republican governor and a Republican controlled State Senate, had caused concern about budget cuts. But the extent of the proposed cuts for the State University could have been scarcely imagined. Governor George Pataki projected a multibillion-dollar deficit in state revenues and promised to reduce the tax burden. Pataki proposed a $289.5 million (31.5 percent) cut in state assistance to the state operated campuses of the SUNY system. The governor expected SUNY to compensate for losses in state subvention with a massive tuition increases while at the same time financial aid programs would be reduced and, in some cases, eliminated. Further, the proposed budget, which projected a tuition rescue, expected SUNY to shrink by at least 4 percent, tuition increases or not. SUNY already had lost hundreds of millions of dollars in state support in recent years under Governor Mario Cuomo. It now had to downsize even more. Some private sector colleges viewed SUNY as huge and predatory. Reducing SUNY's size and increasing SUNY's tuition would help restore some balance, it was argued, between public and private education in a highly competitive market.

The proposed Pataki budget, assuredly the first in a series designed to reduce the size of state government, was vexing news for Empire State College. Newly appointed Chancellor Thomas A. Bartlett even spoke of the possibility of closing some SUNY campuses to meet the shortfall in state revenue. For a college still recoiling from the 1991–92 budget crisis, Governor Pataki's proposal raised serious concern about sustaining the College's mission. SUNY supporters took some comfort, however, in the thought that the Democratic Assembly, led by Speaker Sheldon Silver, might convince or bargain successfully with Governor Pataki and the Republican-controlled

Ann M. Galante, mayor of Mineola and 1990 graduate of the Long Island Center, meets with a member of the Mineola police force. Photograph by Miller Photography, New Hyde Park, New York.

Senate to restore some funding to the State University. The College took comfort also in the hope that Chancellor Bartlett, recognizing Empire State College's unique contributions to the State of New York and its remarkable stature in American higher education, might protect the College or minimize the impact of the Pataki budget proposal.

The wait to receive final word from the SUNY Board of Trustees was made more agonizing because for two months political wrangling delayed passage of the state budget. The Board of Trustees approved the final budget June 27, 1995. Though it required a major cut in Empire State College's funding, the $632,100 was manageable. Nevertheless, the budget reduction came at the very time that the College had hoped to invest heavily in its technological infrastructure. This left the College with a need to generate approximately $1 million in revenue by identifying new sources of income and reducing expenditures through reductions in nonpersonnel expenditures. The College projected new revenues by increasing the assessment fee and charging students a telecommunications fee for VAX usage and related services. In addition, early retirements saved almost $100,000; and moving four staff from state lines to Income Fund Reimbursable lines saved approximately $200,000. The increase in undergraduate tuition by $750 was bearable while much of the state's financial aid was kept intact. Graduate students faced a much greater increase in tuition, going up by $1,100 per year. Nonresident tuition bounced up sharply as well, increasing by $1,174 for undergraduates and by $1,100 per year for graduate students.

The College avoided what it feared most, retrenchment, though a number of contracts of valued colleagues were not renewed. In effect, the academic program would be sustained with little damage to its structural integrity, though grim thoughts about what state budgets would bring over the next three years made the collective sigh of relief in July 1995 the briefest in the College history.

The impact of contracting state revenues on the Empire State College's budget, as illustrated on the next page has been dramatic. In the top chart, which provides a historic overview from fiscal year 1985–1986 to fiscal year 1995–1996, we see a dramatic plunge in state subvention. Falling state revenue has been replaced by increasing tuition and other revenue sources.

In the second chart, we see that by fiscal year 1995–1996 state subvention has been reduced to 30.3 percent. The chart illustrates how the College dramatically compensated for the loss of state revenue with external sources of funding through contract programs, special academic programs, and fund-raising. As we see from the graph, direct state support and state provided benefits account for less than a third of the revenue base. Revenues from Income Fund Reimbursable programs such as FORUM/East and revenues from the Research Foundation and the Empire State Foundation account for 34 percent of the total.

This development points to a future in which Empire State College will carry out a public mission almost wholly with private funds. This may be, after all, good for the College. As state revenues contract Empire State College will have more incentive to develop revenue generating programs. In effect, the College will have the potential to grow and be of greater service to the citizens of New York.

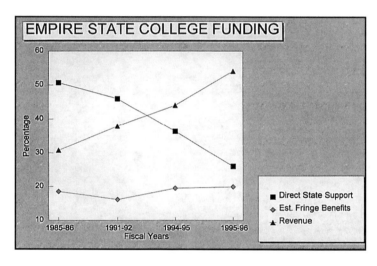

Empire State College Funding

Source		1985-86	1991-92	1994-95	1995-96
Direct State Support		$7,807.9	$10,145.3	$8,967.9	$6,305.5
		50.7%	**46.0%**	**36.4%**	**26.0%**
Est. Fringe Benefits		2,843.0	3,553.0	4,816.0	4,817.5
		18.5%	**16.1%**	**19.5%**	**19.9%**
Revenue		4,751.1	8,372.5	10,887.0	13,100.0
		30.8%	**37.9%**	**44.1%**	**54.1%**
	cost/c.h.	$45	$72	$88	$113
Total State		15,402.0	22,070.8	24,670.9	24,223.0
IFR:					
General IFR		1,089.0	3,422.0	4,044.1	4,305.9
Sutra		0.0	0.0	2,651.9	4,378.2
Frnige Benefits		336.6	547.6	958.1	1,594.2
Total IFR		1,425.6	3,969.6	7,654.1	10,278.3

Distribution of Funds   based upon 1995-1996 allocations
Empire State College: All Funds

	Total	% Total
Direct State Support	$6,305.5	17.2%
State Provided Benefits	$4,817.5	13.1%
Tuition	$13,100.0	35.7%
IFR	$10,278.3	28.0%
Research Foundation	$1,755.6	4.9%
ESC Foundation	$393.4	1.1%
Total		
	$36,650.3	100.0%

Metropolitan Center Mentor Joseph Washington, a mathematician, meets with a student in 1987. Mentor Washington is one of the many faculty who have served on faculty teams for International Programs. Photograph by Patrick O'Hare.

Smiles of success from Gail Roell, a Hudson Valley Center graduate, and daughter Leigh. Photograph by Linda Cohen.

D. Bruce Johnstone (left), then chancellor of the State University of New York, and President James W. Hall meet Center for Distance Learning graduate John Wheeler and spouse at a 1990 alumni reception in Berkeley, California.

Dr. Marlene Evans (left) joins in the celebration at the 1990 North Central Regional Center graduation recognition ceremony in Saratoga Springs. Mentor Evans is a geographer and coordinator of the Saratoga Springs satellite of the Northeast Center.

Endnotes Chapter 5

1. Empire State College Senate, "Minutes," 7 February 1983, appendix A, Empire State College Archives, Saratoga Springs, New York, p. 1.

2. "Vital Signs," *ESC News,* Summer 1983, p. 8.

3. "Vital Signs," pp. 8–9.

4. Empire State College Senate, "Minutes," 26 April 1983, Empire State College Archives, Saratoga Springs, New York, p. 1.

5. "Vital Signs," p. 10.

6. *Seeking Alternatives XI: Empire State College Annual Report* (1 July 1982–30 June 1983) (Empire State College: Saratoga Springs, New York), 1–5.

7. Michael Andolina, "Innovation and Structure," *Innovating,* vol. 3, no. 2, (Winter 1993): 62–69.

8. Dennis DeLong to Richard Bonnabeau, 20 April 1995, E-mail, Empire State College Archives, Saratoga Springs, New York, p. 1.

9. *Seeking Alternatives XII: Empire State College Annual Report* (1983–1984) (Empire State College: Saratoga Springs, New York), 3.

10. *Seeking Alternatives XIV: Empire State College Annual Report* (1985–1986) (Empire State College: Saratoga Springs, New York), 6.

11. Clifton Wharton Jr. to James Hall, 18 September 1978, Empire State College Archives, Saratoga Springs, New York.

12. *Seeking Alternatives X: Empire State College Annual Report* (1 July 1981–30 June 1982) (Empire State College: Saratoga Springs, New York), 7.

13. Ibid.

14. John Jacobson to John Sawyer, 19 May 1982, Letter, Empire State College Archives, Saratoga Springs, New York.

15. *Seeking Alternatives X,* p. 8.

16. *Seeking Alternatives XIII: Empire State College Annual Report* (1984–1985) (Empire State College, Saratoga Springs, New York), 1.

17. *Retrospect and Prospect: Strengthening Learning at Empire State College 1989,* Self-study Prepared for the Commission on Higher Education, Middle States Association of Colleges and Schools (Empire State College, Saratoga Springs, New York, September 1979), 66.

18. Ibid., ii.

19. Ibid., 36, 38, and 61.

20. "College Welcomes New Year with New Master's Program," Empire State College Exchange, 14 December 1992, p. 1; "New Master of Arts in Liberal Studies Program Grows," *Empire State College Exchange,* 14 October 1993, p. 1.

21. *Empire State College Annual Report, 1993–1994* (Empire State College, Saratoga Springs, New York), 9.

22. *Empire State College Communique,* vol. 12, no. 10 (23 June 1986): 1.

23. *Seeking Alternatives XVI: Empire State College Annual Report* (1987–1988) (Empire State College, Saratoga Springs, New York), 5.

24. *Empire State College Annual Report, 1989–1990* (Empire State College, Saratoga Springs, New York), 15.

25. *Empire State College Annual Report, 1991–1992* (Empire State College, Saratoga Springs, New York), 18–19.

26. Julie Smith, "Continuing Education & Public Service: What's It All About?" *Empire State College Exchange,* 29 August 1994, p. 2.

27. Kenneth Abrams to the File, August 26, 1991, Empire State College Archives, Saratoga Springs, New York, pp. 1–2.

28. National Center on Adult Learning, Brochure, 1995, Empire State College, Saratoga Springs, New York, pp. 1–3; *Annual Report,* 1991–1992, p. 17.

29. *Annual Report,* 1989–1990, p. 17.

30. "Self-study, 1989, pp. 36–37.

31. Ibid., 36.

32. Ibid., 37.

33. Ibid.

34. Ibid., 21.

35. Ibid., 28–29.

36. Ibid., 32.

37. Ibid., 24.

38. "Report to the Faculty, Administrators, Trustees, Students of Empire State College," Prepared by an Evaluation Team Representing the Commission on Higher Education of the Middle State Association of Colleges and Schools, 1979, Empire State College Archives, Saratoga Springs, New York, pp. 4–12.

39. Ibid., 6–7.

40. Ibid., 11.

41. Ibid., 6.

42. Sarah Blanshei to James W. Hall, 16 March 1990, Letter, Empire State College Archives, Saratoga Springs, New York.

43. James W. Hall, "The State, SUNY and ESC-Budget 92–93," *Empire State College Exchange,* 20 February 1992, pp. 1–2.

44. Ibid.

45. James W. Hall, "Budget Plan for Empire State College: Fiscal Year Beginning July 1, 1992," *Empire State College Exchange,* 10 April 1992, p. 1.

46. Ibid., 2–3.

47. Ibid., 4–5.

48. James W. Hall, "Plan for a Streamlined College Administration, *Empire State College Exchange,* 1 June 1992, p. 2.

49. James W. Hall, "Meeting the Mandated Budget Reductions: Personnel Actions," *Empire State College Exchange,* 14 May 1992, pp. 1–2.

50. James W. Hall, "President's Column," *Empire State College Exchange,* 31 July 1992, p. 2.

51. Ibid.

52. Jane Altes, "Empire State College—Performing its Mission with Quality," *Empire State College Exchange,* 14 March 1995, p. 3.

53. Ibid., 4.

54. Richard Bonnabeau, "Notes: Empire State College Winter Administrative Retreat, January 25–27, 1995," Empire State College Archives, Saratoga Springs, New York, p. 1.

55. Ibid.

Sharon Grigsby, a 1978 graduate of the Genesee Valley Center, is the assistant for student affairs at Genesee. Photograph by Reed Hoffmann.

6

First Principles,
Enduring Achievements,
and Summary
Conclusions

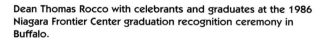

Dean Thomas Rocco with celebrants and graduates at the 1986
Niagara Frontier Center graduation recognition ceremony in
Buffalo.

Historian Robert Seidel joined the Genesee Valley Learning Center faculty in 1974. Mentor Seidel received the Chancellor's Award for Excellence in Teaching for 1979–1980, and in 1990 he was named SUNY Distinguished Teaching Professor. Dr. Seidel has served as chair of the Empire State College Senate and currently serves as the College's representative to the State University of New York Faculty Senate.

First Principles, Enduring Achievements, and Summary Conclusions

The success of Empire State College is deeply rooted in a clear sense of mission, first articulated in the *Prospectus* and then refined by experience. From the mission of providing access to students have come the first principles which inform the spirit and organization of the College. These principles have resulted in a flexible institutional framework which responds to students as individuals, a student-centered pedagogy, a facilitative faculty role called mentoring, a unique system of validating prior learning, and a spirit of innovation. These are the enduring achievements that have kept Empire State College on the cutting edge of American public higher education.

Responding to Individuals: Institutional Framework

The *Prospectus* called for a college built without bricks and mortar that received its substance and purpose from "a process, rather than a structure, of education."[1] The institutional framework that emerged reflected process and pedagogy. This process could harness the prodigious resources of the State University and communities throughout New York State to serve students individually. Rather than having the student come to the College, Empire State College went to the student. It did so in vigorous and bold ways. President Hall quickly broke away from the notion that college locations should be limited to SUNY campuses and created a statewide college.

As we have seen, within the first year of operation regional learning centers, each staffed by a critical mass of faculty representing a wide range of academic interests and in the absence of a departmental structure, were established in major cities. In turn, these centers spawned satellites, staffed by one or two faculty, to serve rural populations or to offer specialized programs. In each instance, including the Center for Statewide Programs, which had satellites all over New York State, the regional learning centers were administered by a dean and an associate dean. Each center had a large degree of regional responsibility, but was responsive to a core administration in Saratoga Springs.

Twenty-five years after the *Prospectus* was drafted, the College holds fast to the principle of providing access, though hefty cuts in state funding have required some streamlining. The number of centers and their satellites now number well over forty, including three programs overseas. And through distance learning, the College has reached a point in its evolution where it has the ability to serve students as anticipated in the *Prospectus,* "according to their desires, interests and capacities," virtually anywhere in the world where telephone, mail, fax and, increasingly, the Internet insure good communication between the student and the mentor.[2]

One might reason that the extraordinary programmatic diversity as well as the geographic amplitude of the College should have been its undoing. But there has been unity in diversity. Early on, the College recruited faculty and deans who were committed to nontraditional education and made it possible for them to work as teams with common goals. Other measures that promoted the development of a unified college included a strong system of governance, clear statements about academic policies, regular gatherings of faculty and administrators, continuous planning, a sophisticated computer-based communications system, and, in the early years, the Center for Individualized Learning, which devoted three and one-half years to gathering faculty on a regional and statewide basis to address important academic issues. These and other activities were vital to creating and maintaining a college culture. In this regard, Empire State College is remarkable for having a faculty and professional staff, though in many instances separated by hundreds of miles, enjoying close and highly productive working relationships. Indeed, technology is drawing us closer together.

Creating a New Faculty Role: The Mentor

Bringing Empire State College to the students and fulfilling their interests with sound programs of study required that they be treated as individuals and not batch processed. To achieve this the College created a path-setting faculty role. The term *mentor,* first applied by Hall, defined a new breed and a new use of faculty. Mentors with extremely diverse academic interests have continued to provide high quality advising in degree program planning. In addition, they serve as tutors to their own students and to students of other mentors as well as find time in busy schedules to pursue their own research interests. A dynamic faculty has sustained the academic vitality and integrity of the College. But mentoring, for the variety of reasons reviewed in this book, is a demanding and sometimes exhausting role. And mentors who coordinate satellite programs have additional challenges as well as rewards.

The workload intensity issue has been echoed in various College reports throughout the years, including the last self-study for accreditation in 1989. While the College continues to move toward making the workload more manageable, by reducing the FTE targets, by providing supportive materials and alternatives, and by easing its clerical and procedural dimensions, the complexity of the mentor role—sometimes referred to as its fragmented nature—will remain essentially the same. It is at the very heart of the College.

Forging a Student Centered Pedagogy: A Broad Spectrum of Options

To honor the principle that students shape their programs of study, Empire State College had to open up an entire universe of learning resources. A traditional college might find difficulty meeting the individual needs and objectives of a single student, even if lecturing were a student's preferred mode of study, but meeting the needs of hundreds or thousands of students would be an impossibility were a college not to seek an alternative to the professorial mode. The learning contract and the mentor role provide this alternative.

Dr. Beverly Smirni is a faculty member of the Metropolitan Center. She joined the College in 1977 as a mentor for the Center for Statewide Programs. In 1991 she was appointed coordinator of student services. In this role, Dr. Smirni has provided vital leadership in focusing the College's attention on cultural diversity and on service to underrepresented student populations. Photograph by Seth Harrison.

Three Empire State College faculty at Mentor Mel Rosenthal's photo exhibit at the SUNY System headquarters in downtown Albany. They are, left to right, Mentors Sharon Villines, Lois Holzman, and Carolyn Broadaway. Photograph by Mel Rosenthal.

Historian Frank Rader served on the staff of the Learning Resources Center and then joined the faculty of the Center for Statewide Programs in 1977. Dr. Rader is an expert on nineteenth-century Irish immigration.

Dr. Diana Worby, recipient of the 1982 Empire State College Foundation Award for Excellence in Advisement, is a mentor for the Hudson Valley Center satellite program in Nyack. Photograph by Seth Harrison.

For Hall and his associates this presented a serious challenge. Primarily, students could not just willy-nilly go off to study. They needed guidance and they needed their progress recorded. The learning contract, which had progenitors at Goddard and Sarah Lawrence, provided the solution. Learning contracts, negotiated between the mentor and the student, and witnessed by the College, bring the student's degree program to fruition. The learning contract marshals the rich and complex resources of local communities to the service of the student, including the faculty from private as well as SUNY colleges and universities who sometimes provide tutorials when cross-registration in not a viable option. Further, the contract reflects the mentor's and, ultimately, the College's judgment about the student's ability to undertake the study and its appropriateness as a subject of academic inquiry.

The *Prospectus* anticipated that the College would serve a wide variety of students whose needs would differ, and recognized the appropriateness of accommodating a wide spectrum of alternative educational programs. *"It will provide the resources both for structure, if necessary, and for individual creative learning."* [3] The *Prospectus* reflected Hall's beliefs about the depth and complexity of the College mission and the need for different major viewpoints. With this in mind, Hall recruited Arthur Chickering as vice president for academic affairs and Loren Baritz as provost for instructional resources.

Today, the range of learning options flowing from the differences between Chickering and Baritz has been preserved. One approach did not vanquish the other. Both survive, indeed flourish, because the individual needs of students determine the mix. The spectrum of learning, as anticipated by the *Prospectus*, remains very broad. At one end, we find the Harry Van Arsdale Jr. School of Labor Studies, which provides classroom instruction, the long established practice of student cross-registration into SUNY campuses and other colleges, and the guided independent study courses offered by the Center for Distance Learning. At the other end, we find completely individualized contract learning and degree programs. In between we find an array of

Dr. Rueben Garner, founding faculty member of the Niagara Frontier Learning Center, retired in 1983. Since 1987 he has served as a history tutor and course developer for the Center for Distance Learning. Photograph by Richard Goldstein.

Mentor Richard Butler joined Empire State College as a business mentor for the Long Island Center. He has been a faculty member of the FORUM/Syracuse program and is currently a mentor at the Central New York Center. Mentor Butler has twice served as chair of the Empire State College Senate. Photograph by Phil Haggerty.

approaches that fulfill student-centered needs. The preservation of this broad spectrum has sustained the flexibility and vitality of the College. It will endure.

Validating Prior Learning: A Student's Formal and Experiential Academic History

Another salient principle articulated in the *Prospectus* is "taking into account fully [a new student's] then current educational experience."[4] To take seriously the charge of fulfilling individual educational objectives, the College has to examine closely each student's academic history, both formal and experiential. Educational objectives have to reflect equally the student's past as well as aspirations for professional competence and intellectual growth. This is especially so for adult students. They bring with them not only prior college study, but oftentimes prodigious amounts of sophisticated learning from their employment, from cultural interests and from other fora. Much of it, because of its specific nature, is beyond the reach of existing standardized testing. Hall and his associates wanted to recognize these accomplishments.

As in other matters, Boyer's task force established the policy of recognizing prior learning, but left the mission of how this would work in practical terms to others. As we have seen, a simple but highly effective system of evaluation evolved through trial and error in the early years and became a national model. The College made the assessment of nonformal experiential learning and other forms of advanced standing part of the individual degree program planning process.

Over the years, assessment has been highly successful, but labor-intensive activity for mentors. To ease the burden, center assessment professionals have assumed more of the task of attending to the prior learning components of degree programs. In addition, to diminish the frustration expressed by students with regard to the length of the assessment process, which has a bearing on attrition, students are now informed much earlier about the amount of transcript credit available for degree program planning. Understandably, students want to know how much advanced standing they have, and as soon as possible. Moreover, students are encouraged to undertake degree program planning as soon as it is appropriate. In some instances degree programs are "approved" at centers prior to a formal evaluation of the student's prior learning. The College is considering other measures to streamline the assessment process and to make it more responsive to student needs and less burdensome for faculty.

The essential policies governing these practices, nevertheless, have remained unchanged: That faculty work closely with students in degree program planning; that the degree programs reflect the educational objectives of the students as weighed in the context of curricular guidelines for the eleven broad areas of study offered by the College; that standardized tests and expert evaluators are employed to assess experiential learning; that faculty committees review and approve degree programs and portfolios; that there is consistency and fairness in assessment practices throughout the College; and that final review and approval is certified by the Office of Academic Affairs. Although credit awards vary from individual to individual, current practice reveals that substantial advanced standing continues to be recognized. The average student receives seventy-four credits, of which forty-seven are for previous college work and twenty-seven are for nonformal learning. Most important, a founding principle of the College, the commitment to validate what adult students already know, remains as fresh, poignant, and educationally significant as it did twenty-five years ago.

Enduring Spirit of Innovation: Constant Renewal

Empire State College has never lost its capacity to experiment. A fundamental principle of its mission is "to create new forms and shapes, new structures and substance, in order to provide and test more effective educational alternatives for individuals of all ages, throughout society."[5] This is a college, as we have seen, that

Below: Dr. Steven Tischler, a historian of sports and society, is a mentor at the Harry Van Arsdale Jr Center for Labor Studies. He poses with his spouse, Barbara Tischler. She is a part-time instructor for Empire State College.

Dr. Keith Elkins, a psychologist and founding faculty member of the Niagara Frontier Learning Center, has served as chair for the Empire State College Senate and in other leadership positions in College governance. In 1977 he served as acting dean of the Niagara Frontier Center. Elkins was appointed SUNY Distinguished Service Professor in 1990. Photograph by Larry Abrams.

thrives on the challenges of launching new programs and constantly renews itself through them.

Learning centers have been the workshops of innovation. In addition to their satellite programs, which provide unique access to individual students throughout New York State, they have created outreach programs serving a host of special constituencies. These range from labor unions to human services agencies, from corporations to correctional facilities, from community colleges to municipal and state agencies. In each instance, programs benefit from forms of educational delivery that best suit local needs. Whatever the form of delivery, face-to-face tutorials, group-based studies, distance learning, or combinations of these determined by the needs of individual students, they express a singular principle and purpose: Providing student access to the College through the mentor, a unique faculty role created twenty-five years ago.

Dr. Thomas Dehner, a chemist and founding faculty member of the Niagara Frontier Learning Center, became associate dean in 1976. In 1979 Mentor Dehner was appointed associate dean of the Public Affairs Center in Albany, New York, and joined the Center for Distance Learning in 1982. He received the Chancellor's Award for Excellence in Teaching for 1990–1991. Photograph by Phil Haggerty.

Summary Conclusions

Empire State College probably would not exist today if it were not for Chancellor Boyer's two early and critical decisions. First was Boyer's decision to launch Empire State College almost immediately after receiving a SUNY Master Plan amendment from the Board of Trustees. Because Empire State College was more chimera than substance, the Board acted greatly on faith that this innovative enterprise would succeed. So, the Board's unanimous support for the resolution creating Empire State College speaks highly of Chancellor Boyer's leadership and the Board's commitment to Governor Rockefeller's vision of a dynamic State University.

The second was Boyer's decision to create a free-standing college. This explains why Empire State College has survived and flourished even at times in the face of fiscal hardship. At first, Boyer's task force gave some thought to a program structurally integrated with the rest of SUNY through a series of campus-based service centers. Boyer wisely decided to establish a new college rather than create another program coordinated by the SUNY System headquarters. One does not have to search far to

Sinologist A. Tomasz Grunfeld, a faculty member of the Metropolitan Learning Center, is author of a number of articles as well as a recently published book on modern Tibet. Dr. Grunfeld received the 1995 Empire State College Foundation Award for Excellence in Scholarship. Photograph by Mel Rosenthal.

appreciate the wisdom of this course of action. State University of the Air, a SUNY-wide program centrally administered, depended on, and failed to sustain, campus-based support. Today, of course, in the frenzy of budget cutting, it is not difficult to imagine dismembering the College and having various units attached to SUNY campuses. Most assuredly, these splintered remnants would die off, one by one, as host campuses pursued other priorities.

The success of Empire State College is best explained by an enduring commitment to the first principles articulated in the *Prospectus*. The *Prospectus* gave the College a strong sense of mission and values. From this emerged an institution accommodating a broad spectrum of alternative educational approaches for a remarkably diverse student clientele. While the *Prospectus* clearly defined the principles that informed the development of the College, it left the forging of specific policies and practices to others. The pioneer administrators and faculty came to the College with a strong sense of purpose. They shared powerful beliefs about the social and pedagogical importance of Empire State College. Creating a student-centered college, one that would fulfill a wide range of educational needs while preserving academic rigor, called for unbridled imagination, sober pragmatism, and a degree of fearlessness.

The College benefited enormously by not being overly planned by Boyer's task force. The most important decision in creating Empire State College was to begin immediately with students and faculty. In this way, policies and practices emerged from direct interaction with students. As Arthur Chickering observed, "At one level it was an expression of the fundamental philosophy of the institution, to pay attention to the students and to be responsive to them, but it was, also, programmatically a wonderful way to create a new institution."[6] In the 1960s and 1970s, a number of

Utica Mayor Louis LaPolla (right) presents a 1988 proclamation in celebration of the relocation of the Utica satellite. From left to right are mentors Crystal Scriber, Kamala Mahauta, and Reed Coughlan. Photograph by Peter Maneen.

innovative colleges were undermined by long and laborious planning and became locked into new rigidities and other orthodoxies.

Because Boyer decided to make Empire State College an autonomous campus of the State University, it was free to experiment. In the first years, the College devised policies and practices governing admissions, the creation of a new faculty role, contract learning, degree program planning, assessment of nonformal experiential learning, cooperative linkages with State University campuses and the resources of local communities, the development and dissemination of independent study materials, the creation of learning locations and the outreach to students with a variety of needs and backgrounds. In effect, an independent college was free to make critical and, in hindsight, productive choices about its fundamental nature and organization. Over the years, Empire State College has refined its policies and practices, but the College is essentially the same institution it was in 1974 when it became the first public nontraditional institution to gain regional accreditation.

In redefining the educational possibilities for adult learners, Empire State College brought to public higher education the kind of personal, interactive, nurturing experience once thought possible only in small residential, usually church-related, liberal arts colleges. In time, this may come to be Empire State College's most enduring achievement.

Dr. Thelma Jurgrau, an internationally regarded scholar on George Sands, is a mentor at the Hartsdale satellite of the Hudson Valley Center. Photograph by Stan Blanchard.

167

Dr. Lee Herman, mentor coordinator of the Central New York Center's Auburn satellite, was the founding cochair with Mentor Miriam Tatzel of the Empire State College Mentoring Institute. In 1986 he received the Empire State College Foundation's Award for Excellence in Teaching, and in 1993 he received the Chancellor's Award for Excellence in Teaching. Photograph by Phil Haggerty.

Dr. Mel Rosenthal (left), a member of the Metropolitan Center faculty, chats with President Hall at Rosenthal's 1980 exhibit of his photographs at the SUNY System headquarters in downtown Albany. Photograph by Ken Wittenberg.

Endnotes Chapter 6

1. *Prospectus for a New University College: Objectives, Process, Structure, and Establishment*, 8 February 1971, State University of New York, Albany, New York, p. 4.

2. *Prospectus*, p. 4.

3. Ibid., 6.

4. Ibid., 18–19.

5. Arthur Chickering, *A Conceptual Framework for Educational Alternatives at Empire State College* (Saratoga Springs, New York: State College, April 1976), i.

6. Arthur Chickering, Interview by Richard Bonnabeau, 16 August 1990, transcript, Empire State College Archives, Saratoga Springs, New York, p. 20.

7

IMAGININGS:
LOOKING BACK
FROM THE YEAR
2021

by James W. Hall

President James W. Hall. Photograph by Mel Rosenthal.

After twenty-five years of extraordinary service to students, it is understandable that the College community should look back and take satisfaction—reward—for a job well done. Indeed, an analytical scrutinizing of that quarter century should yield much information that is valuable to Empire State College, as well as instructive to all of higher learning.

With certainty, looking backward has its benefits. It also holds inherent dangers—traps that ensnare the overly confident in the successes of the past, obscuring the challenges of the present. Perhaps a more liberating strategy is to attempt to imagine the future in the way American writer Edward Bellamy employed in *Looking Backward*.[1] Bellamy imagined the past from a future vantage point and discovered that a gaze toward the past from a point in the future provided a useful lens for fresh, snare-breaking analysis and criticism. Putting on that ocular piece, one can envision SUNY Empire State College looking backward from the year 2021. This chapter contains such imaginings about our progress in the period leading to ESC's fiftieth anniversary.

Kitty Carlisle Hart was a founding member of the Empire State College Council. She appeared on the television show "To Tell the Truth" from 1956 to 1977. She completed her service on the Council in 1981.

Keith Martin (center), former Vice President for College Relations E. Thomas Ezell (right), and graduate Kevin Sweeney, distinguished alumnus, stand in front of 1 Union Avenue. A distinguished artist, educator, and administrator, Keith Martin was a founding member of the College Council. He joined the Empire State College Foundation in 1975, serving as vice chair and chair of its Executive Board. In 1984, he received an honorary doctorate of fine arts degree. Photograph by Phil Haggerty.

A Changed Environmental Milieu

Looking backward from the year 2021, it is striking to what extent the environmental milieu for Empire State College has changed since its founding in 1971. Nearly fifty years ago, relatively few Americans possessed a university first degree. The economic challenges of that period made it increasingly necessary to possess a degree in order to compete for and to hold employment in the burgeoning white collar revolution. As manufacturing declined and formerly manual processes began to give way to robotics and computers, the job market required extensive employee retraining and retooling. Then, Empire State College made it possible for people with busy work schedules to earn a degree while continuing to work. It was among the first institutions to do so, heralding a radical campus revolution in the time and places that a student might pursue learning.

Richard Porter Leach received an honorary doctorate of fine arts in 1986. A former member of the Empire State College Foundation and founding director of the Saratoga Performing Arts Center, he is seen with President Hall (left) and Clifton Wharton Jr., then Chancellor of the State University of New York.

Sal J. Rubino, advocate and trusted adviser, is chair of the Empire State College Council. He has served on the Council since 1976. Photograph by Phil Haggerty.

In the following decades an astounding growth occurred in the numbers of adult students (over age twenty-four) pursuing a higher education. From 28 percent (2,384,000 students) of all higher education enrollments in 1970, by 1990 adult students comprised 44 percent (6,544,00 students).[2] Part-time enrollments increased from 32 percent of the 1970 total to a projected 45 percent in 1995. Moreover, 75 percent of the part-time students were over age twenty-four in 1991.

In 1992, women students constituted 55 percent of all students, while minority populations provided 22 percent. These trends continued unabated well into the present century. In a January 1990 report sponsored by the Pew Memorial Trust,[3] the "new majority" was described as "1) all currently enrolled undergraduates aged twenty-five or older; 2) all currently enrolled undergraduates under twenty-five years old who did not proceed directly from high school to college, who attend part time, or who have 'stopped out' for more than one year." Such enrollments made up 60 percent of all enrollments in the year 2000! So much for the traditional mythical campus of the 1950s!

The State of New York, once the place of second chance for many new and old citizens, has become one of five major international megacenters for telecommunications. Early in the twenty-first century, New York's schools and universities, working with the political and municipal leadership, led a movement to link work and study more closely, transforming the working citizenry into one of the most competent, agile, entrepreneurial bodies politic in the world. New York's businesses rapidly regained the prominent position they had occupied for so many decades in the late nineteenth and early twentieth centuries. Even as the relative level of taxation has declined, the revenue base of the state has increased sharply because of burgeoning economic activity.

Unlike the massive organizations of the 1970s, today most employment is in small working groups, linked through telecommunications to other small groups, themselves part of a network of interrelated employees. While they come together frequently to

accomplish essential group tasks, they carry out much of their work in private homes or small leased spaces. But, unlike the sometimes exploitive manufacturing cottage industries of the eighteenth and nineteenth centuries, the new work requires the mental manipulation of symbols.[4] Often demanding and intense, this new work requires targeted, brief periods of restudy and retooling. Fortunately, the work force is organized so that significant slots of time are programmed into the annual schedule to allow for alternating periods of study as well as planned recreation.

Students in the Year 2021

The impact of this new milieu of work and recreation on ESC's student profile is nothing short of stunning. Today the profile of ESC students is vastly different from the adventurous souls who were attracted to the College fifty years ago. For one thing, a relatively small proportion of ESC's students are seeking a first degree. The largest number, in fact, undertake study with the College faculty as a way to gain a new insight or skill that helps them to undertake new tasks within their place of work. Since for many this place is in the home, they undertake this study under special government tuition grants specifically targeted to the self-employment sector.

Arthur Imperatore (center), recognized for his philanthropic contributions as well as for his personal and professional achievements, received an honorary doctor of letters degree in 1985 at the North Central Regional Center graduation recognition ceremony. He chats with graduate Afi Binta-Lloyd. To the extreme right is Mr. Binta-Lloyd and Edgar Sandman. Mentor LeGrace Benson joins in the discussion.

Dr. Meg Benke, then coordinator of academic services for the Center for Distance Learning, interviews Malcolm Knowles, who participated in the October 1991 advisory committee meeting of the National Council on Adult Learning. Dr. Knowles received an honorary doctorate of humane letters in 1991 from Empire State College. He is one of the leading scholars and practitioners of adult education in the United States.

The second largest group of students is in graduate study, earning recognition for specialized knowledge gained on the job, and pursuing studies in essential new areas. ESC's range of graduate opportunities has increased commensurate with this enrollment. Although a significant number of students are pursuing advanced studies in Business and Management, a far greater number of students are interested in the Masters in Health Services, a program that combines management, public health issues, and human behavior. Both programs are designed to examine and credit the competencies that students gain through independent, interactive, self-paced study.

The next largest group of students are "young" retirees, students whose mental vigor and curiosity lead them to work with a mentor, not for a degree, but for the discipline and feedback that are possible when engaged with an "intellectual coach." Although the Academy for Learning in Retirement had been highly successful in the 1990s and had spread throughout the state under ESC's sponsorship, the very large numbers of healthy, intellectually active retirees today has made the College's direct involvement critically important. From 20 million Americans over age sixty-five in 1970, and 40 million in 2000, we are approaching 65 million retirees over age sixty-five in the year 2030.[5] Indeed, retired persons eagerly seek out these ESC programs because they are the most responsive, tailored-to-the-student programs available anywhere.

A Special Role for Empire State College in a New SUNY

A beneficial result of the State's economic resurgence has been a renewed public understanding and support for post-secondary education to a level not seen since the 1960s. Indeed, the State University of New York is itself vastly different from the sprawling, duplicative organization of the 1970s. Organized regionally around university communication centers, SUNY is truly a statewide, fully interactive university system, capable of sharing its impressive faculty, information resources, and pedagogies with students wherever they may be physically located. Empire State College, as SUNY's pioneering distance learning organization in the 1990s, pointed the way for SUNY's reorganization into tightly linked regional clusters. Today, each region of SUNY is fully linked electronically to the faculty and literary resources of each campus access point in the region. And Empire State College acts as a statewide coordinating organization, providing the many essential services in close cooperation with all of the campuses. This unique role also enables ESC's own students to work with mentors and other SUNY faculty tutors at any of these campus sites as well as in their homes and places of work. The College is superbly organized to interface with the dramatically changed work and study environment.

Mentors: Independent Entrepreneurs

Empire State College is the locus of work for a highly talented faculty. Called mentors, a term first used by Empire State College in the 1970s, they are widely recognized as having been the pioneers in evolving a new and more effective approach to student learning. Today's mentors are independent entrepreneurs, working from their homes and from a number of small offices throughout the state and, in some cases, beyond. Each is able to communicate with students and with colleagues wherever they may be physically located, and the quality of the communications is immediate, realistic, and easily interactive.

Mentoring, the vastly changed faulty role, was ESC's most important innovation. By enabling a student to plan a program of study, then pursue it by drawing together a wide range of study activities, the mentor wrought a structural transformation in the way students and faculty teach and learn. By the 1990s not only some universities, but especially corporations and government agencies were using the concept of the mentor, finding it to be a much more effective way for people to work and to learn. Today, the faculty as mentor is part and parcel of most undergraduate educational institutions. For ESC, this has meant a loss of its uniqueness. On the other hand, ESC remains known for its distinguished reputation in linking mentors to every student effort, irrespective of the study materials that a student may be using at a given point. Moreover, ESC mentors are known throughout the world, engaged as consultants to help others learn how to bring human intellectual coaching into the learning dyad. Mentoring remains ESC's most celebrated and central contribution to higher learning.

About six years ago, the last of the original faculty mentors of the College retired from full-time service. When she retired, she reflected on the shape and character of a career that spanned the most radical transformation ever experienced by the academic community. She noted the crisis that had swept education at the turn of the century when lecturing in classrooms, as had been central to university education for centuries, was replaced by student self-learning, guided by a mentor. She wondered, in retrospect, how lecturing as the primary mode of teaching had lasted so long, been so persistent.

A Changed Academic Framework

Of course, the College pioneered other unique reforms. Some have flourished while others have declined in importance. For example, individual degree programs were critically important in the early years of ESC. Most adults, having already gained some college-level learning through formal study or assessment of informal learning, needed to define an individual curriculum that matched the studies yet to be completed for the degree. But as the numbers of students seeking undergraduate degrees has declined, and as assessment of prior learning has lost its centrality in program design, more and more students have focused on the means of completing academic requirements rather than on gaining advanced standing. In a sense, every student completes a unique set of expectations, but this is now true at all universities. Universities are in the business, not of providing general instruction, but of providing intellectual guidance and expert evaluation of student competence. This has changed the whole framework for a college degree.

Contract learning was also one of the most innovative reforms introduced at Empire State College. In the late 1990s that descriptor was changed to more simply describe a "periodic study plan" (PSP). Although the notion of a "contract" between student and faculty was useful in defining the responsibilities and tasks of each party, it was often confusing to others, implying a legal obligation or, especially in the case of the Van Arsdale School, a negotiated agreement that could not be abrogated. The concept remains central to study at ESC, despite the name change. The PSP describes a unique plan to be undertaken by an individual student for a defined period of time. Building on what is known in learning theory about student motivation, knowledge retention, and mastery, the PSP helps to ensure that student work at ESC is purposeful, efficient, and rewarding.

Assessment of Prior Learning leading to recognition of advanced standing was another of the central features of the early ESC academic program. It helped degree students to gain recognition and credit for what they already knew, avoiding the redundancy then encountered as a necessity at most universities. For adults, it was often a critical factor in the decision to pursue study at ESC, saving them substantial time and money in completing a degree. In the ensuing years, this feature has declined in importance. Since a very large proportion of students are not degree students, and many others are pursuing an advanced degree, the relative amount of advanced standing awarded has become less central to a student's decision about study. The old student query, "How much credit will I get?" has been replaced by new questions, such as "Will I be able to maintain contact with my mentor while I am in Buenos Aires?"

Another important innovation, the year-round academic calendar initiated at the very outset of the new College in 1971, has proven absolutely critical to effective linkage to the adult working population. Moving the academic calendar from one derived from the annual cycle of crop planting and harvest, to one that is continuous, permitting students to begin study at virtually any time their schedule and work requirements demand, has now been adopted by most institutions.

On the other hand, experiential learning, once a central aspect of ESC students' study strategy, has re-emerged as a key part of student work. The recurrent character of study, interspersed closely with the student's work, has given new currency to a close relationship between theory, work, and practical application. Empire State College's

Left: Janet Jones joined the College in 1972 as a stenographer. She is now an information processing specialist for Central Services. Photograph by Larry Abrams.

President James W. Hall participated in a teleconference via satellite with the new chancellor of the California State University (CSU) system in November 1992. The CSU chancellor's staff organized the conference as part of joint efforts with SUNY to apply technology to education. The cameraman is an alumnus. Photograph by Lloyd Woodcock.

experience in managing advanced study through work and application has proven invaluable and is an integral part of most students' PSPs.

International Study

International study is a far more significant activity for students than it was in 1996. Then, a very few domestic students arranged learning contracts with the College's mentors on site in Jerusalem, Nicosia, and Athens. But the change in work schedules, combined with significant opportunities for intermittent study and recreation, has encouraged large numbers of adults to seek out short-term learning opportunities abroad. The international character of the workplace, given New York State's global economic enterprise, requires that corporations and businesses provide extensive international training for employees. Although language training used to be the most important part of such study, today, voice-activated microprocessors provide instant translation. Thus, the importance of intercultural study, knowledge of international business and finance, and world economic and ecological trends, is the most important study. Nearly 20 percent of ESC students engage in some form of international study during their college careers.

Educational Uses of Technology

In all of these features, the College anticipated long ago the potential for integrating educational uses of technology and direct engagement with faculty. Although the broadcast video and computer driven technologies of the 1970s had proven inadequate, by the late 1990s the high quality, video interactive capacities of communications technology began to transform the entire educational experience. The most advanced benefits occurred initially in the very traditional area of library services.

Vice President for Administration William Ferrero has been with the College since 1974. Empire State College's complexities—a statewide campus composed mostly of leased facilities and an extraordinary range of programs—have called for a chief financial officer with exceptional resilience. Photograph by Larry Abrams.

Although ESC students (and the larger community) have always been able to use all SUNY libraries, the capacity of the libraries to meet this need declined sharply as smaller budgets and higher costs for books, access to electronic data and storage reduced the scope and range of each library. With the advent of interactive, on-line bibliographic search capability, and high-speed electronic retrieval of actual texts at any location, the concept of a single, systemwide, library system became possible. By the end of the last century, the SUNY system acquired access rights to books, periodicals, databases and distant library holdings, paying a small fee for each faculty or student use. In this way, the scope and practical value of the system library was infinitely increased even as the need for new storage space, for purchase and cataloguing of items, disappeared. Today, librarians are adept at helping users understand the rich resources at hand, and in helping users navigate the system. For Empire State College, this transformation has meant that its students and faculty have no disadvantage in rapid availability of all needed information. The system serves the distant, at home, or

A 1988 Bedford-Stuyvesant open house. From left to right are President James W. Hall, Dean Nancy Bunch, Dorothy Burnham, and Mentor Coordinator Rudolph Cain. Photograph by Hakim.

night-working student equally as well as the resident student. No single change has made such a dramatic difference in the way a campus functions as has the transformation of the library.

Distance learning was the fashionable term in the 1990s, and ESC was a leading proponent, helping to coordinate the sharing of courses throughout SUNY. But by the turn of the century, every student in SUNY, whether resident on a campus or at some remove from the campus, had become adept at utilizing study materials delivered through electronic communications. Asynchronous learning, allowing student and faculty to interact at times and places convenient to each schedule, became the most used practice. The term, "distance learning," was replaced in the late 1990s by the more accurate and descriptive term, "networked learning." For ESC this represented a significant challenge, because once it had had the distance field to itself. Rather than continue to serve most of the "distance" students itself, ESC was designated by the SUNY Board of Trustees to perform a systemwide coordinating function, maintaining the electronic inventories of available materials for study, coordinating the student election of courses, transferring appropriate academic credit and revenue to the sponsoring SUNY campus, providing training to faculty and staff, and monitoring

Dr. Daniel Granger (right), director of the Center for Distance Learning, discusses the British Open University (BOU) tutorial support system with the BOU's Southeast Regional Director Peter Princep. Princep has been a frequent visitor and consultant to Empire State College since 1979. Photograph by Larry Abrams.

Dr. Hugh Hammett, vice president for external affairs, joined the College in 1978 as the associate dean for the Genesee Valley Center. In 1985 he was appointed executive director of the Office of Continuing Education and then dean in 1987. He became vice president for external affairs in 1989. Photograph by Stanley Blanchard.

Dr. Patricia LeFor, dean of the Long Island Center, at a meeting with President James W. Hall. She was appointed dean in 1982. A former Woodrow Wilson Fellow and recipient of the Chancellor's Award of Excellence in Teaching, Dr. LeFor was a founding faculty member of the Long Island Center and had served as its associate dean since 1979. Photograph by Phil Haggerty.

Dr. Jane Altes succeeded John Jacobson as vice president for academic affairs in 1987. Before coming to Empire State College, Dr. Altes had been the associate vice chancellor for academic programs for the State University of New York System. She guided Empire State College through a successful 1989 self-study for reaccreditation by the Middle States Association and has supported a number of important initiatives, including the Mentoring Institute. Photograph by Mel Rosenthal.

academic quality through systemwide faculty panels. In this relatively new role supporting networked learning throughout the state, ESC has become more central to the overall mission and operation of SUNY.

Technology has transformed, as well, a wide range of University administrative functions that once required many highly specialized offices on each SUNY campus. ESC, from its beginnings, had been required to find new ways to deliver these essential services on a statewide basis, and so was, early on, a model for administrative efficiency. Formerly time consuming operations such as student admissions, course registration, financial aids, purchasing, and student accounting, are now routinely available to students and other users at secure work stations available throughout the state.

At ESC, telecommunications has been instrumental in restructuring the functioning of the entire institution. Indeed, the faculty and administration of the College function across the entire state. No longer are administrators housed in large numbers in Saratoga Springs, which used to be called the Coordinating Center. Today, that center forms the nucleus of a fully linked network of staff who live in many areas of the state while carrying out College-wide duties. The result has been a fully integrated college without boundaries of distance.

Back in 1971, then President Hall described "Greta the weaver" as a typical Empire State College student.[6] Greta, a practicing artist who had initially little interest in a traditional college liberal curriculum, ultimately completed a remarkably well-rounded, intellectually challenging individual curriculum that emerged branch by branch from the conjunction of her natural curiosity and the mentor's creativity and responsiveness. Fifty years later, such students continue to seek out Empire State College and they find a conducive, stimulating learning environment. But it happens that Greta's grandson, James, recently enrolled at the College. Like Greta, he had found it necessary to work immediately following his high school graduation. But unlike Greta, he realized early on that he would require substantial additional education if he were to be able to grow with his small, technology driven employer. That organization, heavily committed to interactive on-line support to a variety of smaller clients throughout the world, relied on James to understand the market's needs, devise and communicate elegant new solutions to very specific, globally diverse problems, and to maintain a knowledge base that anticipated the competition. For James, that meant testing his current technical knowledge periodically against that of the best theorists in the field. Moreover, it demanded increasingly broad mastery of ideas, languages, and culture. By linking skilled tutors who could guide his study, even when he was abroad, Empire State University was able to provide the most up-to-date, convenient, and intellectually timely education possible. James will be one of next year's graduates, as Empire State University celebrates its golden anniversary. He and his late grandmother, and sixty-five thousand other graduates, represent the beginning, the present, and the future of this constantly evolving, ever renewing, educationally responsive institution.

President Hall saluting Long Island Center graduates. Photograph by Gene Luttenberg, New Hyde Park, New York.

Endnotes Chapter 7

1. 1888.

2. Timothy Lehmann, "Demographic Trends and Policy Implications," (A Draft Background Paper), Empire State College, August 1995, p. 1.

3. "Breaking the Mold," *Pew Policy Perspective* (January 1990): 1.

4. See Shoshana Zubbof, *In the Age of the Smart Machine: The Future of Work and Power* (New York: Basic Books, 1988).

5. Harold L. Hodgkinson, "A Demographic Look at Tomorrow," (Washington, D.C: Institute of Educational Leadership, June 1992), 12.

6. James W. Hall with Barbara L. Kevles, "A Model Education," in *Opposition to Core Curriculum: Alternative Models for Undergraduate Education* (Wesport, Connecticut: Greenwood Press, 1982), pp. 212–214.

Bibliography

"A Report on the Electronic University of the Future: A Planning Colloquy." Presented by Empire State College, 16–17 May 1985. Saratoga Springs, New York.

Access, Innovation and the Quest for Excellence: Empire State College in 1979. Self-Study Prepared for the Commission on Higher Education. Middle States Association of Colleges and Schools. Empire State College. Saratoga Springs, New York. September 1979.

Abrams, Kenneth. Interview by Richard Bonnabeau. 17 May 1990. transcript. Empire State College Archives, Saratoga Springs, New York.

Andolina, Michael. "Innovation and Structure." *Innovating* (Winter 1993): 62–69.

Benson, Ann and Frank Adams. *To Know for Real: Royce S. Pitkin and Goddard College.* Adamant, Vermont: Adamant Press, 1987.

Baritz, Loren. Interview by Richard Bonnabeau. 20 March 1990. transcript. Empire State College Archives, Saratoga Springs, New York.

Barylski, Robert. Interview by Richard Bonnabeau, 25 March 1993. transcript. Empire State College Archives. Saratoga Springs, New York.

Bedford Stuyvesant Unit Evaluation. Saratoga Springs, New York: Empire State College, Office of Research and Evaluation, 1973.

Boyle, T. Coraghessan. *The Road to Wellville.* New York: Viking, 1993.

Boyer, Ernest L. Interview by Richard Bonnabeau. 31 August 1990. transcript. Empire State College Archives, Saratoga Springs, New York.

Bradley, Paul. *The Empire State College Mentor: The Emerging Role.* Saratoga Springs, New York: Empire State College, Office of Research and Evaluation, September 1975.

"Breaking the Mold." *Pew Policy Perspective* (January 1990).

Brockmann, Jeanne. "A Study of the Impact of Mission on Selected Aspects of College Administration." Ph.D. diss., University of Massachusetts, Amherst, 1980.
Cardozier, V. Ray, ed. *Important Lessons in Higher Education.* San Francisco: Jossey-Bass Publishers. no. 82. Summer 1993.

Carr, Edward to James W. Hall. 24 March 1975. Memorandum: Report of the New York State Education Department (NYSED) Evaluation Team. Empire State College Archives. Saratoga Springs, New York.

Chickering, Arthur. *A Conceptual Framework for Educational Alternatives at Empire State College,* Saratoga Springs, New York: Empire State College, April 1976.

Chickering, Arthur. Interview by Richard Bonnabeau, 16 August 1990. transcript. Empire State College Archives. Saratoga Springs, New York.

Clark, F. Thomas. Interview by Richard Bonnabeau. 16 March 1990. transcript. Empire State College Archives. Saratoga Springs, New York.

Corwin, Ronald. Interview by Richard Bonnabeau. 21 June 1990. transcript. Empire State College Archives. Saratoga Springs, New York.

Dodge, William. Interview by Richard Bonnabeau. 26 February 1991. transcript. Empire State College Archives, Saratoga Springs, New York.

Dalhberg, Jane. Interview by Richard Bonnabeau. 30 May 1991. transcript. Empire State College Archives. Saratoga Springs, New York.

Drury, George. Interview by Richard Bonnabeau. 24 July 1991. transcript. Empire State College Archives. Saratoga Springs, New York.

Goldberg, Joseph. Interview by Richard Bonnabeau. 30 May 1991. transcript. Empire State College Archives. Saratoga Springs, New York.

Grant, Gerald and David Riesman. *The Perpetual Dream: in the American College.* Chicago and London: The University of Chicago Press, 1978.

Jacobson, John. Interview by Richard Bonnabeau. 8 April 1993. transcript. Empire State College Archives. Saratoga Springs, New York.

Jerome, Judson. *Culture Out of Anarchy: The Reconstruction of American Higher Learning.* New York: Herder and Herder, 1970.
Lehmann, Timothy. Interview by Richard Bonnabeau. 14 January 1991. transcript. Empire State College Archives. Saratoga Springs. New York.

Hall, James. *Access Through Innovation: New Colleges for New Students.* New York: Macmillan, 1991.

Hall, James W. Interview by Richard Bonnabeau. 16 March 1990. transcript. Empire State College Archives. Saratoga Springs, New York.

Hall, James W. Interview by Richard Bonnabeau, 13 June 1990. transcript. Empire State College Archives. Saratoga Springs, New York.

Hall, James W. Interview by Richard Bonnabeau. 6 September 1990. transcript. Empire State College Archives. Saratoga Springs, New York.

Hall, James W. with Barbara L. Kevles, "A Model Education." In *Opposition to Core Curriculum: Alternative Models for Undergraduate Education.*

Wesport, Connecticut: Greenwood Press, 1982.

Harold L. Hodgkinson, "A Demographic Look at Tomorrow." Washington, D.C: Institute of Educational Leadership. June 1992.

Lipkin, R. "Strong Vast Amounts of Data in Tiny Spots." *Science News.* April 1992. vol. 147, no. 16.

Mather, John. Interview by Richard Bonnabeau. 2 February 1990. transcript. Empire State College Archives. Saratoga Springs, New York.

New Models for Career Education: An Assessment. Saratoga Springs, New York: Empire State College. Office of Research and Evaluation. April 1976.

Palola, Ernest and Paul Bradley. *Ten Out of Thirty: Studies of the First Graduates of Empire State College.* Saratoga Springs, New York: Empire State College. Office of Research and Evaluation, 1973.

Perry, Walter. *The Open University.* San Francisco: Jossey-Bass Publishers, 1977.

Prospectus for a New University College: Objectives, Process, Structure, and Establishment, 8 February 1971. State University of New York. Albany, New York.

"Report to the Faculty, Administration, Trustees, Students of Empire State College." Prepared by an Evaluating Team Representing the Commission on Higher Education of the Middle States Association. 1974. Empire State College Archives, Saratoga Springs, New York.

"Report to the Faculty, Administrators, Trustees, Students of Empire State College." Prepared by an Evaluating Team Representing the Commission on Higher Education of the Middle State Association of Colleges and Schools. 1979. Empire State College Archives. Saratoga Springs, New York.

Retrospect and Prospect: Strengthening Learning at Empire State College 1989. Self-study Prepared for the Commission on Higher Education. Middle States Association of Colleges and Schools. Empire State College, Saratoga Springs, New York. September 1989.

Riesman, David. *The Academic Revolution.* Garden City, New York: Doubleday & Company, Inc., 1968.

Rosenberg. "An Examination of the Development of the First Accredited Labor College in the United States." Ph.D. diss., Rutgers University, 1989.

Serling, Albert. Interview by Richard Bonnabeau. 7 May 1990. transcript. Empire State College Archives. Saratoga Springs, New York.

Spindler, Harry K. Interview by Richard Bonnabeau. 1 February 1990. transcript. Empire State College Archives. Saratoga Springs, New York.

Trow, Martin. "Reflections on the Transition from Mass to Universal Higher Education." *Daedalus: Journal of the American Academy of Arts and Sciences,* vol. 99, no. 1 (Winter Edition: The Embattled University, 1970): 1–35.

Zubbof, Shoshana. *In the Age of the Smart Machine: The Future of Work and Power.* New York: Basic Books, 1988.

Index

About the Author

ichard F. Bonnabeau joined Empire State College in November 1974 as a mentor intern. Supported by a post-doctoral fellowship from the Eli Lilly Foundation, Bonnabeau was a member of the pioneer faculty of the Niagara Frontier Regional Learning Center. He came to Empire State College from Eleanor Roosevelt Developmental Services in 1974, an innovative program of the New York Department of Mental Hygiene, nationally recognized for its pioneering accomplishments in the field of developmental disabilities.

Professor Bonnabeau received his Ph.D. from Indiana University, where he studied history and anthropology. At Empire State College he has been both a mentor and administrator. Besides having served as assistant to President James W. Hall, Bonnabeau has been an area coordinator, associate director, and twice acting director for the Center for Distance Learning. Bonnabeau is currently associate director of International Programs, and the College Historian and Archivist. He has held the latter position since 1990. In this capacity he has directed the Empire State College Oral History Project. In 1991, Bonnabeau received the Arthur E. Imperatore Community Forum Scholarship which supported much of the project's work. In 1993 he received the Empire State College Award for Excellence in Mentoring.

On loan to the New York State Education Department in 1987, Bonnabeau served as an associate consultant to the Center for Multinational and Comparative Education, a cabinet-level office reporting directly to Education Commissioner Gordon Ambach. In 1990 he served as a distance-learning consultant to the Egyptian Supreme Council of Universities through the United States Agency for International Development. In 1993 Bonnabeau served as a consultant to Baruch College's distance learning project in the People's Republic of China.

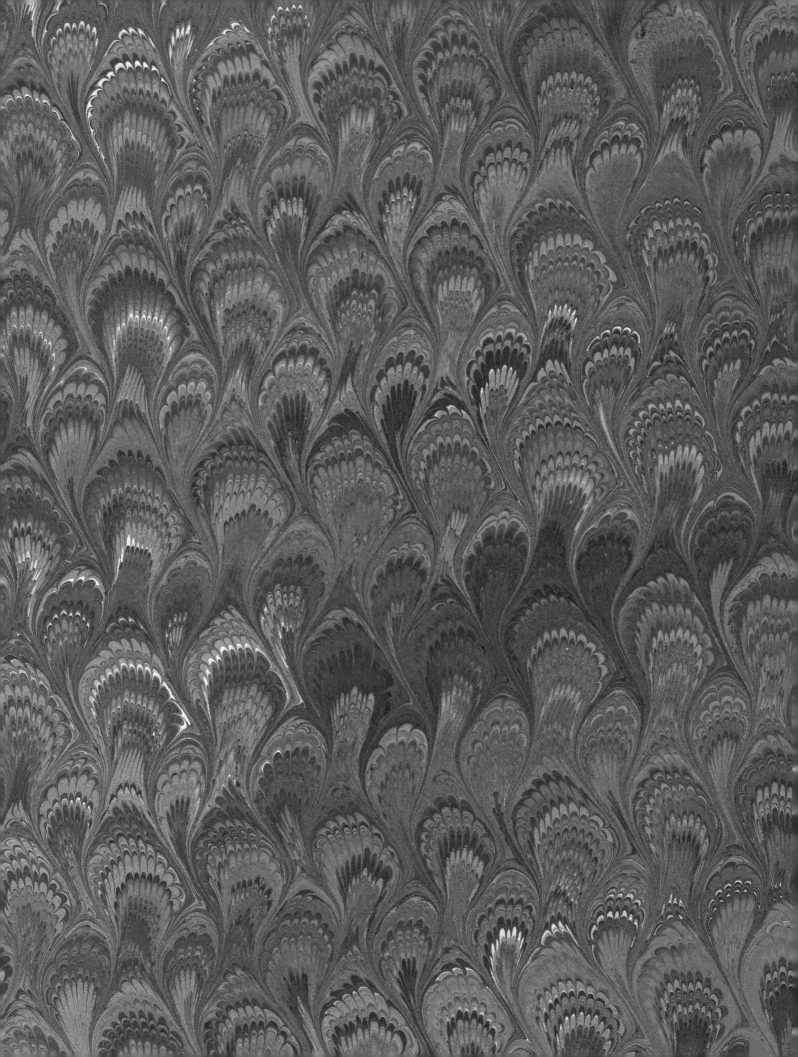